PRAISE FOR *READY OR NOT*

T0089738

"Levine offers eye-opening stats and welcome wisdom to parents raising children in an increasingly unpredictable world. If this book finds its way to those who most need it, surely we will all benefit."   —*New York Times Book Review*

"A practical, wise manual. . . . With empathy, Levine explores the valid anxiety parents and children feel about facing a 'world of disconcerting unpredictability and upheaval' and lays out the 'foundational' skills children need to develop. . . . Plenty of parents will benefit from her treatise on how to prepare children for an uncertain future."   —*Publishers Weekly*

"[Levine] imparts a strong and convincing message: Parents must let their children develop their independence in order to greet their futures with confidence and the skills necessary to survive. Rock-solid advice for harried parents in a world that shows no sign of slowing down."   —*Kirkus Reviews*

"Thoughtful, relevant guidance. . . . With thorough research backing her up, Levine delivers advice with intelligence and compassion, but also with realistic expectations of what it's like to parent as well as grow up in today's world. Best of all, she masterfully balances this realism with positivity. Another invaluable resource from Levine."   —*Booklist* (starred review)

"When I wanted to understand what was going on with the students I had taught at Yale—dazed survivors of the achievement machine—I turned to the work of Madeline Levine . . . [who] has been our leading voice against the culture of overparenting and status obsession. In *Ready or Not*, she once again brings her unique combination of wisdom, clinical experience, and profound compassion . . . to bear on the daunting task of raising young adults in the twenty-first century."

—William Deresiewicz, author of the *New York Times* bestseller *Excellent Sheep: The Miseducation of the American Elite and the Way to a Meaningful Life*

"Thank goodness for Madeline Levine, who proves that there is such a thing as too much parenting. Levine's path forward necessitates that we first address our own anxiety so that we can allow our kids to exert control over their own lives and persevere at the things that matter to them. *Ready or Not* is without a doubt the most important book for these precarious parenting times. Put down your kid's homework and read this book!"

—Julie Lythcott-Haims, author of *Your Turn*

"Informed by a lifetime of clinical practice, wide-ranging research, and a powerful moral sensibility, Madeline Levine's latest book paints a compelling picture of the challenges parents and educators face in an uncertain world. But her greatest contribution is her wise and compassionate advice for all of us committed to helping kids thrive in the twenty-first century. *Ready or Not* is one of the most important books I've read in a very long time."

—Tony Wagner, bestselling author of *The Global Achievement Gap* and *Creating Innovators*

"All of Levine's books hold a place of honor on my shelf, and *Ready or Not* is a worthy addition. It's an invaluable guide to defusing the anxiety and worry faced by today's parents as they navigate raising their kids in an uncertain and rapidly changing world. I love this book. It's a game changer."

—Jessica Lahey, author of *The Addiction Inoculation*

"*Ready or Not* is a great book for helping today's families deal with the incredible impact of technology and media in our rapidly changing reality. One of the leading experts in the field, Madeline does a terrific job of offering support and wise counsel to overwhelmed parents. This is an excellent book."

—James P. Steyer, founder and CEO of Common Sense Media

"Read this now! Dr. Levine's prescience illuminates the challenges of these uncertain times and reveals hard truths about how current approaches to educating and parenting are failing our children. Her ability to illustrate research with real-life stories and offer sage advice is spellbinding and bound to inspire readers to let go of outdated paradigms and actually prepare kids for the unknown future. In these uncertain times, this is the one parenting book that addresses what is happening right now and the ways in which parents and educators need to shift their focus as they advise and guide this generation of young adults."

—Catherine Steiner-Adair, EdD, author of *The Big Disconnect*

"Madeline Levine is a gift to parents, and her books should be required reading. Her latest book, *Ready or Not: Preparing Our Kids to Thrive in an Uncertain and Rapidly Changing World* couldn't be more timely or essential. Dr. Levine makes a clear case that our parenting techniques are not doing our children any favors. In fact, our narrow focus on GPA and test scores is proving disastrous. She is clear that we are raising our kids in a different era—Mayberry is long gone. The world is uncertain and accelerated, and we need a different parenting approach to help our children thrive. Levine provides it. If our children are to flourish in this uncertain world then we better heed her advice. *Highly recommended.*"

—Michele Borba, author of *Thrivers* and *UnSelfie*

Ready or Not

Also by Madeline Levine, PhD

Teach Your Children Well: Why Values and Coping Skills Matter More Than Grades, Trophies, or "Fat Envelopes"

The Price of Privilege: How Parental Pressure and Material Advantage Are Creating a Generation of Disconnected and Unhappy Kids

See No Evil: A Guide to Protecting Our Children from Media Violence

Viewing Violence: How Media Violence Affects Your Child's and Adolescent's Development

Ready or Not

Preparing Our Kids to Thrive
in an Uncertain World

Madeline Levine, PhD

HARPER PERENNIAL

NEW YORK • LONDON • TORONTO • SYDNEY • NEW DELHI • AUCKLAND

HARPER PERENNIAL

A hardcover edition of this book was published in 2020 by HarperCollins Publishers.

The names and identifying characteristics of some individuals discussed in this book have been changed to protect their privacy.

READY OR NOT. Copyright © 2020 by Madeline Levine. All rights reserved. Printed in the United States of America. No part of this book may be used or reproduced in any manner whatsoever without written permission except in the case of brief quotations embodied in critical articles and reviews. For information, address Harper-Collins Publishers, 195 Broadway, New York, NY 10007.

HarperCollins books may be purchased for educational, business, or sales promotional use. For information, please email the Special Markets Department at SPsales@harpercollins.com.

FIRST HARPER PERENNIAL EDITION PUBLISHED 2021.

Library of Congress Cataloging-in-Publication Data has been applied for.

ISBN 978-0-06-265778-7 (pbk.)

21 22 23 24 25   BR   10 9 8 7 6 5 4 3 2 1

To the ever-expanding blessing that is my family:
Loren, Lauren and Emery, Michael and David,
Jeremy and Magen. Roll up your sleeves kids.
There's work to be done.

CONTENTS

Part III · Thriving in the New Normal

PROLOGUE

History is interesting. Living through it, not so much.

As I write this prologue, we are in various states of recovery from a period of historical chaos on multiple fronts: a pandemic accompanied by political, economic, educational, and social disruption. We are all witnesses to a year of despair, profound disorder, dangerous political dynamics, and hovering death—a year that was impossible to imagine, and one for which we were completely unprepared.

Ready or Not was originally published in February of 2020. Three weeks later, the United States was locking down in an attempt to control the Covid-19 pandemic. Now, a year later, half a million American lives have been lost. Worldwide, the loss of life runs into the millions. Economic costs are incalculable, as are the mental health, social, and educational costs to our children who haven't seen a classroom in more than a year. If nothing else, we have come face to face with how essential it is for parents to somehow prepare our children for change, for dislocation, for the unimaginable.

Ready or Not was written to underscore the urgent need to rethink the skills, values, and notions about success that parents and educators have been advancing for decades. Years before the pandemic, it was clear that a sea change was coming and that our children needed to learn a new set of competencies to thrive. In this new, constantly changing world, uncertainty would be prominent and adaptation essential. Well, I was right about a sea change coming, but like all the rest of us, I had no idea that it would be a tsunami.

The relentless pressure on kids to "succeed" at the cost of their mental health, the overvalue placed on prestigious universities, prioritizing grades over character development were all failing educational and healthy parenting paradigms. The unyielding emphasis on "me" versus "we" was not providing a strong enough academic or moral foundation for the world our children are inheriting. Clearly what was needed to navigate this crisis were skills like flexibility, collaboration, critical thinking, curiosity, and empathy. In short, the bundle of competencies that, taken together, produce resilience. We and our children would all have been well served by developing those skills before the pandemic.

Of course I had no idea that a virus, one related to the common cold, was about to upend our lives when I subtitled this book *Preparing Our Kids to Thrive in an Uncertain and Rapidly Changing World*, although I did anticipate a need for change, even radical change. Education is clearly due for a reset. The skills that high-prestige universities and employers are valuing have become increasingly multifaceted and people-centered. Rates of mental illness, particularly anxiety and depression among children and teens, continue to accelerate. I looked forward to the launch of *Ready or Not*, believing that my rather predictable emphasis on raising good and healthy kids, not just good students, would now have the added weight of the support of university admissions directors and heads of hiring. Writing about the downside of our overwrought emphasis on performance and grades, I was certain that there was a compelling case to be made for what have been wrongly labeled "soft skills" (with its whiff of antifeminism) and what I have called foundational skills. For example, curiosity, creativity, flexibility, critical thinking, and perseverance were highlighted as crucial skills by mental health workers, admissions directors, and employers alike. Part of the "ah-ha" moment embedded in this book is not just that the most valuable skill set has changed, but also that these skills are eminently teachable. There is no "resilience gene." The ability to make it through challenges and rapid change is *taught* by parents, educators, and the environment.

At one of the talks I gave during the pandemic, I told my (Zoom) audience that their goal was "to get through this time with you and your family relatively intact." While answering questions afterward, I was asked, "Dr. Levine, why have you set such a low bar? Is that the best we can do—just get through?" That comment surprised me because I actually thought that "getting through" was a very high bar given the tectonic shifts in our lives. But when I thought more about it, I realized that "getting through" might have sounded too much like not doing anything. Being passive, maybe even fatalistic. But "getting through" challenges in life is quite the opposite of being passive. It actually requires a polished set of assorted skills that, together, constitute resilience. And unsurprisingly, the skills that have allowed many of us to make it to the pandemic's finish line are pretty much the same skills that I have advanced in this book— creativity, self-regulation, critical thinking, and flexibility, to name a few. Many of our prior concerns—what our kids' grades were, where they'd go to college, how popular they were, how popular we were—have given way to the realization that life going forward is irrevocably changed, and that brings with it a realization that much of what we thought constituted success in the world would have to be redefined and aligned with the demands of rapid and unpredictable transformation.

My reasons for promoting these skills had been focused on helping our kids to become better, more empathic people with the kind of skills and character that the job market was likely to reward, and that friends and eventual partners would value. I was convinced by CEOs, heads of hiring, college admissions directors, army generals, and naval admirals that our old paradigms of valuing product over process and "right" answers over critical thinking and curiosity would doom our kids when it came to employment and self-sufficiency.

But now, it's clear to me that my vision was too narrow. The issue is no longer whether Harvard prefers stellar grades or a superlative transcript or whether Facebook puts a higher value on technical skills or people skills. The relative value of a long-neglected set of skills has come into focus. And the need is huge. What the pandemic taught us is that massive unemployment, loss of life, disrupted education, and economic free fall are previously unimaginable challenges that will continue to be with us for the foreseeable future. In order for our children to flourish in a world that has shown itself capable of annihilation on a dime, it is exactly the critical and highly teachable skills described in this book that our children will depend on in our clearly interconnected, ferociously unpredictable world. We can no longer avoid the cost of unremitting self-interest. This book will help you learn how to reinforce what will matter most to your child's future. Ready or not, if we want our kids not just to survive but to thrive, we are going to have to adapt our parenting, our teaching, and our everyday concerns to a different kind of preparation, one that values a different kind of outcome. We change, or we and our children will most certainly be left behind.

In between changing diapers, wiping noses, folding laundry, dialing for takeout, rushing to work, going to parent-teacher conferences, driving carpool, and obsessing over whether your parenting skills are in line with the latest findings on child development, you've undoubtedly noticed that the world appears to be unraveling. Not literally, of course, but what with previously unimaginable political friction at home, increasing tension abroad, deteriorating climate conditions, and the ever-advancing tech revolution, the world, as most of us have known it, is becoming ever more uncertain, unfamiliar, and disturbing. This past year's pandemic, school shutdowns, and economic meltdown have exposed the magnitude and unimaginable disruption of the continuing challenges we are likely to face.

Most of us have been busy trying to keep our families functioning reasonably well while we juggle home life, work life, and something resembling our own lives. This leaves us little time to process the daily onslaught of calamitous headlines the twenty-four-hour news cycle depends on. Cybersecurity may or may not protect our identities. Our kids won't have jobs. The robot apocalypse is on the way. We weep at the worst of it: another mass shooting at a school, a church, or a synagogue. We cringe at the debasement of dialogue that has become the new normal in politics. We fight feelings of distrust, anger, and helplessness about a future that too often feels dystopian. Increasingly, we turn our attention to our children out of love, fear, and the consolation of being able to exert some control when so much feels out of control.

Amid this drumbeat of disruption, when we take a deep breath, we can see that the changing world actually offers tremendous opportunities for innovation, growth, health, and greater equality. Babies with birth defects can be cured while still in the womb. Paper microscopes that are cheap and easily transportable can help revolutionize health care in developing countries. Headsets that read brainwaves can allow paralyzed patients to control their wheelchairs by simply thinking about movement. CRISPR allows the editing of genes and may soon be eliminating some of our most lethal diseases. Life-saving vaccines developed in months not years or decades. We are at an extraordinary moment in time that offers equal evidence for concern, caution, and optimism. Great for scientists and researchers. Not so great for parents and grandparents.

The surreptitiously curated information most of us get is piecemeal, anecdotal, and designed to further addict us to our particular worldview. While it plays to our biases, it does little to actually inform us. We are aware that the world is changing, but experts seem to be short on consensus and it is the velocity of change that we find truly head-spinning. Change has always been with us humans, measured in millennia, centuries, or decades, not in years or even weeks. How do we move ourselves and our children forward when our impulse and our anxiety make us look to the past for solutions that are now outdated? We have always been concerned with the forward trajectory of our children's lives. Anxiety is nothing new. Historically, it has hummed along in the background. But our anxiety is no longer background noise. Not for us. Not for our kids. *Anxiety is now the number-one mental health disorder for both adults and children.*[1] And, not surprisingly, rates of anxiety (along with depression, substance abuse, domestic violence, and suicide) have skyrocketed during the pandemic. With all efforts going into "getting through" this period of time, most of us have had little time or bandwidth for developing a more extensive repertoire of anti-anxiety tools.

Ready or Not is about addressing that anxiety. It is about the damage unchecked anxiety does to parents' decision-making at the very moment we need greater, not lesser, clarity about everything from which preschool will best nourish our toddler to which university will be the best fit for our high-school senior. Will coding camp, soccer camp, adventure camp, or plain old camp-camp help set up our kids for future success? Oh, and what will that success look like? Will it come from the metrics we've always used—well-respected universities leading to in-demand professional jobs with high pay and status? Or will it depend on our child's ability to adapt to ever-changing work requirements, perhaps even the requirement to find purpose while lacking any sort of work in the traditional sense? This book is also about how anxiety (theirs and ours) impacts our kids' well-being and hinders their ability to develop the muscular mental health they'll need in a world that is volatile, uncertain, complex, and ambiguous, or VUCA, as the military calls it. A world where change comes on steroids. Anxiety does not have to stifle our judgment or our children's development. By understanding and taking charge of uncertainty and anxiety we can turn our increased awareness into an advantage.

Parents are faced with many challenges over the course of raising children. But at the moment, we face the usual challenges of parenthood compounded by the uncomfortable feeling that we're not really sure which childrearing rules apply and which have passed their expiration date. It's tough to make plans when we aren't sure what we're planning for. I've spent the last three years speaking to a wide range of experts around the country—captains of industry, military leaders, scientists, academics, and futurists—and their projections of our near future, say ten or twenty years down the road, range from life pretty much the way we know it, perhaps with tweaks in self-driving cars and package-delivering drones, to what is called the singularity, in which human intelligence and artificial intelligence combine in some sort of cyborg mash-up. I can't change this lack of consensus on what the future will bring. But I can help you to understand the price uncertainty exacts from us—from our ability to make good decisions, exercise our optimal parenting skills, and nurture our children's healthy development.

The more we know about how vulnerable our thinking can be under uncertain conditions, the more capable we'll be of making decisions that are clearheaded and in the best interest of our children. That's not to say that there is a single solution for all kids and all families. Every child is different, just as every family is different. However, child development is one of the more mature fields in psychology. We're not at a complete loss here, and the evidence suggests that we'll need to adjust some of our traditional assumptions about good parenting. We can look at the data, consider the science, and decide whether we want to shift our attention and intentions or not. As it stands, we are not preparing our children (or ourselves) very well for confronting an unpredictable, rapidly changing future. Just the opposite: in our efforts to protect our children from experiencing distress, we are unintentionally setting up the circumstances that nurture distress today and will surely exacerbate it tomorrow. We are unintentionally diminishing our children's capacity for resilience at the very moment that they need more of it than ever. Ways to help nurture that capacity, the various skills that, taken together constitute resilience, are at the heart of this book.

Fortunately, while there is a lack of consensus about what exactly the future will look like, there is far greater consensus about the kinds of skills our kids will need to flourish in the coming decades. As Darwin discovered more than 150 years ago, adaptability is the sustaining feature of those who not only survive but who thrive. If you have more than one child, you know that kids seem to come into this world with different degrees of adaptability. One child will only eat grilled cheese or spaghetti for a year or two and another seems to go from baby food to tacos and sushi with great enthusiasm. So can we cultivate adaptability? And what about those other attributes that are likely to give kids an advantage in our uncertain future—things like creativity, flexibility, curiosity, and optimism? As we learn about the science of epigenetics—the intersection of genetics and environment—we will see that we can, to a far greater degree than we assumed, cultivate these protective traits in our children. We'll learn how to inoculate our kids against the most disconcerting aspects of an uncertain future and maximize their ability to find fun, challenge, and fulfillment in exactly this kind of environment.

We will need to develop in ourselves a shift in attitude about how, in fact, most people become successful. I've spoken at hundreds of venues to a number north of 250,000 people about trajectories of success. I'm using "success" in a broad sense here. There are folks with large amounts of money and little self-worth. Others are "just getting by" but have fulfilling, happy lives they feel good about. Ultimately, success is an achievement that can only be defined by the person who feels successful. It's not about grades, colleges, salaries, or employment. It certainly can be, but not necessarily. And the vast majority of adults who consider themselves successful have had winding (what I call "squiggly") life paths. So we'll look at the benefits of a squiggly path going forward, the pressing need for moral clarity, as well as how to incorporate a more robust sense of community for all of us who too often feel isolated and alone.

In a popular quip, the scientist Alan Kay said, "The best way to predict the future is to invent it." If I remember right, when I had three children, a private practice, an ailing mother, a husband on too many on-call nights, and an ever-expanding list of responsibilities I never seemed able to meet, "inventing the future" was about the last thing on my mind. Since most of us find the demands of the present crowding out our ability to fully invest in the future, let's at a minimum commit ourselves to preparing our children for that future. Every generation adds to the repertoire of previous generations in fresh and unexpected ways. That is how we adapt, how we innovate, how we continue to move forward. In a time of great uncertainty, if we can raise children who know how to optimize that climate and who greet it with anticipation, optimism, and enthusiasm, we will have done our best to prepare them for a hopeful future they will gladly inherit and invent.

Ready or Not

PART I

Stuck

CHAPTER 1

Why the Needle Hasn't Moved

Doubling Down on the Past
When We Fear the Future

It was bad enough when I had to choose between attachment parenting, tiger parenting, authoritative parenting, and just following my gut. With everything changing so fast I'm more bewildered than ever.

—Sara, mother of a 9-year-old fourth-grader

I'm on another stage somewhere in the Midwest. For almost fifteen years, I've been crisscrossing the United States talking about rising rates of anxiety and depression in our kids, and more recently, about parenting challenges in our rapidly changing and uncertain environment. I've had the privilege of meeting with groups of all stripes: public, private, liberal, conservative, rural, urban, and most everything in between. But what has genuinely surprised me is the uniformity of concerns, regardless of the community I'm in. Parents want to know what to worry about and what they can safely take off their plates. They want to know how to prepare their kids to be successful in a future that seems so unpredictable. How to deal with the endless alarming news about children and teenagers. Most of all, they want to know how to protect their kids and ensure some stability for them in a world that seems anything but.

I'd begun my lecture with the latest numbers on anxiety and depression in adolescents, a subject sure to resonate with parents who are no strangers to anxiety themselves. "Statistics show an ongoing decline in the mental health of our kids," I told them. Anxiety disorders occur in almost a third of 13-to-18-year-olds.[1] From 2005 to 2014 the number of teenagers who experienced a major depressive episode increased more than 30 percent.[2] This translates into about 13 percent of teens suffering from full-blown clinical depression.[3] In the last ten years, the number of young people committing suicide has steadily increased as well. Suicide statistics, while profoundly disturbing, only begin to tell us how demoralized and hopeless many kids are feeling. For every completed death by suicide in young people aged 15 to 24, there are somewhere between 50 and 100 attempts that (thankfully) fail.[4]

The trends are upsetting but not irreversible, I say: "We know how to lessen our kids' distress and achieve better outcomes for them." And I share what an abundance of research reveals about how to raise children to be emotionally healthy and productive adults. *Engagement*, that is, optimism and enthusiasm about learning, coupled with high levels of motivation, is highly correlated with academic success.[5] Many types of workplace success depend heavily on *emotional intelligence*, the ability to recognize, understand, and manage one's own emotions and the emotions of others.[6] And few things predict emotional health as well as *self-regulation*, the internal guidance system that allows us to direct our behavior and control our impulses.[7] Finally, it is *parental adjustment*, especially mom's well-being, that has a critical and continuing impact on our children's well-being.[8]

I tell the assembled parents that if our children are to thrive in a world that is rapidly evolving and full of uncertainty, they need less structure and more play. They need to become comfortable with experimentation, risk-taking, and trial-and-error learning. Shielding them from failure is counterproductive. Our kids need to spend less time burnishing their résumés and more time exploring and reflecting.

I reassure the parents that I'm not downplaying the value of academic success or a financially rewarding job. On the contrary, I'm telling them how to make those outcomes more likely. There are only twenty-four hours in a day, and focusing primarily on one facet of a child's progress—typically academic or athletic performance—limits the attention paid to other important aspects of child and adolescent development.

The audience listens politely, but impatience is in the air. Well-educated and attuned to the latest in child-rearing theories, most of them have heard some version of this talk before, either from me or from like-minded colleagues. They're waiting for the Q and A. When it arrives, I brace myself for the questions I know are coming:

"My daughter loves art, but everything seems to be about technology. What should I encourage her to do?"

"I keep seeing that 'soft skills' like curiosity and creativity are the new hard skills. But can you even teach those things to children?"

"OK, so kids will need soft skills. But I don't see lots of high-paying jobs where the qualifications are 'compassionate problem-solving communicator.'"

"We don't pressure our son. We never have. He *wants* to take all those AP classes. Why should we stop him?"

"No matter what happens, a degree from Brown can't hurt, right?"

"What should my kid major in? Can't you just give me a list?"

These queries, full of societal angst, are the new normal. Parents are worried sick about their children's prospects in an unstable world teeming with threats near and far—whole categories of jobs disappearing, not just to other countries, but everywhere, forever; global financial upheaval; terrorist attacks; refugees in misery; the environment under assault from poisons and rising temperatures, and more recently, a whole year of missed in-person schooling. Their concern is not merely about career counseling or even happiness. It's about survival. Which is why it's so difficult for parents to reconsider the metrics that served them well in their own formative years—test scores, college admissions, that degree from Brown. They rightly ask, "What are we supposed to do instead?" And the answers I've been able to provide, while developmentally sound and emotionally beneficial, often don't strike them as enough fortification against the unknowable future their children face.

It's not that individual parents haven't been listening to messages such as mine. Mental health professionals and educators have helped many families turn down the heat on the high-pressure, high-stakes environment that has been throttling the creativity, engagement, and emotional well-being of too many children for the last few decades. More parents have become willing to enforce reasonable bedtimes, to see the wisdom of backing off on that one extra AP class, to tolerate the less-than-optimal GPA without insisting that their kid needs therapy or medication, or at the very least tutoring. Yet the statistics on our children's mental health remain grim.

While a good number of families—and even some communities and school systems—have introduced infinitely saner schedules and expectations for their children, the prevailing cultural norm remains singularly focused on nabbing the "gold star" regardless of cost. Parents (and too often their kids) see life as a zero-sum game with only

winners and losers. No parent wants his or her child to fall into the lat-
ter category. Our increasingly bifurcated economy adds plausibility to
this concern. The fallacy though is that pedal-to-the-metal living and
learning are likely to produce successful children. In fact, the opposite
is true. For most kids, having something resembling an old-fashioned
childhood—playing outside, meeting challenges without constant parental interference, being bored, having chores, taking some risks—is
far more likely to build the kinds of competencies kids have always
needed and that will be particularly important in the future.

But there's a wide gap between intellectually grasping that concept and committing oneself and one's child to it. Dads still tell
me their kids "can relax once they have a job." Moms fret that "we
can't swim upstream when the stakes are so high." As someone who
has put the well-being of children and teenagers at the center of my
professional life, watching parents and kids continue to struggle is
frustrating and painful. After every lecture I find myself thinking,
*What piece of the picture am I missing? There's a whole new set of
challenges demanding new solutions to be faced in our rapidly changing
world, and yet parents remain anxiously preoccupied with grades and
high-prestige colleges. Why won't the needle move?*

This book is my attempt to answer those questions, a quest that
took me far outside my comfort zone. I sought out not only my
usual sources of information, but also looked for people who had
spent much of their lives dealing with change. It meant talking to
naval admirals in addition to developmental psychologists, corporate CEOs in addition to clinicians, and neuroscientists in addition
to teachers. I wanted to suspend my assumptions and take a fresh
look at what might be the root causes of so much distress among
families, the unseen impediments to improvement, and most especially the strategies that work best to improve outcomes when living

in an unstable environment with little precedent. In many ways the journey I traveled to write this book was emblematic of the solutions I discovered. Stay open. Be curious. Collaborate. Get out of your comfort zone. Challenge your perspective.

With the Best of Intentions

Parenting today is full of ironies. Consider the fact that we're just as addicted to devices as our kids are, but we have much less fun: instead of obsessing over music or fashion blogs, we're drawn to doomsday news feeds reporting the latest food recall, deadly virus, or mass shooting. Adult anxiety has risen along with that of children and teenagers,[9] in large part because of the cultural tumult to which we're constantly exposed. Alarmed and unsure, we overprotect and overdirect our children even more than parents did a decade or two ago, turning our kids into risk-averse rule-followers. Yet that's exactly the opposite of the mindset they'll need if, as experts from multiple fields agree, adaptability, curiosity, risk-taking, and flexibility will be the survival skills of tomorrow. We reward young scholars for memorizing all the right answers, but in a rapidly evolving world it will be more important to ask incisive questions. Why? Because content is available with the swipe of a finger. What to do with that content, how to evaluate it and stitch it together with other content in new and important ways, is what will matter. Students are encouraged to compete for awards, trophies, and a few slots at top universities, but in the coming years a talent for collaboration will be far more valuable than a habit of ruthless competition. Time and again, I observe parents making decisions they hope will benefit their kids yet are more likely to debilitate them. In my clinical practice I see well-intentioned parents reflexively pushing their children toward metric success, unintentionally crowding out curiosity, creativity, and flexibility. These need not be either/or propositions. A healthy balance would serve most kids far better than a singular preoccupation.

At the root of this paradox is our "flat," technology-driven, climactically unstable world. No one, including the many experts I interviewed for this book, knows exactly what the future will hold. This unsettling reality has had a profound but subtle influence on parents' approach to child-rearing. Forces just under our radar are driving our decision-making. Parents know the world is changing but are largely unaware of how these changes are already affecting the way they make decisions about their kids. Besides, they reason, this isn't the first time our country has had to adjust to rapid change. True enough. But there are aspects of our moment in history that make it singularly challenging.

It Really Is Different Now

While every era may feel like both the best and worst of times, rarely have conditions across so many categories accelerated at the rate we're now experiencing. Within the past several decades, climate change has morphed from a distant Arctic threat to extreme weather conditions affecting every continent and spurring mass human migration. Globalization means that countries are increasingly specialized, which limits the range of valuable job skills and employment opportunities here and abroad. Technology that didn't exist ten years ago has altered how we communicate and form relationships, forcing change on the most intimate psychological level. Science plunges forward into areas that are at once exhilarating and

terrifying—genetic modification, biomedical engineering, and artificial intelligence, to name a few. News delivered via multiple portals
offers more information than we can possibly absorb. And because
the portals are driven by a profit motive, the news focuses far more
on the terrifying than the exhilarating. We're human: fear still sells;
optimism not so much.

Today's social change feels cataclysmic, so we look to the past for
perspective. The shift from an agrarian to an industrialized society
in the nineteenth century, waves of immigrants adjusting to the New
World at the dawn of the twentieth, World War I, the murderous
Spanish flu, the deep trauma of the Great Depression, the horrors
of the Second World War and the nuclear age, the upheaval of the
1960s and the Vietnam War—each of those eras, it could easily be
argued, was as challenging or more so than our own. Knowing that
those generations endured and thrived, we can feel fairly confident
we will too. But the dramatic disruptions of the last century—say,
from working on a farm to toiling in a factory, or from fighting in a
war to returning home—did not demand lifelong, continuous adaptation to a swiftly evolving environment. Our own age will. It's not
the fact of change, it's the velocity and relentlessness of it that makes
our era unique.

In this world, the old tropes about education and job security
become slippery. A degree from a top school is invaluable, but only
if you don't incur massive debt, and only in certain fields, and those
fields are shifting. There are fewer jobs for lawyers because technology has streamlined the research necessary to practice law, and sites
like LegalZoom meet many client needs.[10] The average physician
educated at a public institution accrues $180,000 in student debt,[11]
but the health care system is in flux, rendering potential income

impossible to calculate. Finance seems like a sure bet for now, but not every kid wants to be a hedge fund manager. Silicon Valley wizards who dropped out of the Ivy League are hailed as heroes (a fact every frustrated college freshman will at some point announce to his parents). But 90 percent of startups fail,[12] and of the 10 percent that succeed, only the founder and a few top executives are likely to see a significant payout.[13] STEM fields are supposedly surefire pipelines to employment, but in fact only computer science jobs are abundant.[14] An analysis based on employment forecasts from the Bureau of Labor Statistics concluded that by 2024, 73 percent of STEM job growth will be in computer occupations, with only 3 percent in life sciences and 3 percent in physical sciences.[15]

No wonder so many young people end up pouring beer at the microbrewery or opening an Etsy shop.

Even small children are increasingly anxious that the world they know is in existential danger. A colleague's 8-year-old patient became so convinced that "my dream of driving a truck will never happen" that he was unable to sleep unless he was in his parents' bed. His confused and worried parents kept assuring him that he would someday be able to drive a truck, but he had heard enough about autonomous vehicles to know that they were probably wrong.

In my practice I've seen the cumulative effect of all this instability and uncertainty; family and cultural dynamics that were undermining children ten, even twenty years ago are more entrenched and complex today. While parents may be more aware of the ways in which their kids are ill served, they are also more confused than ever about implementing new parenting strategies. There are five increasingly dysfunctional realms of parent/child interaction we need to correct both for the sake of improving our children's mental health and for ensuring that they have an enhanced opportunity to successfully navigate through rapid changes. They are:

- Unhealthy overachieving
- The false self
- Social isolation
- Feeling powerless
- A shaky sense of morality

Unhealthy Overachieving

Parents continue to harbor unreasonably high expectations of their children in multiple realms: academic, athletic, musical, artistic, social. There was a time when parents were more restrained and discreet when trying to prod their kids to greater heights. Now the pressure is often out in the open, not only from parents but also from peers and teachers. This overt pressure makes kids even harder on themselves and less forgiving of failure. The definition of failure itself has expanded from getting a D or an actual F (I haven't seen one of those in years) to bringing home anything less than an A. No surprise, then, that teenagers have little tolerance for thoughtful investigation as a way to learn. Deep learning and innovation require time and mental wiggle room, and these kids have little.

Much of my work with families is devoted to helping parents and kids dial down the drive to compete and win, instead focusing on activities that build the kinds of competencies kids will need both in school and in life. This means cultivating curiosity, encouraging experimentation, and acclimating children to risk and failure. It means redefining success from purely metrics-based to a much broader notion of what constitutes a successful and well-lived life: physical and emotional well-being, warm, supportive relationships, a sense of meaning and purpose, to name just a few. My concern about this has been so great that in 2007, with Denise Pope and Jim Lobdell, I cofounded Challenge Success, a program at the Stanford Graduate School of Education committed to providing families and schools with the practical, research-based tools they need to create a broader view of success and a healthier, more balanced and academically fulfilling life for kids.

Sadly, the parents who are receptive to this view may find that their teenagers are resistant to slowing down. They've been infected by peer pressure to compete and have internalized what has long been a cultural emphasis on rewarding individual accomplishment and competitive toughness. Increased anxiety about future jobs and resources has caused students—often more so than their parents—to ramp up perfectionism and competition rather than scale it back.

Regardless of how levelheaded parents may be, the culture of many schools (especially those in comfortable communities) is one of intense pressure. Gone is the collaborative spirit that was common when my oldest son was in public school a couple of decades ago, when the more advanced students would assist those who were struggling. A community effort, where kids reached across grades and ability levels to help one another, used to be part of a school's culture. This has been replaced by cutthroat competitiveness among students: "If you get into Vanderbilt, that's one less spot for me."

While high schools say they're attempting to scale back the academic pressure, the fact remains that whether they are public or private, they depend on rankings and scores to attract students, and those are based on test results and college admission rates of the graduates. Only Maryland and the District of Columbia require community service as part of the educational curriculum. Helping others is low on the list of most students' priorities, and schools haven't done much to counter that. As it now stands, despite the progress we've made in broadcasting the unhealthy consequences of an overemphasis on achievement and competition, and a neglect of collaboration and community involvement, many students are more driven toward individual achievement than ever. Let me be clear that this is not an argument against motivation or perseverance. But motivation and perseverance need to be in the service of something greater than simply one's last test score.

The False Self

When children feel pressured to perform brilliantly in the public realm and are rewarded for doing so, they have a hard time expressing or even recognizing what interests they actually enjoy, which friends they prefer, what really matters to them, where they stand. They're stuck in what psychologists call a *false self*: Ivy League–bound! Possible baseball scholarship! Queen Bee! These kids have been so successfully trained to seek external affirmation that they have difficulty turning inward and being reflective. They are overly dependent on the approval of others, including their peer group, teachers, and coaches.

Not only are today's teenagers creating a false self, they're also urged by the culture and their peers to create a social media self that often bears no resemblance to an authentic self. This persona is a stellar student/athlete/artist/musician/budding entrepreneur/social butterfly and also a compulsive chronicler of his or her triumphs. The correlation between social media and adolescent depression and anxiety is well documented: the decrease in life satisfaction, self-esteem, and happiness among teenagers over the past decade correlates with the arrival of iPhones (in 2007), Instagram (2010), and Snapchat (2011),[16] and texting as the most prevalent form of communication (2007).[17] As compared with adolescent boys, adolescent girls use mobile phones with texting applications more frequently and intensively.[18] [19]

The ill effects of social media are not limited to overt events such as online bullying, body shaming, or social exclusion. One colleague told me that his client, a 15-year-old boy, had vowed not to get involved with any girls in high school because of what he called "the audience." Girls would want to post selfies with him, he worried, which would then be rated in likes. The girls would be texting their friends, and the friends would weigh in on the boy's attractiveness, coolness, and whether or not he was texting the girl enough or saying the right things. Dating required a twenty-four-hour performance, no goofy comments or missteps allowed. The public exposure completely unnerved this boy and was delaying his social development. I have to admire his courage, though: he managed to figure out his own values despite intense peer pressure. And what about the girls? They're subject to exactly the same audience, with even greater scrutiny applied to their appearance. As they become more engaged with their online selves and less involved with real-life relationships, their development gets impaired too. A preoccupation with one's social media "self" delays and distorts the development of an authentic self.

Social Isolation

Whenever I've spoken at schools, I always ask middle-and high-school students what troubles them most about being a teenager.

I have them rank three common adolescent issues: developing an identity, feeling that they can make choices for themselves, and feeling isolated. Initially surprising to me, but by now expected, the vast majority of kids list social isolation as their biggest concern. For years before that identity, the previously defining issue of adolescence, came in first.

Technology is at the root of much of this isolation, and the reasons are complicated. There are aspects of tech, such as gaming, that provide lively community, and the Internet offers plenty of options for learning, creativity, and political action. As seen above, the problem is "the audience." For teenagers, especially 12-to-15-year-olds, the only thing that matters is what their friends think. All the traditional horrors of being fourteen are still true: Do you sit with the popular kids? Is your girlfriend going to steal your boyfriend? Do you have a zit? You call those boobs? But instead of being segmented into specific and predictable parts of the day—lunch, the walk home from school, a phone call or two, a whispered taunt when the teacher's back is turned—opportunities for humiliation are now constant, thanks to texts and social media.

There's a more subtle element driving the isolation as well. Texting makes it easy to be hard—easy to break up with someone without looking her in the eye and seeing the hurt on her face. It's not uncommon in my practice for kids to walk into my office crying and hand me their phone. The messages I've read in these situations vary from the merely inconsiderate to the outright treacherous. That's bad enough, but commiseration has also been relegated to text. When your girlfriend breaks up with you, six texts from your buddies calling her a bitch doesn't help all that much. You need a friend beside you; you need the familiar sight of him and the feel of his shoulder bumping against yours as he helps you walk off your blues. Historically, friends could spend hours unraveling hurt, providing support, and simply being a reminder by their presence that all is not lost. But today's kids are busy and have become accustomed to superficial contact. So instead of real consolation, all too often the most a friend can offer is a text full of emojis.

Face-to-face encounters are where children and adolescents learn empathy, diplomacy, and how to listen. Without tough or even heartbreaking real-life conversations, they get less practice at human interaction. In the coming years, which will bring frequent job changes and more collaborative work environments, people who have superior interpersonal skills will be at an even greater advantage than they are today. Those who lack such skills will have a harder time not only forming connections at work but also sustaining relationships with friends and romantic partners.

Given the documented increase in loneliness, depression, and anxiety associated with the use of smartphones and social media among teens, it is important that parents put limits on usage. It may feel good to have our kids at home, know where they are, and know what they're doing. But lying in bed, alone for hours at a time with only your phone for companionship, comparing yourself to enhanced versions of other kids, interferes with working through the developmental tasks of teens: risk-taking, separation and independence, intimacy, and moral development. We know that anything over two hours a day of time on YouTube, Instagram, Snapchat, Facebook (or whatever platform has since grabbed interest) has detrimental effects on kids' mental health.[20] We also know that over half of teens describe themselves as being on social media or the Internet "almost constantly."[21] For kids who have been wired from birth, setting limits on their usage is bound to be profoundly distressing to them. Parents, however, are not in a popularity contest and in the same way that we do our best to ensure our kids physical health with exercise, sleep, and nutritious food, we also have to guard their mental health even if it means tolerating some eye-rolling and slammed doors. Put down your phone for most of the day. Insist that your kids do the same.

The pandemic changed the practicality of much of this advice as kids were on screens for extended periods of time for school, socializing, and entertainment. We have yet to know the impact of this, and it will be hard to tease out given the isolation they were experiencing at the same time. But it is a natural experiment and will ultimately give us more information on what is gained and what is lost when kids are glued to their screens. As life returns to normal, I'm betting that the old rules about screen time will still apply.

Feeling Powerless

Agency is the belief that you have the power to take actions that will have an impact on your immediate environment. The alternative is feeling powerless, which leads to demoralization and victimization. By micromanaging children—not just at school but on play dates, on the soccer field, at grandma's, in the clothing store—parents hamper their kids' ability to discover themselves and advocate for their own agenda. It's true whether it's a 3-year-old who wants to wear mismatched socks or a teenager who wants to quit playing cello even though continuing might give her an edge in college admissions. Constant oversight also means the kids are protected from the mandatory bumps needed to learn that they can be challenged, even defeated, and recover. Or better yet, learn to savor the experience of being challenged. When children are denied the opportunity to figure out their own values, desires, and interests, the outcome is often a despairing dependency, the antithesis of healthy autonomy.

Ten years ago, my young patients were in a fury about the parental yoke: "It's my life! Tell my mom and dad to back off. I'll figure it out myself!" One of the most disturbing developments in recent years has been the fading of youthful rebellion among the teenagers I see. It's been replaced with resignation and a jaded demeanor I'd expect from folks many years older who had to work at jobs they despised in order to support a family or pay a mortgage. "You don't understand," these teens will say, shaking their heads. "There is no way out of the next three years. I'm just going to suck it up. I have no choice." The belief that you can't act on your own behalf is a significant contributor to depression at any age.

A Shaky Sense of Morality

In my sessions with students of middle- and upper-class families from the early 2000s onward, I saw the toll taken by an overly materialistic environment. It was a trend noted in a famous UCLA study called *The American Freshman: National Norms*, which compared the motivations of college freshmen in the 1960s to those of later classes.[22] In 1967, 86 percent of students said it was "important or essential to develop a meaningful philosophy of life." By 2004, fewer than 40 percent felt that way. A majority—73.8 percent— listed being "very well off financially" as important or essential. I saw the same orientation in many of my young patients, who favored the pursuit of money and "stuff" over personal, moral, and intellectual development.

When the Great Recession hit in 2007, families up and down the socioeconomic ladder were impacted. For some it prompted serious reassessment of basic values, and this was reflected in the 2016

American Freshman study. A majority of students (72.6 percent) still identified "making more money" as a very important reason to attend college, but they equally (75.4 percent) valued "gaining a general education and appreciation of ideas."[23] This is promising, but ethical lapses remain. In a 2012 white paper commissioned by Challenge Success, 97 percent of high school students admitted to cheating over the past year and 75 percent confessed to doing so multiple times.[24] Disturbingly, few of these kids saw their cheating as any kind of moral failure. "Cheat or be cheated" was the prevailing ethos, reflecting a teenage version of what unfortunately has too often become an adult credo.

Feeling pressured to achieve makes cheating even more tempting. Researchers who conducted interviews with high-achieving high-school juniors and seniors found that students attributed decisions to cheat to the pressure they felt from parents, teachers, and their peers; to feeling overloaded with schoolwork; and to the pressure they felt to get into elite colleges.[25] For these kids, cheating is a survival skill.

Adolescents would be less likely to engage in unethical behavior without the tacit encouragement of the adults around them. Since the early 2000s, the focus on admission to top colleges has had a corrosive effect on what used to be widely accepted standards of fair play (despite a general acknowledgment that money and connections have always given a small group an apparent advantage). This trend was not slowed by the Great Recession. For while it inspired some parents to reflect on their values, in other families it reinforced the parents' assumptions about how to avoid economic disaster. The only sure path to safety and security, they felt, was to be admitted to the most prestigious institutions, to cultivate a peer group with the highest ambitions, and to accrue wealth. To be sure, this works for a small number of students. But few kids are up to that ambitious path or even interested in it. Most don't belong at Harvard or Yale or anything like those schools. By definition most kids are average, yet many parents believe their kids are far above average. Combine that misperception with unease about future options, and parents feel justified in bending the rules.

In the past decade I've seen a rising tolerance among parents for rule-bending in the form of "editing" a child's papers, trying to get a child identified as learning disabled to gain more time for tests, providing excuses for absences or late assignments, and other varieties of gaming the system in order to enhance their child's academic résumé. It is highly unlikely that, while nationwide only 14 percent of kids have learning disabilities[26] and need additional time on the SATs, 50 percent of Greenwich, Connecticut, students are apparently learning impaired and need additional test time.[27] When parents regularly lie to, evade, and game the system on a child's behalf, it erodes that child's self-esteem, motivation, respect for authority and rules, and trust in institutions. Being urged, however subtly, to take part in the deception can throw a wrench into a child's moral development. We are codifying a preoccupation with individual performance at the cost of valuing a fair and ethical community.

The 2019 "Varsity Blues" college admissions scandal revealed the darkest side of this lapse in ethics. The vast majority of parents and students would never try to cheat and bribe their way into a college, but these crimes are at the end of a spectrum that begins with the rule-bending and paper-editing. Most profoundly disturbing was the impact the parents' behavior might have on their children. How much did the students know? Were they willing participants, or dupes? Some were tricked by their parents into thinking they had earned high SAT or ACT scores, when the parents had hired someone else to take a separate test and submit it in place of the teenager's. There is probably no greater blow to a child's confidence than for a parent to basically say, "No way would you make it into college on your own."

Most discouragingly, schools themselves have been caught cheating. From Atlanta to New York City to Philadelphia, teachers have altered answers on student competency tests, inflated scores on high-school exit exams, applied subjective criteria to math tests in order to raise overall results, or inflated facts about their incoming students.[28] A senior admissions officer at Claremont McKenna College in California admitted to inflating the SAT scores of incoming freshman over a six-year period.[29] The purpose was to boost the school's already high position in *U.S. News & World Report's* annual ranking of colleges. Other colleges were found to have similarly lied,[30] including Bucknell, Emory, and Iona College, to name a few. In keeping with a particularly destructive narrative that has become commonplace in many upper-middle-class communities, it apparently is not enough to be really good; one has to be the best or very close to it.

Children learn right from wrong by watching how the adults behave. Fortunately, many parents are terrific role models of honesty and integrity. Even so, Mom and Dad are just two tiny humans in a seemingly unmoored culture where the moral boundaries are vanishing. It's not just in academia. The anonymity of the Internet has spawned a million ways to cheat, troll, and intimidate without being held accountable. A U.S. president claims, with no evidence, that established news organizations are fake and reporters are enemies of the people. Ever-multiplying websites normalize extreme thinking. Reality seems up for grabs, morality mutable. In this atmosphere, and in a society that has often overvalued material gain and individualism, it's not hard for kids to conclude that what counts is winning by any means necessary.

Without a solid ethical grounding, children risk growing into adults who, however outwardly accomplished, lack emotional depth, have impaired social and family relationships, and are vulnerable to depression and despair. But the danger goes further and broader: in the many interviews I conducted, the recurring theme was ethical accountability. Issues that are critical today will be urgent tomorrow. Who will regulate AI? Who will have access to the extraordinary medical breakthroughs that are surely coming? How will technological research be controlled? What reasoning will shape our decisions about energy production and fossil fuels? How do we prevent democracy from deteriorating under authoritarian encroachment? "Winner takes all" isn't a moral philosophy that can successfully carry us through this century. Our children need to understand how to make complex decisions with moral implications and ramifications. More than any other area of concern I have after researching this book, I've concluded that it is exactly in this area of moral reasoning that the stakes are so high and our attention so lacking.

What Should We Do Instead?

Parents always want what is best for their children. But social currents driven in large part by our uncertain era keep pulling families off course. Not knowing what's coming next, or what to do for our kids in place of the things we've always done, has caused us to double down on the old ways. Uncertainty makes us conservative. High grades were thought to be the first stop on a rise to the top, elite colleges an almost certain ticket to professional and financial success, and competitiveness the mindset most likely to lead up the ladder.

There isn't anything wrong (and a lot right) with high grades, top schools, and a competitive nature. But our assumption that these will continue to be singularly important in the future is already being challenged. Google, Apple, and IBM no longer require college degrees of a significant number of their employees. The bias toward recruiting from "core schools" (Ivy League or similar) among many prestigious businesses, from J.P. Morgan to LinkedIn, is waning or extinct. "Too much talent is being missed" or "potential not pedigree" are the inevitable explanations. Collaboration is often at the top of the list of desirable qualities companies look for in job candidates. Google's Project Oxygen, designed to help the company identify the top ten skills of their most successful managers, discovered that interpersonal skills like the ability to communicate, collaborate, and listen dominated the list. Only a single technical skill made the list.[31] Being enthusiastic, motivated, and an avid learner may soon trump that degree from Yale. Not yet perhaps, but the future requires awareness of the likelihood of change. It requires looking forward, not backward.

Decades of research on the human response to unpredictability, risk, and ambiguity tell us that our brains do not function optimally under any of these conditions. We tend to make compromised decisions when probable outcomes are unclear. We like predictability and still have our savannah ancestors' DNA ordering us to escape or kill as quickly as possible when circumstances become uncertain and threatening. But we don't live on the savannah, and our children will be required to come up with far more complex solutions than fight or flee. How can we prepare them for a future we can barely imagine ourselves?

In attempting to answer that question, I delved into the heart of the dilemma: the nature of uncertainty. I studied how it affects our brains and how that influences our decision-making process, especially when it comes to decisions about our kids. I looked at the strong correlation between uncertainty and anxiety, and at how they amplify each other. I reviewed notes on the many families I've counseled and was able to trace a connection between anxiety, parental overprotection, and a condition called *accumulated disability*: the impairment of life skills and the ability to cope, adapt, and function. *Learned helplessness*, the belief that you are powerless to change your circumstances despite evidence to the contrary, can also be linked to the anxiety-fueled parental overprotection that's a by-product of our unstable age.

With awareness comes insight and a way forward. Psychologists have developed a number of effective strategies for managing anxiety, building tolerance for ambiguity, and restoring the skills and capabilities that our kids may currently lack. We can teach them how to cultivate optimism, encourage their appetite for experimentation, help them reframe failure as trial-and-error learning. If we're going to really walk the talk and serve as role models, we also need to make these emotional and mental adjustments ourselves.

Determined to provide parents with a tangible list of skills that will best position their children for the coming decades, I consulted with my usual array of educators, psychologists, and social scientists. Their input was enlightening but lacked the kind of real-world perspective I felt was essential, so I turned to leading thinkers in the corporate world and the military. This was far outside my expertise and comfort zone and also hugely counterintuitive: what could the goals of generals and CEOs have in common with those of parents and educators? But I was looking for people who have faced a set of problems that are multidimensional, constantly evolving, and unyielding to conventional approaches. These men and women had a wealth of practical and proven strategies to share. Innovators in the field of technology are connoisseurs of rapid change, so I sought their expertise as well. They're the first to get a handle on fundamental skills that will likely be crucial in the coming decades, such as statistics and data science. Their curiosity and enthusiasm for meeting uncertainty head-on can provide valuable instruction for parents.

In the course of interviewing these diverse women and men, I encountered dozens of personal stories about the unlikely paths that brought them to the fulfilling positions they currently hold. Casting my net wider, I searched for testimonies from people in various walks and at various stages of life. Their journeys were rarely a straight and certain road but usually a winding and squiggly one with many false starts and detours. Their stories are included here to offer encouragement for parents who find it unnerving to swim against the stream.

While change and uncertainty swirl around us, there is one fact that has held constant since research began on child development over a hundred years ago: parents have always played an outsized role in their children's development and continue to do so. In spite of an enormous amount of interest in child development, there has not been a corresponding appetite to learn more about the conditions under which parents are most likely to thrive. With the majority of mothers now working, and increasingly spending time and emotional reserves cultivating their children, a better understanding of how to reduce their distress and increase their well-being could be foundational in helping to correct escalating rates of emotional problems in children and feelings of inadequacy, failure, and isolation in moms. Fathers find themselves increasingly involved in parenting, even being primary caregivers, with little precedence or infrastructure to guide and support them. The modern family comes in multiple iterations with complex challenges that have barely been looked at. Helping children adjust to conditions of extreme change means knowing something about how we sustain ourselves while we adjust to change. I've devoted a chapter to this critical topic.

No discussion of turning around the anxiety and isolation embedded in living in uncertain times is complete without a close look at what we value and the state of our communities. We'll consider these in the book's final chapter. When a single swipe or tweet can destroy a reputation or alter a set of data, when "bad actors" and unrestrained technology can threaten our country and our world, we must be certain that our children can face these challenges armed with a well-developed moral compass. Values are cultivated and reinforced in our local communities. We need to explore what we lose when we focus exclusively on our family and turn our backs to our neighborhoods and to the wider world. We need to change that so that we and our children can lead lives that are less isolated and fearful, and so that all of us in our increasingly interconnected world can thrive. Of course, most of our effort goes into taking care of ourselves and our families. But we also must accept the responsibilities of being global citizens if we hope to have our kids inherit a sustainable and just world.

To Bravely Go Where No Parents Have Gone Before

Neurologist Robert Burton, author of *On Being Certain*, says the future is like an Alexander Calder mobile: "Touch one piece and all the pieces move. Now imagine the mobile has thousands of pieces, each affected by the movement of all the others." Whether or not we would have chosen to live in this ever-shifting landscape, it's where we find ourselves. For our children's sake, we'd best learn to navigate its randomness and appreciate its beauty.

The future may well hold remarkable opportunities for our kids to live lives that are longer and more varied, healthy, and productive than those of any previous generation. Along with preparing them for the uncertainty of this century, we need to remind them and ourselves that the experience is likely to be extraordinary. They'll talk about their youth to their own children, perhaps with awe and gratitude that they were raised during such a challenging, fascinating, and unprecedented era.

It's only natural for parents to be more focused on tomorrow's negative possibilities than its positive potential. Fear of the unknown and resistance to change is hardwired into our brains. It's an evolutionary survival response. How do we liberate ourselves? We start by learning how the brain processes uncertainty so we can more easily override these ancient responses and take a fresh and open-minded look at how best to prepare our children for all the uncertainty, opportunity, and astonishing change likely to occur in their lifetimes.

CHAPTER 2

Your Brain on Uncertainty

Why We Make Dubious Decisions

Matthew is a 17-year-old high-school senior; his dad is an engineer and his mom teaches part-time at the local community college. They are smart, concerned, and are active members of the community. Matthew is very bright and extremely athletic (actively being recruited for a football scholarship), but he has had some behavioral problems around authority. He tends to make up his own rules and as a result has spent a considerable amount of time talking with his counselor and the school principal about some of his actions, like painting graffiti on school walls and repeatedly being late for class. His parents have consulted with me from time to time about his behavior, but ultimately they feel that his "smarts" will make up for his "teenage exploits."

On a late Saturday evening I get a frantic call from Matt's mom telling me that her son has been in a car accident and the police found alcohol in his system. His folks had rushed to the police station, posted bail, and called me. They want to discuss next steps. I feel strongly that Matt, with his history of mild antisocial behavior, needs to face the consequences of his actions. His license will undoubtedly be suspended and he may have to do community service.

He has not been held responsible for his actions for too long. In a short year, Matthew will be in college without the (dis)advantage of parents who reliably soften consequences for him. I worry that he has not developed the self-regulation skills he will need in such a loosely supervised environment. After two days of intense conversations with both Matt and his parents, they make the decision to hire a lawyer to get the charges thrown out on a technicality. They report this decision to me quite sheepishly but are clear that "one mistake could ruin his college scholarship chances. Admissions are so unpredictable. We're just not willing to take that risk."

This story is emblematic of the questions that drove me to write this book: Why are smart, well-intentioned parents who know all the latest research about child-rearing giving their kids (and themselves) a pass on issues like honesty, being responsible, and doing the right thing? Matt's parents certainly knew that the right decision was to have their son face the consequences of his behavior, but their good sense was overridden by something I was struggling to understand. Fear? Anxiety? Shame? And, of course, this is not an isolated or particularly unusual scenario. Parents continue to provide alcohol at their kids' parties, complete their unfinished homework, blow off shoplifting, and tolerate the occasional Adderall popping for potentially higher grades. We're all vulnerable to these lapses. And we all know better.

I've come to believe many of our questionable choices are driven by neurological, biological, and cultural influences of which we are barely aware. Not only parents, but most adults, are unfamiliar with the powerful forces that drive the way we perceive threat, process uncertainty, and subsequently make decisions.

Think of this chapter as a user's manual for the brain. It describes the motivating factors behind the pained refrain I frequently hear: "I know she should (eat more, sleep more, relax more, do less), but all the kids are like this and I just can't seem to make the change." It outlines the basics of brain science and connects the dots between unconscious processes and parental decision-making. Choices about our kids are always tough, and we happen to be operating in an era that makes them even tougher. The more we understand about how our brain functions under current conditions, the more astute we'll be when faced with dilemmas such as whether an academic preschool trumps a Montessori school, whether an internship at a global financial institution will serve our kid better than one at a local nonprofit, or even whether to enforce consequences or give our kids a pass for driving illegally.

To Live Is to Predict

The conscious brain's main purpose is to make predictions. Jeff Hawkins, coauthor of *On Intelligence*, explains: "Prediction is not just one of the things your brain does. It is the primary function of the neo-cortex and the foundation of intelligence."[1] To deal with uncertainty, we enlist the neurobiology of prediction—that is, we assess the environment and guess what will happen next. Keep in mind that there is considerable overlap of function among different areas of the brain and that there is still a great deal we don't understand. We're closer to the beginning than the end. Still, there is a lot we've learned about how different conditions affect our thinking and especially our decision-making.

The brain is made up of four parts: the cerebellum, brain stem, cerebrum, and limbic system. The cerebellum and brain stem are devoted to essential body functions like balance, heartbeat, and breathing. The other two parts are what we're concerned with. The cerebrum and limbic system control our thinking and emotions.

The cerebrum is responsible for higher functions such as speech, hearing, vision, and comprehending information. The prefrontal cortex, a part of the cerebrum, is the seat of creative thought, problem solving, judgment, attention, and abstract thinking. This collection of attributes is sometimes called executive function.

The limbic system regulates hormones, processes emotions, forms memories, and ensures survival. It activates feelings such as anger, sadness, and fear. It alerts us to potentially threatening situations, ensures that we remember those threats so we can be safe in the future, and prepares the body for escape or defense. One of its other functions is to act as a relay station for controlling aggression.[2]

The prefrontal cortex and limbic system are at work every moment of our waking lives. To move through the world, we're constantly making decisions based on our prior experiences and the level of threat we perceive. The brain loves predictability because the threat level is already known, so whatever decisions we need to make require less energy and generate less stress than when the degree of threat is uncertain. While once this function was about keeping us safe from tigers, it's now about getting us through the day. Say you're picking up your child from school at three o'clock. Imagine the anxiety if you didn't know which exit she'd be using, whether your car had enough gas to get home, where the nearest gas station was, what currency the gas station accepted? All the things we *don't* have to think about enable us to proceed smoothly through our days and keep our stress levels down.

Moment by moment, we assess our environment. When faced with a choice, we weigh risk against reward. Our brain processes information calmly and efficiently as long as circumstances are not threatening. But if we're presented with a situation that seems risky—physically, psychologically, or socially—the brain perceives it as danger, the limbic system overrides our prefrontal cortex, and we go into *alarm,* the first stage of the stress response. Our heart rate, breathing, and blood flow increase as our energy surges. We're in full flight-or-fight mode. This often happens so quickly that we don't fully "see" the danger, as when we swerve to avoid an oncoming car.

When the immediate danger passes, the second component of the stress response system, *resistance*, is activated. The hormone cortisol is released, keeping us revved up and on high alert. Maybe the car didn't hit us, but we're still shaky, furious, and filled with an urge to confront the driver. We remain focused on the source of the threat. A gorilla could dance across the street and we wouldn't notice it (an oft-cited experiment with a man in a gorilla suit proved exactly this point).[3] As we calm down, our cortisol level subsides, the prefrontal cortex regains control, and we enter the third stage of the stress response: *exhaustion*. Surviving the threat, even when it's just a driver cutting us off, leaves us fatigued and depleted. All this occurs in a matter of seconds or a few minutes.

For most people in the developed world, life-and-death risks are remote or occur very rarely. But for millions of human beings such dangers are still commonplace (for example, refugees or people living in war-torn countries or crime-ridden neighborhoods). Maybe that's why our limbic system is still so sensitive. It can overreact and isn't always adept at differentiating between a minor annoyance and an actual threat. Imagine you're dropping your fifteen-year-old daughter off to meet her friend at the movies. The friend isn't there. You text the friend's dad and he doesn't text back for one minute, then three, then five. Your brain goes into overdrive. Did you get the date wrong? The time? The theater? Did he? Is he not responding because he's driving? Should you leave your daughter at the theater, or wait, or call him again, or . . . or . . . or. . . . It's an exhausting amount of energy spent on something ordinary and certainly not life-threatening. You either wait or not, depending on what you know about your child and the neighborhood. But when we think a threat may endanger our child in some way, we often switch into overdrive in situations that warrant a far lighter level of concern. In my office, teens are often more perplexed than angry about how overreactive their parents can seem.

The cascade of responses that occur when we feel threatened are conducive to survival but not necessarily to good parental decision-making. When we don't have enough information or experience to reliably assess risk, or when the information we do have is ambiguous, a fear response is triggered.[4] The surest way to make it go away is to make a quick decision. Even if our decision is not ideal, it will likely relieve the racing heart, the shortness of breath, the high blood pressure, and the tense muscles. This is where the ability to calm down, whether by taking a few deep breaths or stepping back for a moment or two of meditation, can be invaluable.

Delving into Uncertainty

How the brain makes decisions under conditions of uncertainty has fascinated scientists for nearly sixty years. Researchers from multiple disciplines have contributed to the field, including psychologists, biologists, and behavioral economists. *Repeated studies confirm that people prefer to make choices based on known variables even if making a slightly less certain choice could potentially lead to greater reward.*[5] When there is no pressure at all and the only thing at stake is, for example, winning a gift card, study participants still consistently favor known odds over the unknown, even if unknown odds could result in a much higher payoff. This human response is key to understanding parental decision-making in our unstable era.

We've seen that uncertainty is stressful. In 2016, researchers Katrin and Matthias Brand published a meta-analysis of more than 30 studies (nearly 64,000 people) on the effect of stress on decisions and found that under stressful conditions:[6]

- WE SEEK IMMEDIATE REWARD. Because stress feels bad, we want to alleviate it as soon as possible. Therefore we choose an option we can quickly deploy, even if reason tells us it might be a bad choice in the long run. ("This is driving me crazy. I just need to make a decision and make it now.")
- WE RUSH THOUGH AMBIGUITY. Under normal conditions, when faced with a choice where the details are ambiguous, we seek feedback and do research. Stress compels us to skip over those steps and decide using incomplete data. This increases the likelihood of a poor outcome.[7] ("It's too complicated. I'm just going to trust my gut.")
- WE GLOSS OVER POSSIBLE DRAWBACKS. Eager to justify our swift decision by associating it with a high reward, we make choices we might reject if we weren't stressed. ("It's going to work out fine! No guts, no glory.")

When the Stakes are High and Time Is Running Out

Two other aspects of decision-making are especially relevant to parents. They don't directly relate to uncertainty, but when added to uncertain conditions they can exacerbate our tendency to make poor decisions. One aspect involves how people process high-stakes, rarely occurring decisions. Choosing between surgery and physical therapy following an accident is one example.[8] For parents, this category might include choices like where to buy a house or which preschool to select. The researchers noted, "Life offers few opportunities to train for decisions where the consequences of a poor choice are large and, once made, difficult to reverse." The following responses are common among people faced with high-stakes decisions:

- WE DOWNPLAY OR DISREGARD PROBABILITY DATA. Whether assessing the risk of an investment or of living near a nuclear waste site, survey respondents tended to believe that bad outcomes wouldn't happen to them. Like when a parent says, "I know new drivers shouldn't have other kids in the car. But he's really a good driver and besides they're just going a short distance. They'll be fine."

- WE FOCUS EXCESSIVELY ON SHORT TIME HORIZONS. It's always difficult for people to envision the future consequences of today's actions. Therefore, the glory of getting our child into a coveted elementary school may outweigh the consideration of what a daily commute to its distant location will mean for our family over a period of six years.

- WE FOCUS ON INFORMATION THAT RESONATES WITH US EMOTIONALLY. An easy example: *U.S. News & World Report* college rankings. By now we all know the limitations of the metrics they use, but years of emotional investment in the list makes it difficult for parents to place it in proper perspective among more useful and better-researched data.

- WE RELY EXCESSIVELY ON SOCIAL NORMS. With little personal experience to fall back on and facing a set of complex and uncertain variables, many people make the same choice the rest of the group is making. "My son is doing very well in math, but everyone around here hires a math tutor for their kids. I don't want him to be disadvantaged, especially with the SATs coming up. A tutor can only help. Right?"

- WE MAKE NO DECISION AND STAY WITH THE STATUS QUO. When faced with complex decisions, people will often just continue with whatever they have been doing. This tendency is called a *status quo bias*. "I know Hannah is on her iPad too much, but all her friends have one and if I take it away she'll feel left out. Maybe she'll get tired of it when school starts."

Another wrench is thrown into the decision-making process when time pressure is added. Time pressure increases stress, and like stress it results in people more often making hasty and unwise choices. When the clock starts running down we speed up our processing, which may result in only partially absorbing information. We also filter the information according to our biases, meaning we subconsciously select what we want to hear. Overall, we become more impulsive, relying on gut feelings as opposed to reason so we can quickly reach a conclusion and end our discomfort.[9]

Real-World Consequences

What does all this mean for parents? Your mother is very excited about a program that is supposed to accelerate your baby's learning. She proudly presents you with Disney's Baby Einstein video, certain that this will mark the first step in your son's stellar intellectual development. She instructs you to turn it on every morning.

You're aware that Baby Einstein has been shown to actually slow language acquisition.[10] You don't want to disappoint your mom, you're tired, and besides maybe the data is wrong. You feel pressured because she's standing right in front of you with the video. So against your better judgment you start your toddler's mornings with Baby Einstein.

With performance in elementary school touted as the crucial first step in a successful academic career, you hold your son back a year rather than register him for the age-appropriate kindergarten. "Everyone knows" redshirting will give him an advantage over his peer group because he'll be one year taller and more mature. You overlook (or never attempt to find) research on redshirting, which indicates that the benefits of being older in kindergarten sharply decline by later grades and vanish by high school. Additionally there are long-term benefits to being among the youngest in a class because older classmates model high achievement and good behavior.[11]

When your 17-year-old daughter is frantic that her friends will make other plans if she doesn't invite them to her birthday party *this week* because another girl is having a party the same night with alcohol and a DJ, you agree to let her have a keg at her party too. You tell yourself you'd rather have her drink at your house than at some stranger's, and you disregard research showing that endorsing kids' drinking at home is a risk factor for substance abuse.

All these decisions are made under some sort of external pressure and without enough investigation because we're emotionally and mentally overextended. When we don't have a lot of experience parenting, it seems like every decision is complex, ambiguous, pressing, and critical. Too often we fall back on fear and capitulation, two of the worst filters for making thoughtful decisions.

A World of Risk: Parental Insomnia Edition

Before we take a closer look at how uncertainty affects the way parents make decisions, consider all the sources of fear we typically contend with.

PANDEMIC. Will our kids ever make up the year of school most of them have lost? How will they recover from the disruption and isolation?

JOBS. Which ones will survive? What will be automated? What will be outsourced? What will be irrelevant?

TECHNOLOGY. Will artificial intelligence liberate us or obliterate us? Is tech changing our society in ways we can't comprehend and are not even privy to?

SOCIAL MEDIA. Uncontrollable and addictive!

MENTAL HEALTH. Are all these frightening rates really rising? What are we doing wrong?

SOCIAL SAFETY NET. Will there be one? Or will we all have to fend for ourselves?

SOCIAL UNREST AND DIVISION. Justice inequality. Racism. Sexism. A polarized nation.

INCOME INEQUALITY. A zero-sum game: Am I a winner or a loser? What about my child?

SOCIAL ISOLATION. Lack of community, lack of common cause.

TERRORISM. Domestic and foreign, cyber and nuclear.

GUN VIOLENCE, SCHOOL SHOOTINGS. Politicians' unwillingness to deal with it makes it feel inescapable and inevitable.

CLIMATE CHANGE. Fires, floods, droughts, superstorms, mudslides. Can we stem the trajectory or is it unstoppable?

Some of these fears are overblown: we're not likely to get killed by a foreign terrorist (we're more likely to die walking, biking, or choking). But many parental concerns are legitimate. The overlapping of social media and a twenty-four-hour news cycle makes deciding what to worry about (and controlling our panic) a task in itself. We overestimate some dangers and underestimate others. The term *mean world syndrome* was coined in 2002 by George Gerbner to describe how watching violent content on television led viewers to believe the world was more violent than was actually the case. Two decades later, there are many more news platforms than just television. Constant exposure to distressing images impacts our brains by further sensationalizing and "emotionalizing" bad events. We feel more directly threatened and become hypervigilant.

Curating the flood of incoming data from the media and our assorted devices is an invaluable skill, but most parents don't have the hang of it yet. While our kids are digital natives, we are digital immigrants often struggling to make sense of more information than we can possibly work through. So we worry. This insomnia-provoking list is only a partial one, embellished by each parent with his or her own specific fears. Against this relentless buzz of anxiety, family life plays out. Anxiety makes it hard to accurately assess danger and create plans to address it. It's reasonable to assume that as anxiety accumulates over the years, our ability to evaluate risk becomes less reliable.

We see this in the shift in concerns about allowing children to play without supervision. Parents are hesitant to give their kids free range around the neighborhood, citing fears of abduction and violence. In fact, the rates of both are considerably lower than in previous eras. The truth is there has never been a safer time to be a child in America. Yet it simply doesn't feel that way. And as we've seen from the research above, our gut feeling about something as sacred as our children's safety trumps thoughtful reasoning.

What About Expert Advice?

In days gone by (the last couple of generations), parents relied on a select group of child-rearing gurus to guide them. Dr. Spock from the 1950s through the seventies, T. Berry Brazelton and Penelope Leach from the eighties through the aughts. *What to Expect When You're Expecting* seemingly forever (I read it while pregnant with my second son in 1984 and my lately pregnant daughter-in-law read it recently). Looking back, it's remarkable the degree to which parents were all on the same page. I clearly recall the shelf or two that comprised the entire "Parenting" section of my local bookstore—bricks-and-mortar version, pre-Amazon. The Internet exploded that quaint village.

If a way to alleviate the anxiety of uncertainty is to obtain more information, why doesn't the bottomless supply that's now available solve the problem? There are several reasons. The most obvious is the sheer volume of resources is too much for the average parent to digest. Time pressure is a second challenge. We're all short on time, so even if we had the motivation to research every issue, most of us don't have the spare hours. Then there's the matter of figuring out which experts to trust. Instead of a few books and parenting magazines, there are countless outlets featuring everyone from clinical psychologists to researchers to mommy bloggers. Which of these alleged experts have actual expertise? This is where confirmation bias may kick in: we're drawn to people whose opinions align with what we already believe.

The final hurdle is the lack of consensus among the experts we decide are trustworthy. Rapidly evolving research, for example on the effects of tech and social media on the developing brain, make respected professionals wary of taking a stand. Are video games good or bad for children? The inevitable answer is, "Both!" Bad if done to the extreme and potentially good in moderation (but we don't know exactly how much is too much). The same could be said of attachment parenting, being a "tiger mom," encouraging free range kids, and so on.

As we've seen, the more uncertain the circumstances, the more anxious we feel, and the sooner we want to make a decision in order to end the anxiety. A geyser of conflicting information makes us less certain, not more. Still, we must somehow assess risk. So for better or worse, we tend to fall back on our personal history and the advice of people in our immediate circle: other parents, the teacher, the coach, the college counselor. Too often that means simply seeking and reinforcing the biases we started out with.

The Fog of Uncertainty

As children grow, their challenges and responsibilities mount. When they start to show signs of anxiety or depression, competing forces in the parent's mind intensify. They would never risk their child's mental health, but the experts disagree: Are kids today coddled babies or stressed-out overachievers? Do they need grit or time off? Coach says the boy is a talented pitcher, and thousands of dollars have been spent nurturing that talent. Do you encourage your son to take a break when he loses interest or shows significant signs of stress, or do you urge him to tough it out? What about his chances for a sports scholarship? Admission to a school that would otherwise be out of reach?

As the questions pile up, our parental uncertainty rises too. I've watched this scene unfold many times, and the possible outcomes for the child are scary: substance abuse, self-injury, illness, burning out in freshman year of college. Parents of course fear these outcomes, but they seem to equally fear a different outcome: missing the gold ring by just a few grade points, blowing the chance at that top-tier school. Coach, the other parents, the college counselor, and perhaps the grandparents all form a community that may favor "grit" over "quit." With so much seemingly at stake and the future unknown, parents start losing their ability to accurately gauge risk against reward. Most lack a clear concept of the long-term advantages their child might gain by pivoting in a different direction from community standards—advantages such as practice standing up for himself, resisting the status quo, articulating his point of view, investigating other options, and acquiring a sense of agency. All these skills are likely to serve a child at least as well as playing a season of high-school baseball.

Sometimes it's the children themselves who make the situation cloudy. I'm thinking of a high-school junior who was passionately devoted to the debate team and Model U.N. Her parents brought her to me because although she was a skilled speaker and an A student, things clearly were not going well for her. She was eating too much and gaining an unhealthy amount of weight, her back hurt, she was getting sick a lot, and she was often teary. She wasn't falling apart to the extent that she needed hospitalization or even medication, but she was showing enough physical symptoms that her parents were rightly concerned.

The girl refused to scale back her activities or workload. She lectured her parents and me about the sacrifices top scholars must make, and reminded us that if she quit Model U.N. she wouldn't be able to attend the annual conference held in Philadelphia, which would in turn (she believed) hurt her chances of getting into her dream school, the University of Pennsylvania. She begged to be allowed to stay in her clubs. In the end the parents agreed with their daughter: the risk of stopping was greater than the risk of what they decided were tolerably mid-level symptoms.

This mom and dad, like so many I know, were a bit awestruck by their daughter's determination. Her competitive spirit seemed nobler than their misgivings. Undeniably, the daughter was gifted intellectually and had an admirable work ethic. But how much of her drive was a result of having internalized the "college über alles" values of her parents and the school community? Maybe she truly was a born competitor. There are a number of kids who can manage and even thrive on a great deal of pressure and extremely demanding schedules. But when our kids show significant signs of distress, we need to step back from their intense lobbying and see all the possible ramifications of their workload and commitments. Physical symptoms are often the very first indication that a child is not managing stress well. We have to remember that whether it's kid pressure, community pressure, or cultural pressure, caving is rarely our best option. Do not shy away from taking a different point of view. No one knows your children as well as you do. Your first job is to maintain their safety, and this includes their mental health.

This girl's parents held the common misconception that teenagers' poor habits can easily be changed later in life. It's an example of how our environment can radically skew our beliefs. A dad in Atlanta told me, "You can always catch up on sleep and the emotional stuff later, but you can't undo bad grades and low test scores." Every bit of evidence we have actually points in the opposite direction. The prognosis for exhausted and emotionally spent kids is not good. You can always take the SAT or organic chemistry again, but it's tougher to learn life skills that you've skipped over or to recover from substance abuse or mental illness.

Unfortunately, kids buy into their parents' misperceptions. They, too, think they can catch up on the emotional stuff later. A psychiatrist friend told me about a high-school senior whose parents brought him into treatment for trichotillomania (hair-pulling disorder). The young man assured my colleague, "I'll stop pulling my hair out as soon as I get into my dad's alma mater." Unlikely. Reversing poor coping skills is a tricky business. As with most things in life, the development of good coping skills requires practice—and not the kind that involves yanking out hair and plucking eyelashes.

It's not only AP classes and a grueling academic workload that can undermine a teenager's well-being. Sports, music, competitions, and other high-profile endeavors our kids are passionately devoted to may take a toll as well. Parents often assume these pursuits are far more vital to a student's success than they turn out to be. High schools don't dissuade parents from these assumptions—everyone wants kids to go for their dreams. When a child shouts, "My future depends on this!" we may doubt our own instincts. What to an outsider are obvious red flags—eating disorder, frequent crying, poor health—are easier to downplay when we're in an environment that tells us the real risk is removing our child from the club, the team, or the class.

Cognitive Dissonance

If being uncertain makes us uncomfortable, so does the cognitive dissonance that results when we make poor decisions and the evidence starts mounting that we might have been wrong. Cognitive dissonance refers to the uncomfortable feeling we have when we're in a situation involving conflicting attitudes, beliefs, or behaviors. It's an occupational hazard when you're a parent bombarded with conflicting information.

We reduce the discomfort of having contradictory beliefs, or of being confronted with new information that contradicts our beliefs, in a number of ways. Consider a common source of parental anguish: overworked kids getting too little sleep. Here's how we might soothe our stress over allowing the child to stay up late to study even though we know that sleep deprivation is bad for kids:

- We justify our behavior by challenging the conflicting information: *Eight hours? Nine hours? Ten hours? All those sleep studies contradict one another. I'll wait until they have more info.*
- We justify our behavior by adding new cognitions that align with our beliefs: *My friend's kid only sleeps six hours a night and he's doing fine.*
- We seek information that aligns with our existing beliefs and challenges the conflicting information: *One or two Adderall never hurt anyone. I hear the military uses it to keep pilots awake and alert. She's doing well. That's all that matters.*

The worldview that supports these justifications generally reflects the values of the community we live in and our assumptions about what will be best for our children's future. Detach even a little bit from that worldview, and healthy priorities become much easier to set. I want to be really clear that this is a tough ask. Not just the relentlessness of parenting decisions, but equally important, the pace of our own lives has accelerated to a point where it is difficult to make slow, thoughtful decisions. The best advice I was ever given by a psychiatrist colleague when I was wrestling with tough decisions about my kids and my work was "Sleep on it." It's thirty years later. I still do.

Our Kids Learn How to Make Decisions by Watching Us

As we cycle through our decision-making days, our kids are learning by osmosis. Initially they depend on us for everything, so they get a great deal of practice observing our moves and habits. They're attuned to the power structure in our family, just as we were at their age. Who's the best parent to ask about staying home sick? Going to a friend's on Friday night? Buying the new video game? Which parent is more impulsive, guilty, moody, pliable? As you react to the various choices each day presents, your kids often know how you'll respond before you do. They learn how to weigh options by watching you in the throes of indecision. And they learn what to be anxious about by seeing how you respond to current events, unexpected demands, and unpleasant surprises.

Many parents don't seek their children's opinions about critical choices, so the kids are bystanders and gain decision-making skills based on the family's communication style. Is there a lot of discussion in front of them, or do issues get worked out via text and late-night chats out of the kids' earshot? Does the discussion often devolve into a fight or a power struggle? While many parents are committed to teaching their children about manners and sharing, the nuanced process of decision-making often escapes our radar because decisions are complicated, time-consuming, and we'd just as soon not have any additional conflict with our kids.

Once a parent has made a difficult choice that involves the child—or one they know the kid will object to—a common tactic is to offload the decision to a "higher authority" in an attempt to avoid the child's wrath. "Your coach said you need Saturday practice." "Grandma is paying for summer camp and she wants you to learn to play golf." "I've talked to your French teacher and he's sure you can handle fourth-year French." There's nothing wrong with taking other people's viewpoints into consideration, but in the end these decisions should be ours and, to an appropriate extent, our children's. If our opinion is going to hold the most sway, we should own it. Sidestepping responsibility for an unpopular decision is a ploy our kids see through. Ideally, we should be able to explain our reasoning (but we're not required to defend it endlessly in the face of their objections). Whether or not our kid approves isn't the point; it's that we're teaching them by example how to make decisions and explain them to others. When twenty-somethings feel compelled to post Instagrams about "adulting," we have probably missed far too many opportunities to include our children in some of the more challenging parts of growing up, including making tough decisions.

As we become more comfortable managing uncertainty and the anxiety it engenders, we can become more appropriately transparent with our children about our decision-making process: thinking out loud as we decide, asking for their input, and demonstrating ways to interpret, prioritize, and weigh information. We can also take a cue from the SEL (social-emotional learning) programs that have become valuable in so many schools. While our kids are learning about how the brain works and simultaneously developing and applying the knowledge, attitudes, and skills needed to be self-aware and in control of their emotions, we should be working on the same things. Both parents and kids need to take a deep breath and calm down.

Prediction Errors and "Oops" as an Opportunity to Learn

Much of this chapter has focused on the discomfort and dangers of unpredictability. But there's a bright side to it as well because *the brain learns best when its predictions are wrong.* This is called the prediction error signal. It is in that gray space between what we anticipate and what actually happens that we absorb new information, make new inferences, and reach new conclusions. When we "get it wrong" we have the chance to rethink the problem, challenge our assumptions, consider alternatives, and move closer to getting it right.

Think about it this way: a major goal in life is to be able to make accurate predictions of future events in order to be prepared when these events arrive so that we can adapt efficiently. When the velocity of change is extraordinary, as it is now, the best way to help our children become adaptable is to help them become comfortable with prediction errors. Those who see errors as opportunities to learn and try again are the people who will most quickly find new solutions. (This is how our children become resilient.) Those who freeze and panic when they make mistakes will find it much harder to adapt.

I once had a 6-year-old in my office working on a rather difficult puzzle. I worried that she'd be frustrated by all her unsuccessful attempts to get the puzzle pieces to fit. When I asked her if she wanted help, her quick response was, "No, this is way too much fun." You can bet I would have stayed in my office all night just to wait until this eager and confident child completed the puzzle on her own. Actually, it didn't take that long. The fact that she was unfazed by her mistakes allowed her to learn quickly.

This is why the ability to tolerate and learn from failure is so valued by employers. Without failure, we stay hidebound and stuck in the status quo. While that may have been a successful strategy when businesses focused on singular products, it is the worst possible strategy in a constantly evolving environment. Everything from Post-it notes to penicillin to ink-jet printers to x-rays were "mistakes." None of the people working on these projects set out to develop them, but in the process of making mistakes they were able to see alternative uses. One of the positive aspects of the current era is that businesses actively encourage the conditions that will spark these serendipitous discoveries. Many companies, like Sephora, BMW, and 3M, have "unstructured" or "innovation" time for employees to work on untested side projects. When Google allowed its employees a day a week to pursue their own ideas, Gmail and AdSense were born. Embracing unpredictability isn't just a feel-good idea; it's a proven practice that leads to progress and success.

Uncertainty and Decision-Making for Parents: A Recap

Making decisions about our children has never been easy, and the brain has always dealt with it the same way it deals with all decisions: by using past experience to weigh risk against reward and predict outcomes. But today, information overload and a rapidly changing environment result in more decisions falling into the "unpredict-able" category. The brain perceives unpredictability as a threat, and this prompts a neurological response ordering us to make a decision quickly so the stress from the threat can be relieved. We automatically fall back on familiar criteria to weigh risk against reward—like status quo bias, cultural pressure, and gut instinct. These aren't optimal guidelines because they're based on our past experiences, and our past is very different than our children's future is likely to be.

One final observation about the parental brain: I believe the level of uncertainty we live with and our overexposure to toxic national and world events has dramatically weakened our capacity to tolerate anxiety. We're like trauma victims, triggered by every schoolyard rumor and breaking news report. We don't have enough band-width to calmly absorb it all. It's as if we're experiencing mini stress responses—alarm, resistance, exhaustion—multiple times a day, with hardly any recovery time. It's part of the reason that the most common descriptor parents use in my office is "overwhelmed." We're not very good at tolerating our children's anxiety, either. That leads to a cascade of other problems, as we'll see in the next chapter. By understanding how the brain drives our reactions to our environ-ment, we can push past fear and resistance to change. The times de-mand that we develop a more flexible set of responses that will help us, and our children, cultivate curiosity and enthusiasm as opposed to anxiety about the future.

CHAPTER 3

Accumulated Disability

The Real Dangers of Overprotection

I was fine walking to school with my friends, but then my parents read about some perv across the country and said I couldn't do it anymore. Now they drive me.

—Teddy, ten-year-old boy

Most of us understand that we're living in a rapidly changing and uncertain world. As we've seen, this heightens our anxiety and compromises our problem-solving and decision-making skills. In order to fully unwind the ill effects of uncertainty on our thinking, we need a thorough and more nuanced understanding of anxiety. How does anxiety affect us? How does our anxiety affect our children? What can we do to increase our ability to not only tolerate anxiety-provoking situations, but to *learn* from anxiety?

Children's natural instinct is to avoid things that make them afraid or anxious, but if they do, they can't develop courage and competency. This is the worst possible scenario for dealing with uncertainty, because you can't be crazy anxious if risk-taking, rapid adaptation, and comfortably engaging with new people are among the skills you will need going forward.

The Connection Between Anxious Parents and Anxious Kids

Nearly one in five adults in the United States has suffered from an anxiety disorder over the past year, and nearly one in three of us will experience it over the course of our lifetime.[1] Among adolescents ages 13 to 17, one in three struggled with anxiety within the past year, and 8.3 percent had a severe impairment.[2] While no one can claim to know all the reasons for the rise in anxiety, most experts agree that our unstable era contributes to it and that smartphones and social media exacerbate it. As Alex Williams wrote in the *New York Times*, "Epidemiologists consider anxiety a medical condition, but the disorder is starting to seem like a sociological condition, too: a shared cultural experience that feeds on alarmist TV graphics and metastasizes through social media."[3]

Apart from the cultural factors that are causing us to be more anxious, our genetic makeup plays a role. There are adults who are born bold, and others who are born more cautious and fearful. Similarly, some children are active explorers of the world and seem fearless, and others seem challenged just by leaving Mom's side. Studies have indicated that 30–40 percent of the individual risk for anxiety disorders is due to genetics.[4] But having a genetic predisposition to anxiety doesn't mean it's written in stone. The environment, for better or worse, is almost always working right alongside our genetic code.

There is another connection between parents' anxiety and that of their children. *Anxious parents have less tolerance for their children's distress, and this leads them to avoid situations they think will upset their child.* All parents do this to some degree, but anxious parents do it much more frequently.

Childhood is a series of extraordinary discoveries—some delightful, some anxiety-provoking—for both children and parents. Tolerating our anxiety about our children's ventures out into the world requires patience, self-control, and emotional fuel. When we're low on those reserves, we feel compelled to make our anxious feeling stop *now*. When new mom Gina's 3-month-old wailed at night, it seemed unbearable. Her mother told her to let him cry it out, but she couldn't. The shrieking was rattling her last nerve. So she would scoop her infant up at his first protest call and rock him to sleep in her arms. He was no longer distressed, and neither was Gina. In the process, the baby couldn't learn how to soothe himself to sleep. And Gina couldn't learn how to tolerate his discomfort. Our children can't learn if we don't.

This double-edged sword plays out in ways that feel loving and supportive in the moment, but over the years can accumulate, with extremely deleterious effects on our kids. Say you had a bad fall on a bike when you were a child. You're in no rush to get your youngster on a bike—maybe he'll fall and still be thinking about it thirty years later. To make sure that doesn't happen, you delay granting his request for a bike. It's kind of a twofer. You believe you're sparing your son a potentially dangerous and anxiety-provoking experience, but you're mostly sparing yourself reigniting the fear you felt when *you* fell. In this way, instead of helping your child develop bravery and coping skills, you're unintentionally promoting fear and hesitancy.

When we think of protecting our children, we tend to think of rescuing them (from an oncoming car) or shielding them (from online porn or mean classmates). These are, of course, critical forms of protection. But providing our kids with lasting protection requires a longer view. Real and enduring protection is built slowly and incrementally. It comes from the competency and self-awareness children gain as they test themselves physically, mentally, and socially. Responsive parents are very attuned to their children's feelings, and that's a good thing: attunement between child and parent is critical for the development of mental health and empathy. But a parent who is overly attuned to anxiety is not doing their child any favors. This kind of overly anxious parenting typically has deep roots and is challenging to change. But let's look at the unintended consequences of not taming our hyperreactivity to our children's anxiety.

The teenagers and young adults I see in my practice often suffer from what I will be calling *accumulated disability*: impairment of life skills and the ability to cope, adapt, and function.* It's a result of years of misguided protection offered by parents who respond to their children's developmentally normal anxiety by shielding and rescuing them. This would be a shame in any era, but in ours it's a real threat to a young person's life and livelihood. Because if we know anything about the next twenty or thirty years, we know that essential skills will include self-sufficiency, equanimity in the face of change, and enthusiasm for challenge.

Theo: A Cautionary Tale

I first meet many of my patients when they're in middle school. According to their parents, things have been humming along reasonably well, and then the workload gets tougher or the kid transfers

---

* I am indebted to Dr. John Walkup, head of Child and Adolescent Psychiatry at Lurie Children's Hospital in Chicago for introducing me to this extremely useful concept.

to a new school and suddenly he or she is exhibiting serious signs of a disorder. But disorders don't erupt out of nowhere. There's always a backstory, and it often takes several sessions to unfold.

Theo was 12 when his mom brought him to see me. All his early developmental milestones were fine, judging by her recollections. She was a stay-at-home mom and Theo hadn't gone to daycare or preschool, but together they had attended Mommy and Me groups and other similar activities. He was a good baby and a relatively placid child. When he began kindergarten, he had exhibited some separation anxiety: he didn't want to go to school in the morning and his parents would have to pry his fingers off the car seat and carry him into class (where he wasn't the only child sniffling or wailing in a parent's arms). His parents were reassured that his reaction was not unusual, and after a few weeks of distress he acclimated to kindergarten and things calmed down.

In third grade, when Theo was eight years old, he again began to show signs of school-related anxiety again. He felt increasingly shy among his classmates but didn't want to admit that to his parents. He dawdled getting out of the house in the morning, complaining of being tired or sick. By the end of the day he regularly ended up in the nurse's office with either a headache or stomach pains. Theo would beg the school nurse not to call his parents, insisting that he just needed a break and would feel better shortly. His parents were made aware that school was often a challenge for their son. However, he was generally able to return to class after a brief respite.

Around the same time, Theo began having trouble falling asleep, so his parents started taking turns sleeping with him in his twin bed. They felt that since he struggled so much during the day, how could they let him sleep alone at night and not provide comfort? The family stumbled along this way through third grade, then fourth, with no one suggesting that Theo see a therapist because no one knew what was going on inside the home. While many parents sleep with their babies or toddlers, sleeping with an 8-year-old is unusual in this culture, and they were uncomfortable mentioning it to friends or family. Although they took Theo to a pediatrician for his physical symptoms (the headaches and stomach pains), it didn't occur to them to mention the sleep problems or his earlier separation anxiety.

Come fifth grade, Theo's anxiety got worse. He was terrified of the rumors he'd heard about middle school: cliques, bullying, eighth-grade boys who were as big as grown men. He dreaded school and couldn't sleep regardless of who was with him (by then the parents had resigned themselves to this arrangement and bought him a bigger bed). Theo got up repeatedly during the night to use the bathroom or get a drink of water. He was sleep-deprived and nervous during the day, and his equally sleep-deprived parents were consumed with worry and guilt. What could they do to help their son? The poor kid had so much homework and such high anxiety about being a successful student that Theo's parents, who starting out "helping" him with his homework, ended up doing much of it themselves.

That's what finally brought them to my office. Theo's mom asked if I could diagnose him with a learning disability so he could get more time to complete his homework and take tests. His parents couldn't imagine Theo managing the middle-school curriculum, and they were probably right. He likely wouldn't be able to handle it because he'd had no practice going to sleep by himself, organizing his time, or doing his own homework. This is accumulated disability: heightened anxiety and real limitations caused or exacerbated by well-meaning parents' efforts to shield their child.

Theo's parents agonized: "Will he ever make it through school? What are we doing wrong? What more can we do?" And the message that was so hard for them to hear was "You have to do less."

Getting parents to back off is often very challenging because by the time they seek my help, they're deeply invested in reengineering home life so that it's less stressful for the child. And in parallel, the child's toolbox of skills for managing anxiety is very limited. At Theo's house, mundane routines had become tense rituals: What does Theo want for dinner? For dessert? When does he need help? What game does he want to play before he goes to bed? The family was entirely focused on making things easier for Theo, which actually made things harder for him. The more his parents catered to him, the more fragile and stressed he felt and behaved, which made his parents more anxious, so they looked for more ways to accommodate him.

Often in my sessions with Theo, I found myself thinking, "If only the pediatrician had asked them a few more questions, or they had mentioned a pattern of sleeplessness and separation anxiety. If only the parents had sought help when Theo was eight instead of twelve." Four years is a long time in a child's life, and anxiety disorders are far easier to treat in young children. In teenagers, the problems are more entrenched. By the twenties it's even worse. That isn't to say they can't be helped. They can, but it will be harder on them and take longer.

Parallel Treatment: Parents and Kids

What should Theo's parents have done differently? The most direct answer is that instead of helping him avoid the things that caused him anxiety, they should have helped him face his fears. Easy to say; very difficult for parents to do. But somewhere between dads of yesteryear yelling at their sons to "Man up!" and parents of today sleeping in their fifth-grader's bed, there has to be a better approach.

In our effort to defend our kids from forces that feel threatening to them, we overprotect them and unintentionally make them feel even more vulnerable. Every time we intervene for our child, it temporarily quiets their anxiety before upping it. Same goes for us. Supporting this viewpoint is research showing that when parents of anxious children are treated for anxiety disorders along with their kids, the children do much better than when they alone are treated: 77 percent improve as compared to 39 percent when parents are not included in treatment.[5] Genetics certainly plays its role in the transmission of anxiety disorders, but the parenting style typical of anxious parents seems to be as great a risk factor.

Here's how it typically plays out in everyday life. Say your daughter is afraid of dogs, and while taking a stroll with her you see a dog across the street. You can take her hand, cross the street, talk to the dog's owner and ask if the pet is friendly, hold your hand out for the dog to sniff, pet the dog, and finally ask your little girl if she would like to touch the dog's soft fur. If you do this enough times, especially if you get to know a few of the dogs and their owners, your daughter is likely to touch the fur, pet the dog, and overcome some or all of her apprehension. The clinical term for increasing exposure to the source of anxiety in this way is *progressive desensitization*; we'll explore it in detail in Chapter 5. A mantra I teach both parents and kids for remembering the importance of exposure in anxiety-provoking situations of all types is, "Don't avoid the dog." Like everything else you will learn about in this book, changing behavior takes practice. Lots of it.

The other option is to stay on your side of the street. If you do that, your daughter (and you) are momentarily relieved, but neither of you has learned anything about how to overcome fear except by avoidance. Your daughter can't stretch her bravery muscles and find out what it feels like to conquer fear. But this is only half the story: Think of your own reactions. Now whenever you're with your daughter and see a dog, *your* anxiety shoots up as you anticipate her fear. If you walk across the street and pet the dog, you and your child will be exercising the same muscles: tolerating anxiety and building competency.

A friend told me a story that illustrates a different side of this dynamic. While growing up, she flew across the country every year with her family to visit relatives. After she left home, she didn't travel anywhere by air with her mother until she was in her thirties. As the plane was taking off on their first trip together as adults, her mom suddenly grabbed her hand.

"What's wrong?" asked my friend.

"I'm scared of flying," her mother confessed.

"You're kidding! I never knew."

"I didn't want to make you afraid too." And it worked. The daughter patted her mom's hand, grateful for her stoic performance on all those childhood flights. Looking at it from the mother's perspective, she had probably figured out that as nervous as she was about flying, it would be even worse if she also had to contend with a terrified child. Most of our daily stressors aren't that clear-cut, but when we're aware of the emotional benefits to everyone of managing our anxiety, it can change how we choose to behave.

We all need to adjust our behavior to lessen the possibility that our kids' normal anxiety will morph into a disorder. We can do that by insisting at every age that anxiety be met with courage. Anxiety is part of growing up, but normal anxiety is proportional to a challenge. A kid with a peanut allergy may be understandably anxious about peanuts in his food since that can be life-threatening. A child who refuses ever to go to a sleepover because she'll have to sleep in someone else's bed is responding disproportionately to a normal developmental challenge. Lots of kids are anxious about sleepovers, especially the first few times. So as parents, we also need to teach our kids about evaluating reasonable risks and the value of making it through anxiety-provoking situations. This is providing support in its truest sense. We need less of "Are you okay?" and more of "Hey, I think you can handle this." Our kids get better at things when they practice. Having faith in their ability to handle age-appropriate challenge helps build both competence and confidence.

When it comes to managing our kids' anxiety, there's an interesting difference between this generation of parents and earlier ones. In times past, most parents assumed they were their children's teachers by dint of experience and knowledge. They felt their job was to tame their kids' fearful, anxious, rude, or impulsive instincts. Then, somewhere in the 1970s, the trend among parenting experts and psychologists began to shift. Some theorized that maybe children's instincts were all for the better. It became popular to have babies wean themselves, toddlers learn how to toilet themselves when they "were ready," older children select and reject the foods they ate. It was a rare parent in the '80s or '90s who couldn't recall being forced as a child to eat meals they didn't like because, as their parents said, "There are children starving in Africa!" They didn't want their own kids to have to choke down food they hated. And yet, forty years later, we find ourselves at the outer reaches of that philosophy. Parents have become gratifiers of instinct rather than tamers.

To prepare our kids for the future and protect them against

unforeseeable challenges, we'll have to learn alongside them how to overcome fearful instincts and tolerate anxiety—theirs and ours. Anything less is unfair. We parents already have the skills we need to earn a living, form relationships, and support a family, but our kids don't. They're genuinely at risk if we let our own anxiety prevent us from helping them grow into brave and capable adults.

Sowing the Seeds of Anxiety and Avoidance

Anxiety disorders tend to start early in life, usually somewhere between ages six and ten. There are warning signs long before our kids throw up their hands and say, "I can't take school anymore," or cut themselves because they're feeling anxious. Because of our desire to protect them, early warnings are often overlooked. We ferry our children across the street to avoid the crabby neighbor who doesn't like kids. We say, "That party makes you uncomfortable? You don't have to go." The dysfunctional two-step of "It makes me feel bad!" "Let me help you avoid it!" has not been given adequate clinical investigation. It should, because childhood anxiety is predictive of adolescent anxiety, and adolescent anxiety is predictive of adult anxiety.

The kind of avoidance that goes unremarked upon? There were plenty of examples in my house, with three kids (and an anxious mother). I suspect you'll find more than a few in your own home once you know what to look for. No single one of the situations described below guarantees your child will develop an anxiety disorder. What we need to pay attention to are our patterns of dealing with anxiety. *Repeated* capitulation to our children's anxiety is what sets them up for the kinds of limited coping skills we find in anxiety disorders.

SLEEPING

When my first son couldn't fall asleep at night, I would lie with him until he did. Lots of parents sleep with their babies and toddlers, and there are many societies where the "family bed" is part of the culture. It's not the act of sleeping with young children that's problematic, it's sleeping with them in an attempt to reduce their anxiety or your own. It's also worth pointing out that in Western culture, as diverse as it is, sleeping with a child past the age of four years old is generally considered to be outside the norm. (For the sake of full transparency, however, my youngest would come up to our room regularly well past the age of four and sleep on a comforter next to our bed. He is now grown up and is one of the least anxious young adults I know. I used to reassure my husband that "no kid goes to college sleeping in their parents' room." I've included this just to underscore that none of us does everything according to the book, and in an otherwise healthy household, parental gaffes are generally well tolerated.) In retrospect, it was mostly exhaustion, not a hypersensitivity to anxiety, that drove my questionable tolerance. We need to be clear about what motivates us.

The American Academy of Pediatrics recommends against bed-sharing in infancy because research has shown that it increases the risk of sudden infant death syndrome (SIDS). A 2017 study indicated that room sharing (but not bed-sharing) in infants from birth to one year had no ill effect on SIDS rates, but "room-sharing with infants at ages four months and nine months was associated with less nighttime sleep, shorter sleep stretches and unsafe sleep practices." So although the parents may sleep easier with the infant in the room, it isn't necessarily better for the child.

Every baby will do some crying before learning how to self-soothe, and some are absolute terrors about napping or falling asleep at night. However, somewhere between the ages of two and four, children should learn how to sleep alone in their bed every night with only occasional exceptions. Refusing to sleep alone after this age is one of the earliest signs of a potential anxiety disorder. It's also an opportunity to nip the problem in the bud. "I need you to sleep with me; I can't sleep alone" is a common lament among young children. Unfortunately, it often leads to more "cant's": "I can't sleep at my friend's house, I have to be in my own bed." "I can't go to that slumber party, the bed is so messy." "I can't go to sleepaway camp. There'll be crawly things in the bed." And much later on: "I don't know my roommate. I can't sleep in the dorm with a stranger."

EATING

Kids can be finicky and fierce. They'll swear that a certain food disgusts them and they'll throw up if they have to eat it. Parents are tired and dinnertime comes after a long day. Is the kid being manipulative or is she really extrasensitive to certain foods? In the end, the response should be the same, because the way to deal with an anxiety disorder is by exposure and the way to deal with manipulation is by calmly refusing to play: "This is our dinner tonight. Eat what you want and leave the parts you don't like. I'm not making anything else."

The parent's response is crucial. I had a client whose 9-year-old daughter didn't like to eat "sauce," so whenever she went to a friend's house, Mom called and requested that she not be served anything with sauce. Not much chance to gain more exposure there (or more dinner invites).

Sometimes you'll get a peek into what's going on in other families' food skirmishes. A woman told me about a sleepover she hosted for a few of her 7-year-old son's pals. At around 1 A.M., she and her husband heard knocking at their bedroom door. One little guest,

Adam, called out, "I want toast and jelly." The mom told him to go back to sleep. He threatened to phone his mother and have her pick him up if he didn't get the midnight snack. Highly irritated, the mom complied. As they sat in the kitchen together, Adam informed her, "I'm a stress eater. I need toast at night."

Because it's hard to pinpoint kids' motivation for refusing foods, and because we're worried they won't get proper nutrition, the food dilemma is especially anxiety-provoking for parents. When we're fatigued, it's easier to say "Fine, I'll make you a burger." But capitulating to children's unreasonable demands (only white foods, no leafy vegetables, nothing with "texture," no sauce) has the potential to cause more serious long-term damage than occasionally letting them go to bed hungry. They're not going to become malnourished at your house. They're more likely to end up with an eating disorder. Most kids outgrow their finicky eating habits and can tolerate a little tough love when it comes to not being served customized meals.

USING THE BATHROOM

Another common issue is refusing to go to any bathroom outside of the home. It often starts when a child won't use the bathroom at a restaurant, so we have the food packed up and the whole family has to leave. This behavior may expand to not going to the bathroom at friends' or relatives' houses or in a public facility. It can be a sign of social anxiety or, occasionally, of OCD (obsessive-compulsive disorder). If such children aren't exposed to using the bathroom in a variety of locales, the results are predictable: play dates are cut short, outings are restricted, and when the child starts school, he may not relieve himself all day. Now the anxiety starts affecting his physical health. If a child consistently refuses to use public restrooms or the bathrooms at his friends' houses, it's a sign his anxiety is overwhelming his ability to learn coping skills. A couple of sessions with a therapist skilled in desensitization, either with your child or preferably with you if your child is young (to teach you the desensitization protocol—believe me, it's not rocket science), helps head off bigger problems down the line at camp or at college. In Chapter 5, I'll give you a crash course in the technique.

PLAY DATES

Play dates are where kids get to practice tolerating all sorts of potential anxiety triggers: different house, parents, kids, siblings, habits, manners, food, toys, bathrooms, perhaps a babysitter. No wonder some children are a little wary: "I like playing at my house better." And many parents are happy to oblige. I was one of them. I never saw it as an anxiety issue, I just enjoyed having all the kids at my house, getting to play with them, feed them, and overhear their casual conversation. When you're the mother of three physical rather than verbal sons, words are precious commodities.

When a child prefers having play dates at her own home, it's not a sign that anything's wrong. But it's a huge missed opportunity to develop strategies to relax in the face of anxiety and to recognize and challenge anxious thoughts. Social anxiety is a big problem for children and teenagers, and it's often blamed on social media, texting, and gaming. Before any of these are likely to be an issue, parents who encourage children to only have play dates at their own homes are contributing to the problem. It's not just the other children your kid needs exposure to, it's the other environments. In addition, when all the play dates are at your house, you're sending the message that it's the only safe place in town.

The Trajectory Continues: School Days

Between the ages of 18 months and 2-and-a-half years, most children will experience normal separation anxiety when a parent leaves them with a babysitter or in daycare. Skilled caretakers know that distraction is a good antidote. The separation anxiety may return for a bit when the child enters preschool or kindergarten.

Children who have a lot of practice tolerating new places and people will likely make the transition to school with just a little fuss (depending on their temperament, of course). The kids whose parents have avoided the dog more often than petting it will have a tougher time. It'll be more of a sink-or-swim experience for them.

For moms, too, it's a difficult transition. As our child is weeping at the playground fence and jerking away from the remarkably tranquil teacher, it's easy to doubt ourselves: "Did I do the right thing? I'm not sure." "He needs me! If I stayed there today, he'd probably be better tomorrow." In my experience, most children who have separation anxiety at preschool or kindergarten get used to it within a couple of weeks if mom maintains a calm demeanor and the conviction that this is in her child's best interest. But that can be a very hard place to come from, particularly for a first-time parent, so we waver. At the preschool my boys attended, as often as a distressed child had to be pried off a mother, I saw a shaky mom being led out by a teacher.

The years between kindergarten and third grade are critical ones for parents, kids, and anxiety. This is when you can make up for lost time if you've been too protective. With each grade, children face new social and academic challenges. The two are intertwined, but it's social anxiety more than academic pressure that causes a kid at age 8 or 10 to say, "William was teasing me again yesterday and he's going to tease me again today. I don't want to go to school."

You may be worried about bullying, and if it's a pattern, you'll absolutely have to find out more about it, but it's a really bad idea to respond with "OK, honey, you can stay home. I'll call the teacher and get your assignments." This may allow you both to feel better in the moment, but your child will pay for it later if you protect him from peer group interaction. It's the peer group that forces kids to become more open-minded and flexible ("It's stupid that you don't like sauce") and prepares them for the larger social world of middle and high school. Your job is to help your child develop strategies to deal with occasional teasing.

Third-, fourth-, or fifth-graders who haven't learned how to manage anxiety about being in a group are at a great disadvantage, since one of the primary developmental tasks of elementary school is learning to navigate the intricacies of social relationships and to practice the art of making friends. It's essential to identify and treat anxiety at this age and to get your child out into the world to experience a range of situations so that anxiety doesn't balloon into a disorder in the coming years.

Parents of grade-schoolers often use the kids' youth to rationalize shielding them from social situations or providing excessive help with homework: "He's a *young* nine. He needs more time." But if a child in elementary school gets too little experience managing anxiety and meeting challenges, middle school will be like drinking out of a fire hose. They won't be able to keep up, and that's why so many parents first seek my help during the middle-school years.

Middle School: "Now It Counts"

Middle school has always been a challenge. I've always thought that if you took a group of child and adolescent psychologists, psychiatrists, pediatricians, and developmental experts, put us all in a room, and asked us to come up with the worst possible learning scenario for kids ages 11 to 14, we'd come up with something that looks pretty much like today's middle schools. Give kids just forty-five minutes to digest difficult content while they stay glued in their seats. Make sure they have no time between learning physical science and advanced algebra. Have them raise their hands to pee. Force them during the most physically awkward stage of their development to get naked with other kids. Make sure that some of them are the size of full-grown men and women and others pint-sized. Finally, surround them with other kids, the same age, who are positively Shakespearean in their love of drama. And that's before we started bothering them about preparing for college. They can barely prepare for their day, given the tortuous social and academic demands of middle school.

It's not unusual for seventh-graders to be told they should start planning for their college careers, including choosing a major. Putting aside the lunacy of this and its neglect of basic child development issues, let's focus on what it means for kids whose parents have shielded them from the comparatively mild social and academic stressors of elementary school. In addition to the cranked-up workload, with middle school comes puberty (if it hasn't already started), zits and lots of body shaming, bullying, separation from parents, cliques, seven teachers instead of one, cell phones, and the constant presence of social media and all the miserable comparisons it inspires. Most of us know that there has never been much solace in being a middle-schooler. And that was with considerably less in the way of pressure, technology, and general panic about grades and college admission. Even parents who've restrained themselves from intervening too much with homework or projects before now may find themselves offering more and more help to take the pressure off their kids. There's a whiff of panic in the air and the warning, "Now it counts!" can be heard at the dinner table.

It's not just schoolwork parents do for their children, although that's a big item on the list of interventions that can lead to accumulated disability. Middle school is when preteens should be taking on more responsibilities for their own care and helping around the house. Too often, nothing changes or they do even less than they did before. Worried their kids won't have enough time for schoolwork, sports, and friends, parents make their 14-year-old's bed, excuse them from household chores, allow mealtimes to devolve into multiple-choice food preparations. They repeatedly replace lost gear and cell phones (no consequences for carelessness), relax the rules around sleeping, leave technology running until late at night, and make those phone calls to teachers in order to clear up "misunderstandings" about missing homework or poor test scores. These actions on the part of parents keep kids from learning life skills such as time management, self-care, meal preparation, self-regulation, and personal responsibility. This is where accumulated disability takes root and spreads. Success in school or on the field can blind parents to deficiencies everywhere else.

When I bring up chores and responsibilities, parents often respond with "It's easier to do it myself." I completely understand. It's easier (less stressful) for parents with depleted emotional resources *not* to have to listen to their kids freak out about, for example, balancing homework, friends, and babysitting their little sister. Parents call it "keeping the peace" when they do all the chores rather than fighting about it with their kids. But learning how to do household chores and being responsible for their own clothing and hygiene is how teens build real-world competency. As utilitarian and unsexy as laundry, basic cooking, and sewing on a button may seem, these skills will provide a bedrock of self-confidence when our kids move into the freshman dorm.

High School: A Perfect Storm

With college on the horizon, parental intervention continues and ramps up during the high-school years. Teenagers respond in a variety of ways, some very healthy. I've spoken to plenty of kids who, by the age of 15, have figured out their boundaries and have no problem articulating them: "Everybody here is doing the STEM program. It's not for me," or, "I decided I was going to stop track because I liked it but knew I couldn't handle it all."

It's the parents who may resist down-shifting to a less involved role. They attend every practice and game. They regularly monitor their kids' grades via the school web portal. They continue to text teachers, often late at night, to protest grades or make excuses for their kids' late assignments. They accompany their teens to the doctor or dentist and sit in the room with them during the exam or procedure. Many parents discourage their kids from learning to drive until they're eighteen or older; using a ride-share service is safer and less nerve-wracking for Mom and Dad. Tutors are hired, and if a kid can't juggle his or her academic and extracurricular commitments, some well-to-do families even hire a time-management coach.[6] "Homework therapists" are brought in to help with both studying and the stress it causes.[7]

Even students who gamely tackle the most demanding classes may find their parents don't trust them. One father wanted his son to bring his calculus grade up, so he decided to graph all the boy's tests and quizzes. This would be bad enough, but he didn't allow his son to keep the graph! Dad wanted to make sure it was absolutely accurate. The kid ended up with an A in calculus, but his anxiety was through the roof. Graphing every single test and quiz implied that each one was a matter of life and death, and the fact that Dad kept the graph suggested he thought his was son was too impaired to do it himself (remember, this kid was taking *calculus*). At the very least, the father could have handed over some control to his son by suggesting that he keep a record of his test scores so he could track his own progress. Giving appropriate control to your child is key to decreasing his or her anxiety. Parents' interference and the criticism it implies—*You're not doing this correctly, you're incapable of doing it on your own*—can lead to an unwarranted sense of failure in kids. Competence, of course, is built over many tries and that includes any number of mistakes. The young man may have had an A in calculus, but he had an F in self-esteem and confidence. Accumulated disability can affect even the brightest students if their competence is consistently challenged by overly involved parents.

In junior year, parental interference and our complicated college application process combine to create a maelstrom of fear, anxiety, and pressure. Preparing to apply for college is so multifaceted and confusing that many parents hire an expert to walk their family through the maze. The familiar list of hurdles includes SAT/ACT prep and testing, AP prep and testing, researching colleges, planning campus visits, financial aid, scholarships, summer programs, and the actual applications and college essays. This is on top of the student's academic and extracurricular workload. (More than a few colleges and universities are phasing out SAT requirements. This trend is likely to continue, so progress is being made against the old, notably immaterial, metrics.)

Parents and students grind away, eyes on the prize. When kids begin to show obvious signs of emotional distress (anxiety, depression, cutting, substance abuse, eating disorders, somatic symptoms, academic disengagement, emergency room visits), their parents bring them to see me. Some of them remind me of disaster survivors. Teaching these teenagers how to calm down, how not to be on high alert, and how to analyze threat level is where our therapy begins. People who have lived through trauma, and particularly those who suffer from PTSD, become hypervigilant about threat. Likewise, these kids see danger everywhere: "I got a B, I'll never get into Stanford now." "I took AP Calc 1, but I've been told to be really competitive you have to take AP Calc 2. This is going to be a disaster." If anybody had told me when I was getting a Ph.D. that half my future work time would be spent doing breathing exercises with 16-year-olds, I would have said "Not in a million years." But I am.

At this point many of my young patients are genuinely incapable of managing their own lives. Their parents have taken the reins. No matter what prized school they may get into, I know that I will be seeing a substantial number of them before the end of freshman year. They have reached the conclusion that not only are they poorly equipped to deal with life, there's nothing they can do about it. They have no options or sense of agency. The term for that is *learned helplessness*: the belief that nothing you do can impact your environment. Accumulated disability is "I don't have the skills to do this." Learned helplessness is "It doesn't matter what I do. I'm powerless." These two conditions are intertwined—the teenagers' accumulated disabilities give credence to their belief that they don't have the skills or courage to change their situation. The consequences are far-reaching, as we'll see in the next chapter.

CHAPTER 4

Learned Helplessness and Delayed Adolescence

A Stalled Generation

Not that long ago teenagers weren't beaten down—they were pissed off. Overwhelmed by excessive homework or parental pressure, they stomped around my office, tossed off a colorful inventory of swear words about their parents, and threw textbooks on the floor. They begged me to get their folks, teachers, coaches, and tutors off their backs. In family therapy sessions, they fought to draw a clear line between their own interests and their parents' plans for them. They pushed back against overinvolved, overinvested moms and dads. Akin to the 2-year-old's anthem "You're not the boss of me," teens were quick to declare "It's my life, not yours!"

But now teenagers are much more likely to display a disturbing absence of the bravado and even rebelliousness necessary for accomplishing the tasks of adolescence. Under normal circumstances teenagers live in the moment, consumed with carving out the emotional space they require to become independent. They need to establish their own moral code. They need to noodle around with different experiences, find those they enjoy or have a talent for, and practice like mad so they can get better. *They need to celebrate success, and to endure and learn from failures.* That's how they develop competence and become confident. Three psychosocial achievements—a sense of self, the belief that we can have an impact on our circumstances, and the ability to regulate our emotions—allow us to handle challenges, setbacks, and disappointments. These attributes are the scaffolding upon which intimacy, meaning, and mental health are built. Ultimately, autonomy—being capable of both healthy separation and healthy connection—signals the successful completion of adolescent tasks. In almost all cultures, adolescence begins with a bold psychological move away from parents and ends with a mature return to the family relationship and an expanded repertoire of friendships and intimate relationships.

In the teenagers I've been counseling for the past two decades, anxiety and accumulated disability have stalled the push toward separation. Parents' takeover of the agenda of adolescence has led to a joyless, "Let's just get this over with" attitude among these kids. They may excel at their studies, but learning doesn't excite them. (One of my Challenge Success cofounders, Denise Pope, accurately described them as "robo-students.") The internal work of separating from parents, made more manageable by a spirit of rebelliousness shared with peers, has been thwarted. They constantly feel at the mercy of other people, especially their parents and teachers, on whom they depend for a sense of self. They seem more like spectators than participants in their own lives.

Just as troubling as the passivity, disengagement, and demoralization I often see in my young patients is the fact that many parents regard their teenagers' persistent reliance on them as proof of how admirably close they are to their children. High-school kids allowing parents to choose their elective classes, college students speaking daily with their moms to solicit advice on everything from laundry to dating—these aren't signs of closeness but of unhealthy enmeshment. Research shows that college students who have overinvolved parents are more likely to be depressed and to have low life satisfaction than students with more appropriately involved parents. This is probably because, while parents may feel that they are being supportive, they are in fact reducing their child's sense of competence and autonomy.[1] Studies have also found that college students who are self-regulating do better academically than those whose parents continue to control them from afar.[2]

All forms of parental control are not equal. The behavioral control that lets kids know their limits and the consequences of their actions has been found to be helpful for adolescents: "Curfew is eleven o'clock. Be home by then or you'll lose driving privileges." This type of overt rule-setting makes teenagers feel safe and allows them increasing freedom as they show responsibility: "You've been super reliable about the car all month, so if you want, you can drive it into the city now."

But psychological control is usually covert. It involves intrusively manipulating a child's thoughts and feelings, especially through the spoken or unspoken threat of withdrawing love if he or she defies the parent's plans: "Rice is my alma mater. It'll break my heart if you don't get in." Parents who use psychological control with their children cultivate a sense of helplessness. Helplessness leads to depression. Psychological control, whether your kid is three or thirty, is a nonproductive and harmful approach.

Adolescence is an inside job. In the 1990s, Suniya S. Luthar, Ph.D., studied adolescents and found that ninth-graders with an internal locus of control—those who felt they had some command over the forces shaping their lives—handled stress better than kids with an external orientation—those who felt that others had control over forces shaping their lives. "People who believe they are powerless to control what happens to them . . . become passive and restricted in coping abilities," Luthar writes. "On the other hand, when individuals believe that events and outcomes are controllable, learned helplessness is avoided, and, instead, active attempts are made to overcome aversive situations."[3] Locus of control is not an all-or-nothing concept. None of us are entirely reliant on one or the other. We may work a little harder for our bonus (external motivation), but ultimately it's how we feel about our work (internal motivation) that counts most.

But more and more often, the teenagers I observe aren't even partially internally motivated. They persistently turn outward toward coaches, teachers, and parents to remove roadblocks and facilitate solutions. They have no experience with weathering setbacks, and they aren't really capable of mastering challenging situations. A startlingly large number of these teens are behaving like younger children. They're stuck performing the chief psychosocial tasks of childhood—being good and doing things right to please adults— instead of taking on the developmental work of separation and independence that is appropriate for their age. When faced with teenage-sized problems, they often have nothing more than the skills of a child.

Enraged but Powerless

In the spring of 2018, the Centers for Disease Control and Prevention released a harrowing report on suicide in the United States: Between 1999 and 2016, rates had increased by at least 30 percent in more than half the states. Among people ages 15 to 35, it was the second leading cause of death.[4] A year earlier, the CDC had released figures specific to adolescents: between 2007 and 2015, suicide rates doubled for girls between 15 and 19. There was an increase of 30 percent for boys in the same age range. Of special concern were girls ages 10 to 14, among whom suicide increased 200 percent between 1999 and 2014.[5]

Close to home, I had been following with alarm a rise in suicides among high-school students in wealthy enclaves of the San Francisco Bay Area and Silicon Valley. These tragic acts naturally generated a great deal of media attention, reflection by district officials, and heartache among teachers, parents, and students. In newspaper editorials and at community meetings, some of which I attended as an invited expert, adults and teenagers blamed the suicides on pressure at home and at school: parents obsessed with getting their child into a top-tier college, educators more interested in test scores than in student engagement, an unremitting emphasis on competition, too much homework, too little sleep. A Harvard study of over ten thousand middle- and high-school students confirmed that over 80 percent of students believe that their parents value achievement over kindness.[6] I don't really believe that most parents value their child's personal achievement over their character. But kids draw their conclusions from what we pay attention to. More than a celebratory dinner over a soccer win, we need to be sure we are celebrating the small acts of kindness that we can see daily in our teens if we're looking—helping a sibling find a toy, carrying groceries in from the car, checking in with an elderly neighbor.

In an angry online open letter that went viral, a high-school girl ended her lacerating commentary by saying, "Suicide continues while our parents value wealth and success over our lives. We cannot wait for change. We need it now."

I found this young woman's *cri de coeur* painful—and her sense of betrayal and powerlessness even more so. Her honest distress was compelling, but she didn't seem aware that she, and her classmates, could begin to initiate the changes she yearned for. She could say no, take fewer classes, cut out an extracurricular activity, get to bed on time, refuse pressure to do more, to *be* more.

When I was interviewed for "The Silicon Valley Suicides," a cover article in *The Atlantic* by Hanna Rosin, I pointed out that studies show teens identify school as the greatest source of stress in their lives. Rosin astutely observed that this finding "may suggest a submission of sorts—the unquestioned adoption of parental norms."[7] This mirrored my experience with my anguished young patients. Despite their outrage at parental and community pressure, they felt powerless: unable to change their circumstances, affect their own fates, or act on their preferences. In place of rebellion, I found compliance and a compulsion to please that put these teenagers' health and sanity at risk.

A phrase I routinely hear from adolescents is "Whatever. I have no choice." What I haven't heard recently is what echoed a decade or two ago among the fired-up teens I talked to: "It's my choice, not theirs!" Where's the protective defiance? In order to move on to the next stage of development, young adulthood, our kids have to successfully navigate the challenges of adolescence. Many of them haven't. As a result, young adulthood, historically a time of exploration, commitment, and identity consolidation, looks more and more like a stunted adolescence.

The "Emerging Adult," or Making Up for Lost Time

The beginning of adolescence is reckoned from the onset of puberty— the stage at which a person is physiologically capable of reproduction.

Kids in industrialized nations are reaching that point at increasingly younger ages. In 1860 the average age of the onset of puberty in girls was 16 years; in 1920, it was 14.6; and in 1950, 13.1. By 2010, it had dropped to 10.5 years.[8] The same thing is happening to boys, but they're about a year behind girls in development. Some scientists attribute the change to a spike in childhood obesity, which triggers hormonal surges at younger ages. Others blame environmental toxins, especially endocrine disrupters, chemicals in food and household products that also affect the production of hormones.

While the reasons are complex, the fact is that kids are reaching physical sexual maturity earlier than ever before. The World Health Organization now defines adolescence as covering ages 10 to 19. "Most aspects of emotional and intellectual maturity reach adult levels sometime between 15 and 22," says Temple University psychologist Laurence Steinberg, the author of *Age of Opportunity: Lessons from the New Science of Adolescence.* "Adolescents' judgment in situations that permit measured unemotional decision-making and consultation with others—what psychologists call 'cold cognition'—is just as mature as that of adults by 16. In contrast, adolescents' judgment in situations that evoke 'hot cognition'—situations in which their emotions are aroused, time pressure is a factor and they are in groups—is not fully mature until they are older."

Neuroscientists using functional MRI to study the brains of teenagers and young adults have found that the frontal lobes, the regions of the brain in charge of executive functions such as self-regulation and judgment, aren't fully on line until the mid-twenties. Steinberg is more interested in a part of the brain called the nucleus accumbens, a pleasure center that reaches peak activity in adolescence. In general, research suggests that teenagers do goofy, risky things because their judgment isn't totally functional, and because

doing goofy, risky things feels good. Furthermore, among our pre-
historic ancestors, risk-taking was rewarded with reproductive success; venturing afar to find a suitable mate took guts. Teenagers
are evolutionarily primed and neurologically wired, Steinberg says,
to feel deeply, take chances, and bump up hard against the world.
And, research shows, they're staying in that condition well into their
twenties.

Findings like these have led to the concept of "emerging adulthood," a term proposed by Clark University psychologist Jeffrey Arnett to describe a new stage between adolescence and full-fledged
adulthood. He believes that in a prosperous industrialized society,
young people aged 18 to the mid-20s now have an exciting extended
opportunity to pursue experiences and explore their identities before taking on adult roles and responsibilities. He labels this period
of time "emerging adulthood" and calls it "the age of possibilities."
That's one way to describe it. Another might be "perilously pro-
tracted adolescence." Perhaps the concept of emerging adulthood
makes sense not because it's a time for additional growth and extensive self-evaluation, as Arnett seems to believe, but because it allows
time for some catch-up—a remedial period during which the work
that was supposed to have been accomplished in adolescence stands
a chance of being realized.

I'm among those who worry that a do-over may not be optimal
or easily achieved. Another is Meg Jay, a psychologist at the University of Virginia who warns against thinking of the twenties as an
extended adolescence. She considers those years to be a critical stage
of *adult* development that can't be fruitful unless you've successfully
completed the work of traditional adolescence. Telling people they
have ten extra years to launch adulthood, she says, robs them of psychological momentum.

Too many of the teenagers I encounter in my practice and across the country are late in developing what it will take to function as an adult and create adult relationships: agency, independence, intimacy, fortitude, and self-reliance. Often it's because their community (not just parents but also peers, teachers, and extended family) is focused exclusively on the high-school paper chase and fails to encourage these qualities. I try desperately to convince these teens and their parents that delaying the emotional work of adolescence is dangerous.

"We're discovering that the brain during adolescence is very malleable, very plastic," Steinberg says. "It has a heightened capacity to change in response to experience. That cuts both ways: On the one hand it means that the brain is especially susceptible to toxic experiences that can harm it, but it also means that the brain is susceptible to positive influences that can promote growth. That's an opportunity we're squandering." [9]

This finding deepens my concern about the particularly noxious experience of learned helplessness, so powerful that it can override a teenagers' biologically determined propensity toward risk-taking, savoring novel experience, and personal growth.

Chris: Undermined by Anxiety and Too Much Protection

Chris was 26 when he came to me for therapy. He hadn't finished his B.A., though he'd spent eight years on campus. He was unemployed. He was drinking too much, smoking too much dope, and true to the stereotype that's becoming an archetype, living in his parents' (well-furnished) basement. As they had been since Chris left for college at 18, his parents were giving him an allowance of

$6,000 a month in addition to paying his housing costs and tuition (on those rare occasions when he was actually in school).

When I first met with Chris, his parents were demanding that he get a job, but he refused. While his glib charm kept him from looking particularly helpless, this young man had no skills for beginning the journey into responsible adulthood. His insistence that every job available (Starbuck's barista, for example) was beneath him, his surface narcissism and sense of entitlement, masked how inadequate he felt to meet the basic requirements of work. I know the word "entitlement" gets thrown around a lot to describe kids who seem "spoiled." My experience tells me that many, if not most, of these kids are extremely insecure and deficient in an array of basic coping and life skills. When I questioned Chris more deeply, I discovered that he didn't know how to stick to a schedule, and that he had social anxiety about talking with strangers without the lubrication of alcohol. He accurately concluded that he wouldn't last a week at even the most routine job.

Chris is the oldest of five children. His father, a hedge fund manager, was busy and distant; his smart and exacting mother was a lawyer who stopped working when she had children. Chris was a bit dreamy and absent-minded as a kid. He loved to spend time outside, especially exploring the woods near his home, and hated sitting down to do homework. Both of Chris's parents were afraid he'd never excel at school, and his father, whose work exposed him daily to the increasing chaos of global financial markets, was already worried about Chris's ability to cut it in the world of work. He ignored Chris's real interests in the natural world, which were very different from his own. Because of their fears about their son's future prospects, Chris's parents made so many accommodations and spared him so many responsibilities and challenges that ultimately their prophecy was fulfilled. Young Chris picked up on his parents' concerns, and not only came to think of himself as incompetent but truly *was*.

The pitfalls of accumulated disability and learned helplessness started early. Chris recalled that when he was eight, he was bullied at school by an older kid who pulled some classic maneuvers— name-calling, lunch-grabbing, shoving. Frightened, Chris told his mother about the problem. His parents kept him home for a week, then moved him from his upscale public school to an independent school. They had researched bullying and learned that it can be very detrimental, and they "didn't want to take any chances." Chris resisted the move but eventually adjusted to his new environment, which, of course, was not bully-free either. Without appropriate guidance from adults, the strategy Chris developed to preempt bullying was to become the charming class clown and dispenser of gifts—first treats like cookies and candy; later, in high school and college, drugs and alcohol.

I pointed out to Chris and his parents the kinds of steps that would have been more helpful to him—talking to his teacher, asking the school for a conference with the other boy and his parents, or teaching Chris various strategies for dealing with the bully. But none of those things happened. Chris felt his parents had no confidence in him, and as a result he had no confidence in himself. By failing to help Chris tackle this problem and many others head-on, his mother and father ended up unintentionally promoting anxiety, avoidance, and poor coping skills. This is a toxic combination which ultimately led Chris to substance abuse.

Chris's struggles as a young adult illustrate what happens when parents don't intervene early to help a child face his or her anxieties. For their own reasons, each parent shielded Chris from having to conquer his fears, which in turn led to his being even more anxious and fearful, which led to the hopelessness and lack of agency that characterize learned helplessness.

Kids aren't served by being kept away from what makes them anxious, and neither, by the way, are college students. The advent of trigger warnings—professors giving notice to students that some reading material may be troubling (for example, "Trigger Warning: The assigned chapter contains references to physical violence") is a particularly misguided trend. A 20-year-old who is anxious about something is not helped by being shielded from it any more than 8-year-old Chris was helped by being pulled out of school. To treat young adults as if they're so fragile that they can't tolerate exposure to distressing words is to make the college experience perversely anxiety-reinforcing. It's certainly not preparing them for the slings and arrows of the typical work environment or the unknowable challenges of the future.

Eventually, Chris decided that he was ready for rehab. His mother and I agreed that his funding would be cut off, and when he finished his program he would have to find work and an independent living situation that he could afford. While he was in rehab, I worked with his parents to help them fully understand why their protection of Chris hadn't been good for him, and what they should reasonably expect from a young adult.

After he completed the program, Chris got a job in the landscape maintenance division of the local parks department. In treatment, he began to see that during his youth he hadn't had the opportunity to learn how to manage his feelings, take responsibility for his actions, or cope with frustration, but that he could work on those life tasks now. In his late twenties, he's starting to understand the requirements of adulthood.

Emma: Insisting on Independence

There's more time for Emma to get things right. A new patient of mine, she's 15, depressed, and anxious. She copes with those feelings by cutting her arms with a razor. From the day she was born, Emma's parents were committed to shielding their only child from discomfort. Her mom was willing to cook three different entrees for dinner to make sure that toddler Emma would eat one of them. In middle school, Emma was upset when she wasn't invited to a friend's party. Rather than have Emma talk things out with her friend or just sit with the disappointment, her mother arranged a spectacular spa-day party at the same time so that many of her classmates came to Emma's gathering instead. Emma had no opportunity to face challenges herself and came to feel that this was because her mother believed that she was "incapable of living life." Every time she tried to handle a situation on her own, her mother subtly intruded and ultimately took over.

When Emma hit puberty, she tried to distance herself from her mother and find the space to foster independence. Her mother felt betrayed. "After all I've done for her!" she said to me. She said it to Emma too, often, and these declarations made Emma increasingly anxious and depressed. Her mother had trouble tolerating these feelings in Emma and repeatedly told me, "I just want my daughter back." For Emma, the feeling was not mutual. In the fraught process with her mother, Emma gave up trying to be a capable, independent young person, and when her anxiety and depression became unbearable, she began cutting to block out the painful emotions. It hurt, she said, but at least she was making a choice about her own life.

The parents of both Chris and Emma felt they'd done everything possible to help their children by trying to keep disappointments, anxieties, and sorrows at bay. They were hurt, baffled, and extremely angry when they ended up with troubled kids, one a young-adult substance abuser without motivation, one a depressed teenage cutter. This pattern of protecting kids early in life and then being disappointed and finally furious when they don't grow up has become one of the most common problems I see in my office.

I had to convince Emma's parents that she needed to practice bouncing back from disappointment on her own, and that ending childhood requires friction. Emma and her mother needed to be reassured that conflicts between parent and teenager could ultimately lead to authentic closeness. I also emphasized that Emma needed to learn how to take risks. Many of the teens I treat feel they can't take a chance, even a small one. "I wanted to take life science class," a high-school junior told me. "It sounded interesting. My mom said, 'You're not great at that; it'll bring down your GPA.'" This inquisitive boy is beginning to shut down, to succumb to the message, "If you can't be great right away, why try?" No wonder teens become terrified of risking "achievement failure" and instead prefer the passivity and safety of predictable outcomes.

Extremely risk-averse parents communicate their own anxiety to their children through catastrophizing. They're always suggesting the worst possible outcome of everyday challenges: If you don't bring your math grade up, you'll never get into a good school. If you don't get on the select team, you'll never play soccer again. If you don't have a date for the prom, everyone will think there's something wrong with you. This kind of thinking is contagious—and paralyzing. Combine it with the adolescent penchant for self-dramatization, and you might end up with a kid like one of my patients, a high-school senior who announced to me that she was suffering from PTSD because she was rejected by her dream school. While she did not have PTSD, her coping skills were so limited that in fact she did display some of the symptoms of this disorder (being startled by a ringing telephone, having nightmares), which generally develops only under the most extreme kinds of exposure to violence. Depending on the child, a college rejection might be sad, disappointing, upsetting, or expected. It should not be a trauma.

The Intimacy Gap

Neither young Emma nor older Chris was in a relationship. In my work, I'm finding that the adolescent task of developing the capacity for intimacy is often delayed until adulthood. A too-close attachment to parents seems to give kids fewer chances to experiment with forming bonds outside the family. Could that be why a hook-up culture prevails among millennials and why only 26 percent of them are married, compared to the 50 percent of baby boomers wed by the same age? Other forces may be affecting the millennial marriage rate—the sad lessons of their parents' divorces, a dearth of jobs that could support a family, paycheck-devouring levels of student debt. It could be a by-product of the digital age: left to their own devices, and I mean electronic devices, teens spend twice as much time communicating via text as they do in face-to-face encounters. They have less practice accurately reading the cues of disappointment, hurt, and anger, or of hopefulness, interest, and playful flirtation—the language of intimacy. Many young people in their twenties seem at a loss as to how to move past being someone's friend and into the more nuanced adult romantic partner role.

Undoubtedly a major factor in delayed intimacy is a slow-down in the development of emotional regulation, especially the ability to handle another person's feelings and to survive loss. Kids need room to experience and negotiate their first love, first sexual experiences, first heartbreak. Parents must allow them to feel bad so that they discover they can survive emotional crises. Many of the teens and young adults I work with are undone by feeling bad. They've had no practice, because adults have always stepped in to right the ship.

Rebels with a Cause

We disregard the imperatives of adolescent development at great risk to the emotional health of our teens. They are *supposed* to protest, make noise, experiment, and challenge the authority of the adults around them. That's how they engage in the process they're wired for, the process of figuring out who they are and who they are not.

You might not be able to tell from the outside that adolescence as we've known it is imperiled. In many ways teens today still act like the teens we've always known. They lie. They say they're going to the library but instead hook up with a girlfriend or boyfriend. They drink too much, smoke weed, drive with friends in the car when they've promised not to. They maintain some of the peer-pressured behavior of teens, so they have some experience with risk. But these experiences aren't the same as the psychological work of separating from the family in order to craft and test an authentic self.

A common parental refrain these days is "I can't stand to see my child unhappy." My response is always, "Then you're in the wrong profession." Adolescents learn to regulate their emotions by meeting an increasingly complex set of challenges, some of which they'll handle well and some they'll handle badly. We want our children safe, of course, but they can't mature until they know what they can handle and which skills need work. That knowledge isn't always pleasant. Parents have to be willing to return to their roles, not as friends or enablers, but as knowing, thoughtful adults who can provide the kind of security and stability that kids at any age need in order to learn from challenging experiences.

Adolescents ought to be a natural match for our age of uncertainty. Traditionally, they've been risk-takers and creative thinkers who work well in groups and aren't satisfied with the status quo. These are characteristics that come in handy when things are unpredictable and rapidly changing. If curiosity and productive insubordination are suppressed, adolescence is altered and adulthood is delayed. Fortunately, parents and teenagers are becoming wise to the dilemma and starting to reverse some of these unhelpful trends.

PART II

Course Correction

CHAPTER 5

Unlearning Helplessness
and Restoring Capabilities

Despite the alarming rise in teen anxiety and depression, and the stream of demoralized young people who come through my office, the spark of adolescence is impossible to extinguish. I see it flicker in the kids who push back against their parents' insistence that a tutor would help bring that B in physics up to an A, or that while a class in photography is nice, it won't bolster their résumé for college. And sometimes we all get to watch the spark ignite a bonfire.

In February 2018 a group of teenagers in Parkland, Florida, captivated the nation with their furious and far-reaching response to the shooting and killing of seventeen of their classmates. Harnessing social media, the students at Marjory Stoneman Douglas High School created a movement (#NeverAgain) to protest gun violence. They held news conferences and founded #MarchForOurLives to advocate for stricter gun control laws and energize young voters. They spent spring break organizing a nationwide protest that attracted more than 2 million people to 800-plus marches across the United States (and more overseas).[1] They adroitly handled reporters, politicians, and crowds of 200,000. We parents marveled at how empowered they were, how boldly they denounced the status quo and demanded change. In the speeches that went viral, in the plans they swiftly implemented, in their defiance and ambition, we saw a thrilling fearlessness. "What we must do now is enact change because that is what we do to things that fail: We change them," said Lo-renzo Prado, a Parkland school shooting survivor.[2] The audacity of these students stood in sharp contrast to our own feelings of futility and to the wariness and weariness of many of our kids.

It's encouraging to believe that inside every high-schooler beats the heart of a warrior. Most of them, we pray, won't be tested by trag-edy. But they'll all be challenged by a future that is sure to reward the type of guts and inventiveness displayed by the Parkland students. Regardless of the age of our child or the habits that have accrued in our family, we can help our kids develop those traits. Children and adolescents can rebuild their tolerance for new environments and learn how to conquer anxiety. They can restore capabilities that have atrophied and acquire strategies for maintaining confidence in the face of increasing demands and ambiguity. Our kids can replace trepidation and helplessness with agency and fearlessness.

Finding the Strength to Embolden Our Kids

It takes a courageous family to raise a courageous child. If facing uncertainty makes us panicky and overprotective, our first task is to regroup and fortify ourselves. As we ponder how we can communi-cate less anxiety to our children, it's worth reminding ourselves that parenting has a long trajectory. We tend to think that every mo-ment, decision, success, and failure is critical, but what's critical over time is that our children become loyal friends, good partners, honest and reliable workers, have a strong moral center, and develop other worthy attributes. Our goal as parents is to be courageous enough to give our kids the time and opportunities they need to cultivate these qualities, and to model them ourselves.

We also need to accept that our children's sense of accomplishment and self-worth will wax and wane along with their successes. One of my young patients was a star basketball player in middle school, confident and popular among his classmates. In high school he was placed on the junior team and didn't do particularly well. He went from being poised and positive to feeling insecure and gloomy for several months (which is when his startled mother brought him to see me). We explored his other interests and talents, and he decided to join a rugby team. As he became more competent, his confidence increased and he went back to being his "normal kick-ass self," as he put it. The human learning curve is full of dips and plateaus, as we all remember. We do our kids a favor when we acknowledge this.

Think of your child's growing up as a movie, not as a snapshot. What looks critical at one moment often becomes incidental over the course of time. The vast majority of our concerns—Daycare at age two or preschool at three? Public or private school? The traveling team or the local team? Summer job or summer school? State college or a private one?—usually end up mattering less than we believe they will. Love, support, curiosity, an emphasis on "doing the right thing," and the ability to tolerate our children's missteps and disappointments are what matter most.

When we shield children from failure or choreograph successes for them, we're distorting the experiences they need in order to grow. In contrast to the basketball player whose parents didn't interfere with his struggle, I can think of many kids whose parents have interfered and unintentionally placed roadblocks in the way. I'm seeing a patient who's gone through the first two years of college without going to class or writing a paper on her own. A paid tutor does it for her. I hesitated to include this example in the book, thinking it was too extreme. However, I mentioned it to a colleague and he countered with a story about a young man who completed all four years of university the same way. When he confronted the student's mother about it, she said, "You don't expect me to allow some grades to get in the way of his success, do you?"

I'm not suggesting we banish tutors from the educational landscape. They can guide students through facets of subjects that are particularly hard for them or through courses that are a punishing but unavoidable part of the core curricula. Hiring a tutor also shows kids that needing help isn't shameful; in fact, it's wise to know when to ask for it. If a child or teenager has learning disabilities, tutors can teach workarounds and how to study more effectively. The problem is not with tutors per se but with our assessment of our kids' abilities and temperament. Few parents will declare, "My child is a B student. That's exactly where she belongs." But a lot of us insist, "If she just worked a little harder, she'd be an A student." Tutors, we believe, will bridge the gap between brain power and effort. But hiring a tutor also sends the message *I'm afraid you're not smart enough.*

A fearful family is one in which the parents don't trust their children's intelligence, competence, or common sense. They don't trust the world to deliver the kind of advantages they feel are necessary for survival. They don't trust teachers or the system; they need to place a finger on the scale because they're afraid that whatever is required of their child, he or she won't measure up. It's a searing and destructive vote of no confidence.

As much money and effort as it takes to manipulate children's successes in this way, we do it because it gives us the illusion of control. It's a lot harder to hand appropriate control to our kids. We can start by acknowledging the emotional fuel that's required for this difficult, often painful, decades-long assignment. The greater our inner reserves, the more tolerance we'll have for all the sources of anxiety in our lives and in our children's lives, and the more effective we'll be at managing and modeling an approach to life that is dictated by thoughtful choices and not reflexive anxiety.

Shoring Up Our Emotional Reserves

There is a simple fact about emotional resources. They are not endless. Every one of us needs to understand that under conditions of high and chronic stress, too little sleep, and not enough opportunities for restorative activities, our judgment will be impaired, our decisions will be less than optimal, and in general we will function poorly.

More than 70 percent of moms work, as do almost 93 percent of fathers.[3] So most households are comprised of two working parents whose most sorely tested resource is time. This reality is even more pressing in the quarter of all households that are headed by a single parent.[4] Competition, as opposed to collaboration, has become the prevailing norm as parents scramble to help their children partake in what are believed to be limited resources. The bifurcation of wealth in this country adds a sense of urgency to our decisions about where our kids go to school, the courses they take, and the colleges they attend. The cost of college is prohibitive for many families, and a hardship for many more. There are days when any one of us would be hard-pressed to find time to take a restorative breath. Yet doing just that is critical to our goal of having the patience and attention span we need to help our kids build their own resilience, competence, and composure.

Meditation is an excellent tool for restoring equanimity. Fifteen minutes of solitude with Jon Kabat Zinn in the background can do wonders if you're so inclined, as I happen to be (although I was a late starter). But it's not for everyone. If meditation doesn't work for you, keep investigating. When *do* you feel calmer, sharper, more patient, wiser? In what environment do you laugh easily? When do you feel good about yourself? What situations, people, or physical locations make you feel relaxed and positive? The answers are highly subjective. When you discover the activities that rejuvenate you, try not to think of them as electives—fun stuff you get to do when all the dreary tasks of life have been completed. They are our refueling stations and deserve a slot in our daily schedule. A good friend in a close-knit family works a long day but always, always cooks dinner when she gets home. She finds it creative and relaxing. She's become such a good and cheerful cook that her grown kids often "just happen to be in the neighborhood" at dinnertime. It's a refueling twofer for her.

When it comes to regulating anxiety specifically about our children, we have more control than we may realize. A lot of angst builds up when our kids aren't even in the room. Take an inventory of your average day and ask yourself when your child-related anxiety spikes. Is it when you talk to other people about your kid? If so, who? Your mom, sibling, partner? Other moms and dads? Pinpoint the sources of anxiety and cut back on those conversations.

Some of us spend a lot of time comparing notes with other parents. What we're often doing is attempting to boost our child's position on this year's academic/social scoreboard. We think of it as healthy competition—we're fighting for our kids! That's what we tell ourselves when we grill other parents about their child's performance; when we ask them for the names of the best tutors, the most gifted teachers, the winningest sports teams; or when we nose around for info about who got invited to whose party. Even though our children may be nowhere in sight, our anxiety continues to rise because we can't stop competing, supposedly on their behalf. We can limit this behavior when we realize how it depletes our emotional resources, leaving less fuel for our relationship not only with our children but also with our partner and friends. Oh, and not incidentally, less bandwidth for our own mental health.

When we're with our kids, it's understandable to react anxiously to their anxiety. Understandable—but not beneficial. Kids worry about a lot of things: *Will I have someone to eat lunch with? Will Kara still be my friend today? Will Clayton text me back? Will I be picked for the team?* These concerns reflect normal phases of social development and aren't cause for alarm. To keep the atmosphere calm for our children and ourselves, we can reframe anxiety-provoking situations as opportunities:

"I might not get picked for the team!"

"I know you'd really like to get picked for the team, but if you don't it will give you more time. What would you like to use it for?"

Or:

"I know you'll feel bad if you don't get picked, but you can handle it."

Those words—*You may feel bad but you can handle it*—signal not only our faith in our child's abilities but also that *we* can handle it if they feel bad.

It's natural for us to empathize with our children. Sometimes, though, there's a blurry line between empathy and overidentification. Our kids, even the youngest of them, are separate from us. We're not always correct about the depth or duration of their anguish, or even its cause. (They don't tell us everything!) We're always going to have strong feelings when our children are in distress, but it's their distress, not ours, and for the most part we don't do them or ourselves any service by taking it on. Instead we can make a conscious decision to scale back our identification with them and say, "I understand that you're anxious. I think you can figure it out. Let me know if you need help."

Finally, there's the matter of sleep. Few of us get enough rest, and nothing drains our emotional reserves as quickly as sleep deprivation. For some reason, playing "Who's more exhausted?" has become a macho badge of honor among adults. High-schoolers have adopted it as well. Kids of all ages are sleep-deprived because of their crushing schedules, overuse of devices, being able to cajole worn-out parents into staying up too late, and because of school start times that experts agree are often far too early. Research is clear that sleep deprivation leads to impaired learning, poorer school and work performance, and emotional problems. We're running around like crazy trying to give our kids all kinds of questionable advantages when the best thing we could give them (and ourselves) is an adequate night's sleep every night.[5]

Lack of adequate sleep is such a pervasive problem among students of all ages that when parents call to tell me they think their child has ADD or ADHD, I rarely see the family right away. Instead I say, "My first appointment is three weeks from now. In the meantime, I'd like you to make sure your kid gets at least nine hours of sleep every night. Call me back then." Half the families never make the call.

Anxiety-Proofing with Progressive Desensitization

The dynamic of anxious parents accommodating their children's anxiety, leading to more anxiety and ultimately to accumulated disability, can begin very early in a child's life. Children are born either more or less anxious, and their natural propensity for it is often genetically related to that of their parents. Regardless of their genetic makeup, if children aren't exposed to challenges and don't learn how to handle them, they are likely to be risk-averse. The science of epigenetics has made it clear that genetics is almost always modified by the environment. When your toddler falls (as he or she will, over and over) are you indifferent, concerned, calm, or frightened? Your tolerance for the anxiety that typically accompanies new experiences is a crucial factor and one that will be tested regularly over the many years of parenting.

Anxiety disorders in children usually fall into one of three categories: social anxiety, separation anxiety, and generalized anxiety disorder (GAD). Lots of children have phobias (about spiders, bathrooms, dirt, food, and so on), but what differentiates GAD is that it involves multiple triggers. GAD is defined as "excessive anxiety and worrying occurring more days than not for at least six months about a number of events or activities."[6] Another part of the official diagnosis is that it causes distress or impairment in the child. Lots of kids can be repetitive or hyperfocused in a way that might strike us as neurotic but doesn't bother the child at all. Think of kids who love to count, are obsessed with the color purple, or only want to wear Batman pajamas day and night. These behaviors are common, usually transient, and of no particular concern.

Progressive desensitization is the standard treatment for children and adults with anxiety disorders. The process involves gradually increasing a person's exposure to situations that are causing the anxiety—like making sure the child who's afraid of dogs gets to come into contact with lots of friendly canines. Parents practice progressive desensitization all the time without realizing it:

"Mom, I'm scared there's a monster in my closet!"

"There's somebody in your closet? Let's take a look."

"No, I'm too scared. You open the closet."

"OK. See? There's nothing there."

The next night: "Mom, I'm still really scared. Open it again."

Most parents will check the closet for a couple of nights and then say, "Let's do it together." In a week or so the child is checking for himself. Eventually he doesn't bother to check because he's become desensitized to the fear. That developmental step is now behind him.

This pattern is repeated hundreds of times as kids are introduced to new foods, clothing, skills, people, and environments. As long as parents don't capitulate to their child's fears, the child moves past his or her resistance. It's when we're too tired or distracted to refuse— when "Never mind, we won't walk past the dog" is easier—that children can get stuck in their fears.

This is not to imply that anxiety disorders can always be laid at the feet of overly accommodating parents. There are limitless parent–child combinations, and anxiety disorders range from mildly inconvenient to debilitating. What I'm hoping we can do is raise our awareness of the little steps that add up to courage and self-efficacy. Ideally, a fallback response to a child's fear or hesitancy will be to reframe their anxiety as opportunity. "Oh, I remember how nervous I was the first time I went away to camp. But then I met Leslie, she was kind of nervous too, so we talked a lot and after a while we became best friends. You're really easy to talk to, so I'm thinking that you'll make some new friends too."

Using progressive desensitization, psychologists can help kids with most anxiety disorders. Sometimes we'll request a psychiatry consult to consider anti-anxiety medication if the child's symptoms are overwhelming. Then it's a matter of gradually exposing the youngster to the source of the anxiety while providing plenty of positive reinforcement for his or her successes. It usually takes from six to twelve weekly sessions. Where therapists have an advantage over parents is that we're not dealing with our own kids, so our anxiety isn't as affected by the youngster's distress. However, it's entirely possible for parents to use progressive desensitization on their own children. They just need patience. They also need common sense: not every aversion requires a twelve-week desensitizing program. Children go through phases. We look for impairment and persistence of symptoms when deciding what to treat and what is likely to resolve on its own.

To give you a general idea of progressive desensitization in action, here's how I treated Lucas, a nine-year-old boy who had refused to use public bathrooms for two previous years. These stages of progressive desensitization can be replicated for most anxiety disorders and phobias. As I've said, with younger children I most often teach the parents how to implement this technique.

I began by rehearsing some relaxation scenarios with Lucas—I taught him some deep breathing and the concept of mindfulness. This is important because he will need to have some tools to help him remain reasonably calm as he confronts his anxieties. Then Lucas and I made a list of things that made him anxious about public bathrooms. We talked about what was most scary and what was just a little scary. I took the least anxiety-provoking thing on his list and started with that. He said that seeing a picture of a bathroom was low anxiety and using a public bathroom was the highest anxiety. We started by having him look at a photo of a bathroom in a magazine and rate his level of anxiety on a scale of 1 to 10. If he had been terribly uncomfortable with that exposure, I simply would have instructed him to take a few deep breaths and maybe say the word *bathroom* out loud." I wanted the first few activities I did with Lucas to be successful. Tackling a phobia takes real courage and I let Lucas know that. I began with low-anxiety exposure and, bit by bit, I increased the salience of it, the in-his-faceness of it. Lucas and I went from looking at pictures of bathrooms, to drawing pictures of bathrooms, to driving in a car past a place where the bathroom makes him nervous, to walking down the hall by the bathroom, to his going in but not using the toilet, and finally to his using the toilet.

Whenever possible, I take my patients out into the world to have real contact with the object of their anxiety. Research tells us that this is a more effective way to desensitize than only being in the office. With each step they rate their anxiety, and we only progress as it decreases. It doesn't have to drop to zero; it just has to go down far enough (say to a 3 or 4) for the patient to manage that level of the experience. If they're getting too stressed, I'll say, "You've been doing really good work. It seems like this has made you a little anxious. Maybe we're moving too fast." And then I'll return to the previous step. The next session, we inch forward again. By the time most kids have completed the sessions, they've learned either to mostly eliminate anxiety or, more frequently, to manage a tolerable level of anxiety. Each successful experience reinforces the desensitization.

Progressive desensitization as a response to children's anxiety demonstrates our belief in their abilities. Day-to-day, we're not going to ask them to rate every blip of anxiety or revulsion, we're just going to calmly inquire about it and gently nudge them forward. "You hate cheese? Have you ever tried shredded cheese? You know, there's cheese on that pizza you love." "You're scared of moths? Did you know they're kind of like nighttime butterflies? I wonder if you'd like the butterfly pavilion at the Natural History Museum." Question, probe, joke around a little, educate, keep moving forward. Build tolerance by encouraging curiosity. Give them a chance to conquer their fear.

Always, our goal is to promote bravery and inquisitiveness. We're not going to win every round. Sometimes we're too tired to tussle with them about the monster in the closet, and that's all right. A general thrust toward fearlessness and engagement is what we're aiming for, not parental perfection (an elusive, manufactured concept that after thirty-five years of personal and professional practice I've never encountered!).

Giving Kids Age-Appropriate Control

Building capabilities eases anxiety: the two are inextricably linked. As our children gain proficiency in meeting diverse people, experiencing new environments, and making transitions, we can simultaneously give them more control over their lives. Like the progressive desensitization parents instinctively practice, there's no need to manufacture special events where kids can take control or experience risk—there are plenty of opportunities in everyday life. The trick is not to shield them from activities and responsibilities as long as those are age-appropriate (or just slightly beyond). If we encourage our children and offer nonjudgmental feedback along the way, they'll get increasingly adept at managing their time, completing tasks even if they're boring, setting ambitious goals for themselves, making mistakes and recovering, and inventing new ways to solve problems.

The following list of age-appropriate chores and responsibilities is taken from Montessori guidelines. These are suggestions, not strict rules. Each task a child masters builds competency and self-assurance. And if chores evolve into routine responsibilities, they also teach what it means to be a contributing member of a community. That's foundational to our kids' growing into good team players, classmates, colleagues, friends, partners, and citizens. While

Ages 2–3	Ages 4–5	Ages 6–7	Ages 8–9	Ages 10–11	Ages 12 and up
Put toys in toy box	Feed pets	Gather trash	Load dishwasher	Clean bathrooms	Mop floors
Stack books on shelf	Wipe up spills	Fold towels	Change light bulbs	Vacuum rugs	Change overhead lights
Place dirty clothes in laundry hamper	Put away toys	Dust/mop floors	Wash laundry	Clean countertops	Wash/vacuum car
Throw trash away	Make the bed Straighten bedroom Water houseplants	Empty dishwasher	Hang/fold clean clothes	Deep clean kitchen	Trim hedges
Carry firewood	Sort clean silverware	Match clean socks	Dust furniture	Prepare simple meal	Paint walls
Fold washcloths			Spray off patio	Mow lawn	Shop for groceries w/list
Set the table	Prepare simple snacks	Weed garden	Put groceries away	Bring in mail	Bake bread or cake
Fetch Diapers and wipes	Use handheld vacuum	Rake leaves	Scramble eggs	Do simple mending (hems, buttons, etc.)	Do simple home repairs
Dust baseboards	Clear kitchen table	Peel potatoes or carrots	Bake cookies	Sweep out garage	Wash windows
	Dry and put away dishes	Make salad	Walk dogs		Iron clothes
	Disinfect doorknobs		Sweep porches		Watch younger siblings
			Wipe off table		

your family may not love the idea of a 2-year-old carrying firewood or a 6-year-old wielding a potato peeler, the list reflects the types of chores children and adolescents can reasonably be expected to master at different ages, according to the educators at Montessori.[7] I've included this list as a tonic to all the assignment lists, ranking lists, and precollege preparation lists that float around our households. Before your child goes off to Princeton or to San Jose State, they're going to need to know how to cook an egg or change a burned-out light bulb.

While some of the tasks listed above may seem a bit challenging, educators are well aware that children benefit from taking on situations that are in their ZPD, or zone of proximal development. Nothing terrifying—tasks just outside their current comfort zone. Kids who learn early in life that they're capable of mastering activities that at first feel a little stressful grow up better able to handle stress of all kinds. Along the way they will have scraped knees, bumped heads, experienced social exclusion and probably imbibed a bit more alcohol than is optimal. This is how they grow, develop awareness of their strengths and weaknesses, and cultivate the self-efficacy that keeps them from feeling helpless. In contrast, when children are given little control over their environment and activities, it lowers their motivation and inhibits their forward growth.

That's what happened in one family that I treated. The parents of 4-year-old Jack came to see me because the teachers at the academic preschool he had just begun attending were worried. Jack had stopped participating and spent lesson time staring into space. "My son has always been happy-go-lucky and full of life," his dad said. "I don't know what's happening to him." When I visited the school to observe Jack, I immediately noticed two key things. First, because there was so much material to be learned—worksheets involving letters and numbers, for example—the preschoolers were expected to stay in their seats. In general, this is more difficult for boys than for girls. So Jack was often gently reprimanded for moving around too much. I saw him become increasingly listless as the morning progressed.

Second, presenting lessons with right and wrong answers meant that the little students were frequently "wrong." What else could possibly be expected from a 4-year-old? I could see the kids instantly deflate when they enthusiastically offered an answer only to be told by the teacher that they were wrong. I felt like I was observing the etiology of learned helplessness as child after child couldn't positively impact his or her environment.

I advised Jack's parents that, like most preschoolers, their son needed an environment that provided lots of opportunities to move around, explore, and learn by trial and error. Tony Wagner, Expert in Residence at the Harvard Innovation Lab, told me that he'd like to replace the word "*failure*" with the term "*trial and error.*" Dr. Wagner celebrates the process of growth through allowing kids to learn from not-quite-there attempts and false starts. "Otherwise," he says, "it's like telling a baby not to talk until he can speak in complete sentences." Jack would thrive with teachers who valued all kinds of responses, not just "right" or "wrong" ones. This is how most young children learn best.

I explained to Jack's parents that the greatest predictor of academic success is engagement. Engagement has emotional, cognitive, and behavioral elements. Young kids like Jack should be enthusiastic about going to preschool, excited about learning, and active in the classroom. Jack wasn't engaged at this school, and he wasn't the only child there who seemed to have shut down. Much of the class was preternaturally quiet. In preschool this is a certain sign of withdrawal and disengagement. A healthy school environment, especially for kids this young, should be active, noisy, bustling with movement and enthusiasm. When I was scouting preschools for my son Loren, one headmaster took me into a classroom of four-year-olds and said, "See? You can hear a pin drop." I practically ran out of the room. It was clear that my active, enthusiastic, extremely motoric firstborn would have spent most of his preschool education being disciplined in the principal's office.

Within weeks of transferring to a play-based preschool, Jack was back to being his happy-go-lucky self. The experience made his parents aware of how important it was to provide Jack with opportunities for success and a school that was a good fit for their active, inquisitive kid. As often as possible, they would give Jack chances to investigate his world, applaud his efforts, and encourage him to keep learning. Instead of telling him he was "wrong" when he didn't answer something correctly, they learned the simple response that psychologists use all the time, "Tell me more." When children are young, whether 2 plus 2 actually equals 4, 5, or 6 is less important than finding out how they think, what is going on in their mind, and how they see the world. There will be plenty of time later to gently let them know the "right" answer. Obviously, at some point, your child will learn that 2 plus 2 equals 4, but that is by far the easier part of education. Establishing inquisitiveness, enthusiasm about learning, and having an open, playful, and agile mind is much more important than memorizing numbers. Every business leader I spoke to about future valuable skills underscored this exact point.

Assessing Risk

An essential part of building children's self-efficacy and independence is helping them venture out on their own. It starts with crossing the street alone and progresses to walking to school with a friend, riding a bike or skateboard around the neighborhood, taking public transportation, going to the mall, learning to drive, and taking a trip with a class, club, or group of friends. At every step parents may be met with ominous warnings from neighbors and other parents, either in person or on overheated sites like Nextdoor.com. The relentless hand-wringing prompted former journalist Lenore Skenazy to found Let Grow, an organization whose mission is to "counter the culture of overprotection." Its website serves as an aggregate for news items with headlines like, "Company Sells Electronic Ankle Monitors to Dept. of Corrections—and Parents of Teens" and "To Grandmother's House He Went: Busybodies Alert Cops to Boy, 8, Walking Alone." One section is devoted to debunking scare stories and providing accurate data about child abduction, sex trafficking, and other parental nightmares.[8]

Inflated crime statistics aside, it's undeniable that each week seems to present a new challenge/opportunity/risk. How do we know if an activity really is too dangerous for our child? As I write this, electric scooters have begun zipping their way onto San Francisco's Uber-crowded city streets. They're a great method of traveling the "last mile" to public transportation. But a friend recently saw four high-school boys, sans helmets, racing the scooters at top speed (15 mph) on the sidewalk in front of her house and using a 10-inch wedge of uplifted sidewalk to launch themselves into some serious air. My own 28-year-old "child" just bought one of these scooters. Do I love it? No. So I bought him a yellow vest, issued some obvious (and probably unnecessary) caveats and wished him well. This is just to let you know that parental vigilance is basically a chronic disorder. We adjust, ratchet down appropriately, occasionally hold our breath, and then get back to our own lives.

The problem is not only how do *we* know if an activity is too risky, but just as important, how do we train our children and teen-agers to think about risk? A simple strategy is the three categories General Colin Powell insisted his intelligence officers use when assessing conditions for his troops. He'd say, "Tell me what you know . . . tell me what you don't know . . . and then tell me what you think."[9] When we're posing these same concerns to our kids, we should let them provide the answers rather than filling in the blanks ourselves. It'll be counterproductive to demand, "What do you know about electric scooters? Do you know how fast they go? Fifteen miles an hour! That's how fast!" More effective would be to suggest that the kids research the scooters online and report back to us. They're likely to come across some sobering facts about the damage that can be done to a skull without a helmet when it meets the sidewalk at 15 mph. Once our kids have collected information, we should encourage them to articulate their conclusions.

I like General Powell's categories because they encourage traits our kids will need in order to evaluate risk throughout their lives: a habit of contemplation and critical thinking that includes collecting information, considering alternatives, research, and finally, drawing reasoned conclusions. It's an elegant template for rational decision-making.

Parents and children will also find it helpful to think about risk-taking as a problem-solving opportunity. Consider this scenario: your 15-year-old wants to go to a party at her friend Daniel's house, and you know his parents aren't going to be home most of the night. You're pretty sure this situation is over your daughter's head and poses an unacceptable level of risk to her. You can simply say, "No way," but that doesn't teach her anything about how to assess risk in social situations where you might not be there to make the call. A better approach would be to talk about the pros and cons of different options. After asking her thoughts about the party, and listening respectfully, you can move into your concerns, which are likely to fall under General Powell's "what you don't know" category.

"Daniel's a nice kid. I can see why you want to go to the party. But my guess is there will be alcohol there, and you know that drinking is not okay with me. Alcohol messes with good decision-making in kids your age."

"Ma, I'll be fine!"

"Sometimes parties can get out of hand quickly and this is a situation you haven't had much practice with."

"Look, there probably will be some drinking and when kids start hooking up maybe I feel a little nervous. But so what? I'll call you if there's a problem."

"The phone is good, but I don't feel comfortable relying on it yet."

"You never let me do anything! When can I just go out like all the other kids?"

"Not this time. I appreciate that you understand how alcohol can impair judgment. That's why at this point a parent needs to be home all night."

I'm offering this sample dialogue knowing that real-life conversations never go as smoothly as they appear in parenting books. I'm not able to include the mandatory eye-rolling and contemptuous looks. However, in exchanges like this, we can respect our teens' point of view (increasing the likelihood that our directives will be followed) while dropping legitimate concerns into their consciousness. Before she says no, this mom is helping her daughter think about risk, options, and unanticipated consequences. The young teen brain is not very good at this type of thinking.

There is a simple rule of thumb parents can use in most situations to help them determine whether their child is prepared to take the next level of risk: look at how well they managed the prior level of risk. Say your 10-year-old has been riding his bike around the block on his own for about a week, and now he's desperate to be allowed to ride around your suburban neighborhood. This request spikes your blood pressure. *What if he falls? What if he has a flat tire? What if some pervert jumps out of the bushes and grabs him?!*

Your first job is to calm your own nerves. Most of us know when we're catastrophizing. Second, take a look at how he did biking around the block. Was he responsible? Did he come back on time as promised? Has he had a flat or been shown how to repair one? Finally, talk to your son and set some appropriate next-step limits. "You can ride your bike around for thirty minutes. Let's see how that goes and then we'll talk about a longer cruise around the neighborhood." This rule of thumb is helpful for everything from when to allow your toddler to go down the steeper slide to when to allow your teenager to drive on the highway.

The ability to organize oneself and assess risk has always been important, and it will be a signature skill during turbulent times. That's why it's so beneficial to be transparent with your children about your decision-making process as opposed to simply issuing a yes or no, or caving in to their demands because you're too tired to argue. Of course we get an occasional pass when all we can muster is a "yes" or a "no." We're human too. But we must tend toward clarity.

Changing Explanatory Styles from Pessimistic to Optimistic

A hallmark of learned helplessness is the belief that we can't do anything to change our circumstances. It's as if there's a narrator inside our head murmuring a steady stream of negative, self-defeating commentary. This is especially insidious when we're interpreting life events. We each have an explanatory style—the manner in which we habitually explain to ourselves why things happen and what they mean. Say you've just blown a presentation at work. An optimistic explanatory style would go something like "I should have been better prepared. They had faith in me to pull this off and I know I can. I just have to put in more effort." This generally leads to a robust sense of agency. A pessimistic explanatory style would be "Just like me. I'm such a loser. I'll probably get fired over this." This generally leads to learned helplessness. We don't explain every life event to ourselves in the same way, but our explanatory style pretty consistently tilts in one direction or the other.

Explanatory style is determined by our responses to three key components: permanence, pervasiveness, and personalization.

PERMANENCE

People who give up easily, who succumb to helplessness, believe that the causes of bad events or situations are permanent—that the way things are right now is the way they'll be forever. "I'll never be able to do this." Those who resist helplessness believe that the causes of bad events are temporary. "Today was a tough day; tomorrow will be better." People with an optimistic explanatory style may get discouraged and give up temporarily, but those with a negative, pessimistic explanatory style (think Eeyore, from *Winnie the Pooh*) give up permanently.

PERVASIVENESS

When failure strikes a single area of their lives, people with a negative explanatory style feel it universally, believing that what's true for one situation is pervasive. They catastrophize, declaring that everything is falling apart (and always will be) when something goes wrong. "I can never do anything right." People with optimistic explanatory styles, on the other hand, can be upset about a specific event without generalizing to all events. "I'm not great at math, but I'm really good in English." They may become temporarily discouraged in the affected area of their lives yet stalwartly march on in others. High-performing kids with an optimistic explanatory style may still get depressed, but in spite of this, they become more determined to keep up with their studies so that when their depression lifts they aren't behind in their work.

PERSONALIZATION

When bad things happen, people with a pessimistic explanatory style consider the problem personal, blaming themselves (internalizing). "I'm an idiot." People with optimistic explanatory styles are more likely to blame circumstances (externalizing). "Guess the boss was in a bad mood today." Persistent internalizing lowers self-esteem.

In a therapeutic setting, we treat patients' negative explanatory styles with cognitive behavioral therapy (CBT). CBT, generally shown to be the most effective therapy for depression and anxiety, is based on the idea that what we consciously think about a situation or condition determines in great part how we feel.

Here's how the members of one family changed their explanatory style. When Ashley didn't do particularly well on her SATs, she became convinced that there was no point in taking them again, even though she was only a junior. She couldn't possibly improve, she said, because she's "stupid" and "a failure." To back this up she pointed out that some of her friends did extremely well. But she overlooked other kids who didn't do well on their first go-round.

She was depressed, teary, and convinced that after high school she'd be working minimum-wage jobs for the rest of her life. Her parents tried to be solicitous, but they added to her anxiety by talking about the test every night at dinner, suggesting prep courses, tutors, and other strategies. Ashley's mother couldn't stop asking her husband what they were going to do if their daughter refused to take the test again, or if she didn't score well the second time. The mom made so many phone calls to the school about improving Ashley's test score that a counselor referred Ashley and her parents to me.

The first thing I noticed was that Ashley had a very limited explanatory style. She was a consummate internalizer. According to her, every unpleasant or uncomfortable thing that ever happened to her had been her fault. She told me, for example, about a time she wasn't invited to sit at her usual table of friends in middle school (typical middle-school trauma), and described it as the day she realized how unattractive and unlovable she was. When I pointed out to her that there are many ways to see a situation, and that maybe her middle-school rejection could be explained another way, she was confused.

We began CBT, which involved teaching Ashley how to observe and question her explanatory style, a task she found difficult at first. She needed a lot of coaching from me to come up with possible alternative explanations (middle-school girls can be mean, maybe they were threatened by Ashley's good looks, maybe they'd had fights at home and were feeling retaliatory). It took about twelve sessions of CBT for Ashley to learn how to dispute her knee-jerk explanation of bad things as pervasive, permanent, and personal by asking herself a series of questions: What happened? How did it make me feel? Why do I think it happened? What evidence do I have that this explanation is the right one? Are there alternate explanations for what happened? Clearly, in addition to limiting and even eliminating symptoms, CBT is also a great reinforcer of critical thinking.

My sessions with her parents focused mostly on helping Ashley's mother to change her own pessimistic explanatory style. (There may be a genetic component to our inherent explanatory style; many of the pessimistic kids I see have one parent or both with the same bent.) Once Ashley and her mother got the hang of confronting their explanatory styles, they began to work together, catching one another in negative thinking and asking for evidence.

Neither Ashley nor her mom is likely to morph into a Pollyanna. They were, however, able to shift their thinking enough so that they could challenge themselves and each other when they slipped into pessimism and catastrophizing. Changing explanatory styles also helped Ashley with her tendency to ruminate—to think repetitively about the causes and consequences of bad experiences, a trait that is found more often in females than males.[10] To her relief, Ashley discovered that she could stop ruminating if she intentionally challenged her dark thoughts or distracted herself. Transforming a pessimistic explanatory style often begins with arguing against one's own negative inner narrator.

Ashley took the SAT again at the end of her junior year; she did better. She took it a third time in the fall of her senior year, continuing to improve enough to be considered for some of her top-choice colleges. She could finally say, rather triumphantly, "What happens once doesn't mean your whole life is ruined."

Cultivating Optimism

The concept of learned helplessness was originated by Martin Seligman, a groundbreaking psychologist who in 1998 developed the concept of positive psychology. He described the new field as "the scientific study of positive human functioning and flourishing on multiple levels."[11] Prior to Seligman, the workings of the human mind were examined almost exclusively in terms of mental illness, not mental health. After researching the factors that contribute to psychological well-being, Seligman came to believe that every one of us carries a word in our heart—yes or no. Optimism is a yes; pessimism is a no. Childhood pessimism is the precursor to adult pessimism and is associated with depression, so dealing with it early is important.

I often suggest to parents that they try Seligman's "ABCDE" method of helping kids conquer pessimism. Here, in brief, is how it played out with one family I counseled:

A=ADVERSITY. A 10-year-old boy came home tearful because he was cut from the baseball team he was hoping to make.

B=BELIEF. The parents asked their son what he believed about what happened. He answered, "Lots of my friends made the team, so I'm a loser. They probably won't want to be friends with me. I'll never be one of the cool kids."

C=CONSEQUENCES. They asked the boy how he dealt with the disappointment. "I just sat by myself in a corner at lunch," he told them, "and I wouldn't talk to anyone."

D=DISPUTATION. The parents educated their son with examples of how he might counter his negative thoughts, assuring him that arguing against his negativity would make him feel better. They guided their disappointed ballplayer through a series of questions, much like the CBT uses to challenge and change explanatory style. The results of a few rounds of disputation were extremely heartening: "Okay, so I'm not so good at baseball. But baseball isn't the most important thing to me. Actually, what I really like best is being good at math. And I was chosen for the Mathlete team, so I do get picked for some things."

E=ENERGY. By the time the boy finished challenging his assumptions, his parents reported, he'd bounced back from his disappointment and was ready to move on. Buoyed by the relief and enthusiasm of feeling more cheerful, he even became something of a wordsmith. "It kind of sucks to not be good at baseball," he said. "I guess I'll work on it. But I'm going to work most on math. I'm mathletic!"

Doing things for other people increases optimism, research tells us. So does the practice of gratitude. These interventions are worth the trouble: optimism is not simply the absence of pessimism; it is a way of thinking and of approaching the world that confers many advantages. Optimists are happier, healthier, and more resilient than pessimists. They're less likely to ruminate, they have better emotional control, and they perform better at school, at work, and on the playing field.

Moving from a Fixed Mindset to a Growth Mindset

Building on Seligman's theories, Stanford psychologist Carol Dweck was interested in how learned helplessness and explanatory style related to classroom learning. Dweck found that children—all of us, in fact—approach problems with what she termed a fixed or a growth mindset. Kids with a growth mindset believe it's possible to get smarter if you work at it; they regard false starts and unsuccessful attempts as opportunities. Children with a fixed mindset try mightily to avoid mistakes; they think that if they can't do something right the first time, improvement is impossible. Fixed-mindset kids as young as four will keep doing the same simple puzzle over and over rather than risk failing at tougher puzzles. Growth mindset kids don't understand why someone would choose to keep doing the same thing when the world holds so many interesting challenges.

Dweck's work is relevant to adults as well as children. It is used in companies all over the world as they try to cultivate a growth mindset in their workforce. Employees can't afford to have a static view of their intelligence, capacity, and competence when adaptability to changing conditions is so crucial to an organization's success. Not surprisingly, preliminary research on the impact of the pandemic shows that college students with a growth mindset were better able to learn, be engaged, perform, and be less stressed than students with a fixed mindset.[12]

Shifting children from a fixed mindset to a growth mindset needs to be a family affair, and the dinner table is a good place to start. Instead of asking about test grades, parents might ask, "What did you learn?" Instead of asking a young athlete about scores and wins, they might ask what worked well and what mistakes she made and what she learned from them both. I also recommend that parents tell their kids about mistakes they've made and how they've turned failures or disappointments into learning experiences and opportunities. Kids don't always see or understand that adults face challenges every day, usually small, sometimes big, and they are reassured by models of parental perseverance in the face of setbacks.

I also think it's helpful to explain what a growth and a fixed mindset mean and how they affect the brain. Kids like learning about their inner workings. I have a young girl who came to me very much with a fixed mindset—not surprising, as it was the dominant mode of thinking in the house. Dinnertime was a recitation of each person's daily failures and how badly they all felt. Mom burnt the casserole. The train broke down and Dad was late for a meeting. Her brother didn't make varsity. The boy she liked hooked up with another girl. So this became a family intervention, and with some work both individually and as a family the idea of the growth mindset took hold. Dinnertime is very different now, with every family member on the lookout for someone regressing to a fixed mindset. I was fortunate that everyone bought into the idea and that they turned it into a fun nightly ritual. But well explained, it's awfully hard to argue against implementing a growth mindset in the home.

To encourage a growth mindset, I urge parents to move away from judging children on performance alone and to praise their openness to risk-taking and willingness to try new things. And I tell them that when they help their children move from a fixed mindset to a growth mindset, they're helping them build a better brain: recent research suggests that kids with a growth mindset are more likely to have a greater number of neuronal connections in the areas of the brain associated with learning than do kids with fixed mindsets. After all, our brains are prewired to learn new things. A good dinnertime question is, "What was something new you learned today?"

Parents and Kids Are Stepping Up

Six months after the Parkland shooting, Marjory Stoneman Douglas High opened its doors to the first day of the fall semester. Among the many parents interviewed by the media for the occasion was Ryan Petty, who had lost his daughter Alaina in the slaughter. He was also father to Patrick, now entering his senior year. The interviewer inquired about the mood at the Petty household that morning— how were the remaining family members handling the difficult anniversary? They had talked about it, Ryan Petty acknowledged, but then he said that his son had been back on campus for several days already: "[We're] so very proud of him. He has really demonstrated a lot of courage in his willingness to go back to school and actually help other students come back and feel safe." The father went on to reveal his own plans for the rest of the year: he would be running for a seat on the local school board. "School boards are literally making life-and-death decisions for our kids and for our teachers. And I decided the best way for me to influence the policies and make sure that the security protocols are implemented correctly is to have a seat at the table."[13]

The Florida families that were impacted by the Parkland shooting are no different from families anywhere. Children and teenagers are capable of changing the way they engage with the world. Adults, too, can make profound changes when jump-started by a threat to their family. Our challenge is to jump-start ourselves and our kids without the push of a catastrophe. We can make all sorts of adjustments in our parenting approach that will help our kids achieve greater competence as well as better mental health. They may not win the Nobel Prize for Peace, like Malala Yousafzai did at 17, or start a movement like #MarchForOurLives. But they can recover the zest, curiosity, proactivity, and comfort with risk-taking that are their birthright.

I believe that all children and adolescents are capable of feats of courage and compassion. My friend's son, Ryan, had cancer and chemo when he was just thirteen. His friends all shaved their heads in solidarity. They talked a lot about wanting to change their classmates' perceptions so that the other kids didn't see Ryan as weird. Teenagers at that age are honing their moral compass. Given the kinds of wrenchingly difficult choices that are likely to present themselves in the coming years—who gets advanced medical care, the ethics of designer babies, how to prioritize our planet and our economy, how to regulate AI—whatever we can do to support our kids as they struggle with moral dilemmas is valuable. Often this means just listening as they wrestle with ethical issues about the planet, the country, and themselves. Patience and a few well-placed questions do more to advance their thinking than any long-winded lecture is likely to do.

In order to meet the challenges that await our kids, it is critical that we help them develop into thoughtful, moral, self-confident, and autonomous adults. In this chapter we've seen the places where they are likely to get stuck and we've learned how to help them regain their momentum. Next we'll explore the specific attributes our children are most likely to need in order to have a place at the table as they enter the unknowable and sure-to-be-remarkable future.

CHAPTER 6

Demystifying
Twenty-First-Century Skills

I know that twenty-first-century skills are what everyone is talking about. Come on. It's so granola. Kids need hard skills, not soft skills. My kid just started an investment club at his high school. Mark my words, that's the ticket.

—James, father of a 17-year-old high-school junior

Two decades into the twenty-first century, parents and educators are still trying to identify "twenty-first-century skills"—and there doesn't seem to be an end to the possibilities. The expertise our kids are supposed to master before they arrive at college has swelled to a to-do list that is more daunting than inspiring. Certainly core curricula like reading, writing, history, geography, math, and science are just as vital to the education of a well-rounded student as they ever were. But in recent years a great deal has been added to the list of academic must-haves. In uncertain times everyone seems to have a pet idea about what skills will be most needed.

Educators are doing their best to get their arms around this predicament, and an extensive, much-read document published by an education think tank in 2015 illustrates what they're up against. *P21 Framework Definitions* featured a set of student outcomes that incorporated traditional subjects and "21st century learning themes."[1]

The themes included global awareness; financial, economic, business, and entrepreneurial literacy; civic literacy; health literacy; and environmental literacy. Information, media, and technology skills were also deemed essential. In addition, the framework included an array of desirable life and career skills: leadership, collaboration, project management, and more, all on top of the basic subjects you and I had to master when we were in school.[2] And what has been removed to make way for this onslaught of new content? Art, recess, music, and PE—the slivers of school that support spiritual and physical health.

I'm not saying this breadth of expertise isn't within the reach of certain students. But a 2017 article in *Education Week* pointed out the drawbacks of such sweeping recommendations: "One fear is that the bar for making today's students future-proof is unrealistically high. And even if America's schools could churn out a steady stream of [extraordinarily high-achievers], some experts worry it might not matter," because automation and AI are primed to alter or eliminate so many jobs. [3]

I would agree. The more I investigated the ballooning list of twenty-first-century skills, the more skeptical I became of the overkill. Consider a skill that was widely touted just a few years ago: coding. Experts advised that all kids should learn to code, just like learning their ABCs. If nothing else, coders would always be employable. By 2019 it was generally acknowledged that artificial intelligence would soon be handling much of its own coding—in fact, some computers were already coding themselves.[4] So what looked like a surefire academic/workplace advantage has been replaced in a mere two years by a new iteration—data analysis—that treats coding as a language requirement. It is likely that shifts like this will continue, probably at an even greater rate of acceleration.

Is it even possible to know which knowledge and capabilities will best support our children no matter what the future brings? Is there a way to step back from the panicky piling-on of more requirements and teach our kids a set of skills they can reasonably be expected to master whatever their natural talents and interests may be and whatever kind of work they may choose? And whom to ask: Educators? Psychologists? Career counselors? Scientists? Putting these questions to the expected cast of characters just added to my confusion. Educators want to expand the "core" curriculum, scientists want more STEM, psychologists want more SEL (social and emotional learning). Like the blind men touching the elephant, experts in each discipline see only a part of the picture. But I wanted to see the whole elephant. Could all these differing views of what matters in education somehow be woven together, or do we need a whole new strategy? Given that our near future promises to be uncertain and unpredictable, and that solutions seemed so varied, I felt challenged to confront what techies call a "wicked" problem. Wicked problems are tough to solve because they're complex, difficult to define, have incomplete and contradictory information, and resist solution. Sounds exactly like the kinds of challenges confused parents and educators are struggling with. I knew I would need to cast a wide net to capture diverse points of view in order to come up with a set of guidelines that are understandable, actionable, and likely to stand the test of time.

Life in a VUCA World

I began my search with a simple question: Who is already dealing with the most extreme types of uncertain conditions? A friend who's an ex–Navy SEAL sprang to mind. Over coffee, I told him about the parents who confess to me that they don't feel equipped to cope with a world of disconcerting unpredictability and upheaval, and I described educators' attempts to meet our era's uncertain but escalating demands.

"Ah—VUCA," he responded. "It's an acronym that pretty much covers life on Earth today: Volatile, Uncertain, Complex, and Ambiguous." While the notion of VUCA began as a description of the unsettled world at the end of the Cold War, the acronym itself was not created until the late 1990s and became popular after the terrorist attacks in 2001. VUCA became standard military lingo for summing up the novel and extreme fighting conditions in Iraq and Afghanistan. The troops on the ground—and eventually the military brass—realized that to be effective in a fluid and often chaotic environment, they would need to create more horizontal chains of command and to rethink traditional training and education.

Researching VUCA, I learned that the term was adopted by business leaders who had to devise new strategies for confronting uncertainty, even pandemonium, in the marketplace, especially after the financial crisis of 2008–2009. Eventually, VUCA conditions created a paradox in the world of business, and then, notably, in the world of technology. Tech mantras like "move fast and break things," "disrupt," and "fail fast, fail often" imply both thrilling invention and thoughtless destruction. Left out of early discussions were the ethical dilemmas that arose along with all that chaotic creativity. Only after the Russian hacking of the 2016 U.S. presidential elections did the moral dimension of unrestrained technology gain the serious attention it deserves. Ethics suddenly moved front and center in our concerns about managing a VUCA world.

The challenges of VUCA were also confronted by a group intimately involved in the future of work: college career counselors.

Tasked with providing guidance that will lead students to fulfilling and financially rewarding careers, the counseling community arrived at a sobering conclusion: there's no longer such a thing as a lifelong career. In 2011, the *NACADA Journal* published a report titled "Career Advising in a VUCA Environment." Drawing from ninety-one sources in fields related to employment, behavioral economics, sociology, and more, the authors stated:

> The expectation for a lifelong career is no longer realistic because the nature and pace of change in the workplace is so rapid and unpredictable that no curriculum can provide students with all of the skills they will need to be employable throughout their lifetime. . . . Employers have also learned that they cannot expect graduates of either high school or college to enter the workforce with sufficient skills and special knowledge to immediately meet job obligations. . . .
>
> In a VUCA work environment, job security does not result from having a job, but from purposely and self-consciously maintaining a currency of skill and special knowledge that assures employability. . . . Career advisors must help students realize that choosing the perfect major or program will not give students the specific knowledge in any occupation that they will need to be successful. They need to see formal, higher education as a preparatory phase of continuous, lifelong knowledge acquisition and skill building that is accomplished by a variety of means and media.[5]

Top executives at LinkedIn echo these declarations on the part of career counselors. Chief People Officer Christina Hall says: "Just having a skill is not enough. We have shifted criteria for hiring. We can teach skills. But we need employees with emotional intelligence, a good attitude, and the ability to keep learning."

If this is what awaits graduates, it means we should rethink the "more is better" approach to academic and extracurricular requirements and instead adjust the school experience so that it focuses on knowledge and mental strategies that will give students the most needed skills in a rapidly changing workplace.

The Gravitational Pull of AI

One of the most interesting parts of writing this book was the lack of consensus among experts about what our world might look like in ten, twenty, or thirty years given the advances in AI. Talking to leaders who range from computer scientists like Peter Norvig, the head of research at Google, to social scientists like Bob Johansen, Distinguished Fellow with the Institute for the Future, the only agreement seems to be that the future will be greatly influenced by AI. Whether that will be an app that can check your refrigerator to make sure you're not out of milk, or a robot apocalypse is unclear. My own take is that it won't be as extreme as the last example. Fingers crossed.

Technology is driven by AI, robots are powered by it, the social media that propels our culture is manipulated by it, our democracy is likely to be impacted by it, medical science is being reinvented by it, climate change may be modified with its aid, the workplace has already been dramatically altered by it, and our common fate will depend on how well humans are able to control and direct it. When trying to establish a set of guidelines for raising kids who will thrive in this landscape, it only makes sense to keep in mind that significant parts of our children's future will depend on the as yet unknowable but hopefully responsible development and use of AI.

This goes to the very heart of the uncertainty we've been grappling with in this book. We have to assume that even areas that seem resistant to AI, such as empathic interpretation of language, will eventually be at least partially mastered. So the game plan for raising our kids must involve not only teaching academic curricula but also helping students develop resilience and a real appetite for lifelong learning and the challenges they are certain to encounter. Perhaps most crucially, they'll need a reliable moral compass to navigate the increasingly complex ethical challenges posed by AI and technology.

Why Soft Skills Aren't "Soft"

Two baskets of skills are essential to our children's well-being and preparation for the future. They are "soft skills," or what I prefer to label "foundational skills" like collaboration and communication, and the more easily quantified "hard skills" of traditional academic subjects and technical education like coding and programming.

If we're serious about equipping our kids to thrive in a very uncertain, accelerated future, the only skill we absolutely know they will need is the ability to adapt. Lifelong learning will be the key to job security. In addition to hard skills in an individual's particular field—for instance biology, economics, or the law—lifelong learning involves capabilities such as flexibility, curiosity, tolerance for failure, and collaboration. These skills are of critical importance, require effort and intelligence, are amenable to teaching, and just as challenging to master as hard skills. By any measure, "soft" is a misnomer, given that word's dismissive hint of gender and easy mastery. Many of the successful women I spoke with were clear that they considered the term "an insult."

Earlier generations may have been hired out of college based on their academic records and gone on to hold corporate or public-sector jobs for decades, regardless of their social skills or ability to evolve. That won't be an option for our kids. They'll need to keep improving in both academic competencies and foundational skills. Employers are clear that a "*hybrid*" skill set is most valuable. Consider collaboration: it's a combination of listening, asking questions, accurately reading the physical cues of others, articulating ideas, and being humble enough to share information and credit. The more challenging the work, the more adept a person will need to become at all those attributes. Collaboration is critical in order to reach success in just about any field, including the sciences.

Writer David Brooks made this point in a funny yet on-the-nose *New York Times* piece called "Amy Chua Is a Wimp." Chua had just published *Battle Hymn of the Tiger Mother*, an occasionally self-mocking yet ultimately serious ode to demanding, relentless, hyper-involved Asian mothers and the supposedly superior students they produce. Chua famously didn't allow her two daughters to go on play dates or sleepovers, play video games, or do arts and crafts. Instead she insisted they practice musical instruments for long hours and, of course, excel at their studies.

"I believe she's coddling her children," Brooks wrote. "She's protecting them from the most intellectually demanding activities because she doesn't understand what's cognitively difficult and what isn't." It's a lot easier to practice a piece of music for four hours, Brooks said, than to navigate the group dynamics and status rivalries of a room full of 14-year-old girls. "Yet mastering these arduous skills is at the very essence of achievement. Most people work in groups. We do this because groups are much more efficient at solving problems than individuals. . . . Participating in a well-functioning group is really hard. It requires the ability to trust people outside your kinship circle, read intonations and moods, understand how the psychological pieces each person brings to the room can and cannot fit together."[6]

Young adults change jobs an average of four times in their first decade out of college.[7] So wherever your child is working, his or her colleagues will be a revolving cast. The authors of "Career Advising in a VUCA Environment" write, "Employers understand that recruits with the right skills and abilities quickly become costly liabilities if they display bad attitudes, especially if they infect other workers. However, capable people with good attitudes and interpersonal skills can be taught new skills by good trainers."[8] While it may sound profoundly old-fashioned, never underestimate teaching your kids the value of a good attitude. That means teaching and appreciating optimism, empathy, gratitude, self-reflection, humility, and enthusiasm around challenges and diverse points of view.

One of the challenges with foundational skills is our confusion about what they are and how to teach them. At first blush they seem fuzzy and insubstantial. "I don't see any job posts for 'a collaborative empath' or an 'optimistic collaborator,'" parents say. We too often assume that hard skills are what matter and foundational skills merely add-ons. This is simply no longer true whether we're talking about work in the nonprofit sector or the historically hard-charging financial sector. Creative problem-solving and persistence are the skills that Byron D. Trott, founder, chairman, and CEO of merchant bank BDT & Company, considers crucial. He encourages his clients and colleagues to "see around corners." He looks for the unique ability to see what others don't, to anticipate the unexpected, and to take a long view. Working with many of the largest family and founder-led businesses in the world, he is not interested in either predictable short-term solutions or stressing academic pedigrees. His employees are just as likely to come from state schools as from prestige schools. He values intellectual curiosity, diversity, conviction in your beliefs, and the ability to form long-term, trusting relationships. Because relationships are always front and center, his company enjoys a degree of loyalty from both clients and employees that is remarkable.

We do our kids a disservice when we insist on one more AP course instead of encouraging work at the animal rescue center. It is imperative to understand that the more we rely solely on an outdated notion of optimal work preparation, the more we are actually reducing opportunities for our kids.

Epigenetics: Nature *with* Nurture

We're all born with certain proclivities: we're more or less outgoing, great at math or crossword puzzles, possessing of a green thumb or the ability to discern by taste every ingredient in a complex sauce. While subjects such as math, languages, and gardening can be taught with lessons and repetition, being extroverted or having the mind for crosswords is less easily transmitted. Where foundational skills like creativity and curiosity are concerned, it's even more mystifying. We tend to think that humans are either born with a high degree of those traits or not.

For much of the twentieth century, research in these areas centered on nature versus nurture: How much did environment affect a person's natural propensity for a given trait? Could we say with certainty, for example, that IQ is 40 percent heritable and 60 percent environmentally determined? With the advent of twin studies, it became clear that there was no way to make hard-and-fast assertions about nature versus nurture. Although limited in quantity, the quality of twin studies—where a set of twins are separated at birth, raised in different families, and then compared when they are adults—suggested that regardless of genetic makeup, environment can affect aptitude and life trajectory. The disturbing documentary *Three Identical Strangers* dramatically illustrates the impact environment had on a set of triplets adopted into three very different households. Exact same genetics but totally different life outcomes. However, there is no way to determine *exactly how much* effect environment has. When I was a graduate student in psychology (eons ago), we talked a lot about nature versus nurture. Later it became nature and nurture. With the advent of more sophisticated technologies we now know that it is nature *with* nurture.

Epigenetics is the study of how environment affects the traits we're born with. *Epi* means "*on top of*"—what happens in addition to a person's genetic proclivities. The science has to do with how the environment switches genes on or off. Genetic makeup establishes a wide range of possible intellectual development, but where a person ends up is also determined by experience. *Ability isn't fixed; it's elastic.* So while it's true that some babies are eager to explore every corner of the living room and others are content to stay put and play with the toys put in front of him or her, each of those babies has the potential to stretch. Are some kids more creative or curious than others? Of course. Can you expand and cultivate creativity and curiosity in any child? Certainly.

At the same time, we all have a limit beyond which, regardless of effort or desire, we cannot go. My son loved basketball and practiced his heart out, but he was never going to end up in the NBA. We should be encouraging our children to push themselves, to develop their talents and passions, but we should also be aware that the bromide "You can do anything" is wishful thinking.

Today's parents are not always wonderful at recognizing or accepting their children's limitations, as we've seen. That's one of the reasons tutors are in such high demand. But it's important for us to be on the lookout for our children's natural talents and interests so we can encourage those and also use them to create an environment that will nourish our kids' other, less "natural" traits. The skills critical to our children's future success can be cultivated within almost any context, but they'll stick better if it's a context your child actually enjoys.

Sometimes children's interests get short-circuited by parents who think that because their kid will clearly never excel in a particular field it's a waste of time, especially in high school when "everything counts." Once we acknowledge that we have only a partial idea about what will count in the future, we can also admit that we don't really know what will be a waste of time. Instead of trying to steer our reluctant kids to "surefire" pursuits, we can ask ourselves how our child's genuine interest or passion might lend itself to cultivating some of the other important skills and life strategies.

If we can take the giant leap of faith our era requires and devote more attention to foundational skills and a little less to résumé fodder, we can help our children develop traits like inventiveness, tolerance for failure, risk-taking, collaboration, and bravery.

I checked in with James Hetfield, lead singer of the band Metallica, about a panel I once sat on where the audience consisted of hard-charging, high-achieving parents. One dad was deeply concerned about the amount of time his son spent playing guitar. I told James I was uneasy with the audience suggestions: "Take the guitar away for a few weeks, strictly limit practice time, allow access to the guitar based on the kid's most recent grades."

"How about having his parents tell him to start a band?" James interjected. How compelling, from one of the world's great guitarists, who spent much of his free time studying chords, not calculus. The boy could have cultivated a raft of valuable skills—creativity, perseverance, collaboration, risk-taking—by forming and playing in a band, and maybe he'd even have developed some entrepreneurial chops as well. All while doing something that he genuinely loved, was motivated by, and engaged in. I know it's common to talk about thinking "inside the box" and "outside the box." Years of clinical practice and a notably creative child of my own has taught me that sometimes it's best not to have a box at all.

After many months researching twenty-first-century skills and talking to as many experts from as many fields as I could, I ended up settling on a collection of academic and foundational skills I feel are particularly important for our kids' future success. In the next chapter we'll take a deep dive into these skill sets and the conditions that nourish them in our children.

CHAPTER 7

Academic and Foundational Skills in an Age of Uncertainty

Michael was always a creative and curious kid. When he was young, this caused him great joy and occasional suffering. He would redecorate the living room so that it became a desert island or, alternatively, a crowded city. Scrounging around the house, he'd find enough boxes, towels, crepe paper, and poster board to build a world that he saw clearly in his mind's eye. In school he did well but was often called to attention by one teacher or another when he stared out the window or doodled in his notebooks. He was terrified by the word "infinity" because he couldn't imagine anything that went on forever.

When he went to film school, his parents tried hard to find out what percentage of kids actually graduated and made films. They never were able to get an answer. So, while they enjoyed their son's talents, they worried that he would have difficulty finding a job. And he did. Cycling through the usual jobs of unemployed actors and directors—waiter, dance teacher, tutor—he became interested in how companies work. He particularly liked the collaboration he experienced doing low-level odd jobs for various production companies and learned the basics of organization, marketing, accounting, and time management. While he had an abundance of foundational skills like creativity, curiosity, communication, flexibility, and perseverance, he understood that he'd need to hone his technical skills if he was to move on to a more satisfying career trajectory. Through a combination of university and online classes as well as jobs that demanded more technical knowledge, he amassed the kinds of skills he needed to open his own production company. Is it still gig economy work? Yes. But then again, about a third of our workforce is part of the gig economy. Have his new technical skills mattered? Absolutely. A client told him recently, "You're really the whole package." And he is.

The academic and foundational skills that will reliably guide our children into the future overlap and support each other. Kids often learn them in slightly different ways. And while there is not a tidy distinction, there are enough differences in these two buckets—partly genetic, partly cultural, and partly family and community-based— that makes it useful to consider them separately. Taken together these skills help to cultivate resilience and a lifelong love of learning which are certain to be essential for success in the twenty-first century.

Core Academic Skills and Technical Proficiencies

This category refers to the basic pool of knowledge students should possess by the time they graduate from high school. Increasingly these will be both academic and technical skills. They include traditional academic core curricula mandated by school systems and required by most colleges: reading, writing, math, history, geography, science, and a foreign language. Technical skills are generally more specific and often refer to mechanical or STEM-related skills like programming or coding. Data analysis, digital literacy, and critical thinking will be essential skills that incorporate both technical and academic skills.

The curriculum for what our kids learn doesn't vary much from school to school. Yet some kids finish high school fully prepared to take on college, while others never have a shot. There are many reasons for this, but a big one is that there's a world of difference among teaching and learning styles. The more effective educational experiences are interactive as opposed to passive, and it's an unfortunate fact that kids in wealthy zip codes or who attend private schools are more likely to receive an interactive education. Learning in an interactive setting as opposed to a passive one is conducive to the mix of soft and academic skills we're looking to develop in our kids.

Marin Montessori Junior High, located in Terra Linda, California, is one school organized on an interactive model and committed to serving a diverse population of students. Here's one example of how it works. The school has a garden where students grow vegetables that are used in their lunches, which gives the kids an opportunity to learn about planting, fertilization, keeping the vegetables healthy, how pests affect crops, and planning crop size. They harvest the extra vegetables and sell them at a local farmer's market, where they learn how to interact with adults, persuade them to buy the produce, and efficiently make cash transactions. They also create spreadsheets and track the sales.

This is obviously a more complicated, costly, and time-consuming process than simple math and earth science instruction, and is beyond the financial reach of most public-school districts. But someone has to pave the way. If these methods of learning are tested and refined in schools such as Marin Montessori, it will be easier for other schools to replicate the process. Even in privileged settings there are crosscurrents that will have to be managed in the transition from passive to interactive learning. For example, AP classes currently gobble up a lot of student energy, and they're anything but interactive.

Much of the student work in forward-thinking schools is project-based as opposed to individual. A friend's high-school junior is taking a course in American history. But rather than focusing on the drudgery of memorizing dates and battles, the teacher helps groups in the class critically evaluate the biases and validity of various source materials and their relationship to historical events. Different groups take a deep dive into everything from textbooks to Fox News. In this context, the arc of history, as well as its assorted facts, becomes far more interesting. Kids learn to work together and teach one another. Embedded in this American history unit are the three other essential academic proficiencies: digital literacy, data analysis, and critical thinking.

DIGITAL LITERACY AND DATA ANALYSIS

Critical thinking is generally considered the ultimate mandatory twenty-first-century skill. In order to master it, students need a robust set of underlying skills. Most important among these are digital literacy and data analysis. Digital literacy is the ability to find, evaluate, and use information across all types of digital media. Data analysis is the process of using logical and analytical reasoning to assess every component of a piece of information.

In terms of information, we are all drinking out of the proverbial fire hose. It's hard to think critically or to parse information when you're choking on news vs. "fake news." Real videos and "deep fake" videos. Trolls and hackers. Information, misinformation, and disinformation. So the first step in thinking critically is to be aware of, and able to recognize, manipulation.

With the Internet's continuous growth and the acceleration of artificial information, manipulative narratives can be created and spread instantly. When a small town in central Macedonia in the

Balkans is capable, for a few bucks per posting on Facebook, of impacting our presidential election as it did 2016, we must make certain that our kids are well equipped to recognize digital manipulation. It is critical that our children, the future guardians of our government, our democracy, and our planet understand that it is human nature to prefer our own point of view, and that when challenged, we tend to double down on our beliefs. Understanding how easy it is for programmers of AI and various algorithms to play to our emotions and our preferences is the first step in diminishing their impact on our thinking. The more information is manipulated by special interests and unseen hands, the more important it is to have the best tools at our disposal for recognizing deception. While we have had a taste of the havoc this kind of manipulation can bring, our kids are likely to have a full meal. Make sure your older child's school has an emphasis on critical thinking skills and a robust digital literacy curriculum. Have your kids teach you about how they've learned to identify bias and misinformation. This is another good dinnertime conversation, far better than the grades/test scores track.

Equally importantly, kids need to know how to recognize and create evidence-based content. For example, it's not always easy to tell the difference between information pulled from scholarly peer-reviewed journals and from "journals" that are pay-to-publish or less than scholarly. Years ago I pulled articles from Google Scholar. Then I came across the following quote from the *Journal of the Medical Library Association*: "Google Scholar is designed to find something good enough for the task at hand. So often, that task is not comprehensive or exhaustive research that requires a turbo-charged database, but is a senior high school assignment, a college paper, or other thing that needs to get done as painlessly as possible."[1] Yikes. Needless to say, I abandoned my Google Scholar searches and did the majority of my research at Stanford University under the tutelage and watchful eyes of highly experienced professional librarians.

Tristan Harris, former design ethicist at Google, reminds us that we are one person in front of a screen, but there are thousands of engineers behind that screen doing their very best to make sure we stay engaged, if not addicted. Kids, especially teens, hate to be manipulated. Having kids and teenagers understand the high-level machinations involved in addicting them to their devices might impact their usage. Similarly, learning how to use connectivity to advance good causes can help turn kids into activists for themselves and for our planet. I asked Cameron Kasky, a Parkland survivor and a cofounder of the March for Our Lives campaign, why he thought the teens emerging from that tragedy were able to mobilize millions of people around the country. His response was succinct: "We're theater kids, we're comfortable with ourselves, we're familiar with being on a platform, and we know how to use the media."[2] It shouldn't take a tragedy to make sure our kids are digitally literate and media savvy.

When considering data analysis and digital literacy, we can focus on the negatives, be fearful of the unknown, and retreat from uncertainty. Or we and our children can embrace change enthusiastically, learn new technologies, make sure they are aligned with our values, and consider it all an exciting learning opportunity with tremendous potential.

CRITICAL THINKING

Why? How do you know? What's your evidence? What's an alternate explanation? For the terminally curious, whether a Nobel Prize–winning scientist or a fifth-grader collecting information on his family history, critical thinking can be the most fun part of the day. It is an opportunity to think deeply, to challenge our thinking, to become familiar with the scientific method, and to simply play with ideas.

Critical thinking is the ability to curate the incoming data and stimuli we receive each day and to make informed decisions about all that information. "Curate" is another way of saying "assess and edit." It means having the tools to analyze the way you think and present evidence for your ideas that is logical and compelling, whether in spoken or written form. Critical thinking is essential in our knowledge-based economy because it increases our capacity to deal with change and uncertainty quickly and effectively. In becoming critical thinkers, our kids are better able to analyze information, evaluate credibility using diverse sources, and justify their thinking. It allows them to separate facts from opinion, examine an issue from all sides, make rational inferences, and withhold personal biases. It includes self-awareness and empathy, making it a perfect tonic for our "post-truth" world.

As an aside, it's my point of view that kids need to do more of their thinking away from the computer. There are advantages to learning information with the swipe of a finger, but there are also disadvantages. Retaining information helps us to construct and hold an enduring sense of self as well as a coherent worldview. The process of reading, thinking, flipping pages, and then rereading takes more "work" than always having information at our fingertips. My concern is that kids' brains are starting to be *deconditioned*, just like any muscle or organ that is not adequately exercised.

To foster your child's critical thinking, encourage questions. Try not to jump in with quick fixes. Let your kids go through the process of thinking through a problem with your guidance but not your interruption or solutions. After about age seven, kids have the cognitive capacity to think about problems in far more sophisticated ways than when they were younger. Let them flex those muscles.

Foundational Skills

Foundational skills are attitudes and beliefs that drive the way we approach the world. These traits will be as crucial to our children's success as academic and technical skills. They are curiosity, creativity, flexibility, educated risk-taking, collaboration, perseverance, and self-regulation.

Each of us is born with these attributes to a greater or lesser degree, and we're each able to build on our genetic foundation to the limits of our potential for improvement. The most powerful way to cultivate them in your children is to model them yourself. Don't under-live your life. Be curious and creative and adventurous. Read as much as you can. Discuss issues of the day as often as you can. Cheer your child's growing independence and competence.

CURIOSITY

Curiosity is the human instinct to find answers and solve problems. We're all born curious, and the environment we're in has a great impact on how our curiosity will flower. One of our primary jobs as parents is to make sure not to extinguish our children's curiosity with an emphasis on right answers rather than on learning. One of my favorite quotes is Picasso's: "It took me four years to paint like Raphael, but a lifetime to paint like a child." Among young children, curiosity is linked to higher math and literacy skills, and among adults it's linked to job satisfaction, social skills, academic success, and general happiness.[3] We simply learn and live better when we're curious.

Erich Fromm perceptively said, "What are the conditions of the creative attitude, of seeing and responding, of being aware and being sensitive to what one is aware of? First of all it requires the capacity to be puzzled. Children still have the capacity to be puzzled." If we want to help them on their journey of discovery, we should allow ourselves to be puzzled as well.

Research has revealed aspects of curiosity that are especially helpful for parents who want to encourage the trait in their children. From a brain science perspective, we need just enough information to be intrigued. Too little information makes it bewildering, and too much robs us of the opportunity to explore because we're over-whelmed. When creating an atmosphere that will nourish our kids' curiosity, we need to stay attuned to their current interests and then not overwhelm them with information we already know.

Parents like to impart knowledge to children (too often in the form of lecturing). At the same time, we get weary of incessant random questions or, "Why? Why? *Why?*" To promote curiosity, we don't need to hang breathlessly on our kids' every query, we just need to listen for the questions that have the potential to lead down an intriguing or provocative road, and then show them the way. What's important is cultivating the habit: feel curious, follow that curiosity to answers, which lead to more questions, more curiosity, more roads to pursue. A powerful way parents can encourage curiosity is by saying "I don't know" when we don't. It signals that it's okay not to know all the answers, and we can follow it up with "Let's find out!"

Parents' curious (as opposed to nervously watchful) attitude toward their children's interests is not only good role-modeling, but also a healthy approach to the long-term relationship. A young friend of mine in his mid-twenties told me he had just gotten his Emergency Medical Technician license and was excited about becoming a paramedic. His doctor parents weren't nearly as thrilled, he reported. "They said, 'Why aren't you going to medical school?'" His parents would have served him better by being curious: *Why did you want to become an EMT? What does the training involve? What did you enjoy about it?* Maybe being a paramedic will inspire this young man to continue in the medical field and maybe not, but either way he'll be practicing collaboration, critical thinking, and risk-taking, all extremely valuable skills. We simply can't graft our own trajectory onto our kids'. But we can bear enthusiastic witness and offer well-timed, judicious guidance as they craft their own.

In theory, and sometimes in practice, corporations understand the value of employees who are naturally inquisitive. Many companies even include curiosity assessments as part of the recruitment process. These tests, which have been validated in numerous studies, measure things like whether the candidate reads widely outside his or her field, gravitates toward learning new things, or has many nonwork-related interests.[4]

"Curiosity is much more important to an enterprise's performance than was previously thought," writes Francesca Gino in the *Harvard Business Review.* "That's because cultivating it at all levels helps leaders and their employees adapt to uncertain market conditions and external pressures: When our curiosity is triggered, we think more deeply and rationally about decisions and come up with more-creative solutions. . . . Most people perform at their best not because they're specialists but because their deep skill is accompanied by an intellectual curiosity that leads them to ask questions, explore, and collaborate."[5]

CREATIVITY

"Creativity" is a widely misunderstood word. In our culture we tend to think of it in terms of artistic talent or, more recently, superior coding ability. Parents often describe their kids as "smart but not creative." Or vice versa.

Creativity is the use of imagination or original ideas to produce something meaningful—someone was being creative when they invented the wheel, the zipper, the hairbrush, the lawn mower, the alarm clock, the iPad. The same child who's "not creative" because he doesn't draw well or write whimsical plays may be posting wildly original life hacks on YouTube or devising a unique method of training the family dog. The urge to find new ways to express ideas or solve problems is highly coveted not only in the workplace but also throughout life as a driver of fun, pleasure, and problem solving.

"How do you teach someone to be creative?" parents ask. For the most part, we don't teach creativity, we cultivate it. Yes, there are educational games that purport to build creativity, but their value is questionable. Just like curiosity, creativity flourishes when it's organic—when it arises from something our child is already interested in, and when the child's environment offers plenty of support for those interests. Try to join in with your child, when appropriate, in their excitement around discovery. Stay awed.

Families who share a vocation shed a light on the importance of environment in promoting creativity. When everyone in the household is engaging in the same field, young children have lots of teachers and tools to help them learn. Bandleader and pianist Jon Batiste was raised in Kenner, Louisiana, a suburb of New Orleans. His extended family included seven uncles and several relatives who were musicians, and growing up he played in the family band.[6] Batiste recalls:

I would do regular kid stuff. I would play basketball, I had tennis lessons, I loved playing chess. . . . Then I would go and play with a literal jazz legend at night in New Orleans. And then I would have to go to school in the morning. So it was a wild juxtaposition. But then, when I was 17, I moved to New York and started my own band. I was playing gigs, I was looking around, and I was like, "I'm really a professional musician!"[7]

When Batiste went to New York City at 17, it was to attend Juilliard. His musicianship had evolved organically in his environment, which still had room for "regular kid stuff." In a perfect world, every child's natural talents would be able to take root in this sort of rich creative soil. But for most families it's different: not everyone is on the same wavelength or interested in the same things. So once we've identified our child's interests, how to we provide the right environment in which to cultivate them?

Our first job is to stay nonjudgmental. I've seen kids interested in things that have easy apparent value and appeal (i.e., computers) and things that left me scratching my head as to what the child found so compelling: ferns (and assorted fern-like pteridophytes), loaches (and other exotic fish), and endless collections of atypical trading cards (ALF, Garbage Pail Kids, Gremlins, along with more expected choices like Topps basketball or baseball cards). If your child's interest is not harmful to himself or others, get interested. "Tell me more about fish." "What is particularly interesting about that fern?" Keep your comments open-ended, curious, and enthusiastic. Learning anything in depth provides the tools for further learning: enthusiasm, curiosity, perseverance, and problem solving. If you can't get into your child's interest in a genuine way, then just don't get in their way!

FLEXIBILITY

Flexibility is the ability to shift one's thinking among different perspectives, from short-term to long-term, from the macro to the micro. It requires being able to absorb new information even if it conflicts with your existing beliefs (something people generally hate doing) and to adjust conclusions accordingly. This takes place on both a cognitive and emotional level. People with mental flexibility can consider multiple points of view simultaneously and are comfortable with ambiguity. They are creative (weaving together diverse points of view), self-aware (they know their own strengths and weaknesses), and efficient (figure out the quickest and most effective way of achieving a goal).

In order for kids to become mentally agile, they've got to start with a certain amount of confidence. They have to have experienced success and both tolerated and learned from mistakes. Parents, along with teachers, hold the keys to this confidence, much of which is cultivated in early childhood. Anxious kids are at a real disadvantage here: they are driven to get the right answer as quickly as possible in order to relieve their anxiety. Learning is rarely fun for them.

We need to make learning playful and engaging. We need to encourage kids to think of multiple solutions without judging their answers. Remember the game of "how many uses can you think of for a brick or a blanket or a rubber band?" That's the general idea. Stretch your thinking. Look at a problem from different points of view. We have research that tells us that part of the reason why kids engage in risky behavior is because they simply don't have a good understanding of the consequences of their actions.[8] In my office, I often will use the phrase "and then what?" It helps kids to think past their immediate answer and consider repercussions. A young girl swipes a pair of jeans from the local department store. She's relieved that she isn't caught. But by asking "and then what?" she realizes that there are outcomes other than being arrested on a shoplifting charge. She starts to think about having to explain to her parents about her new jeans, about her own conscience bothering her at night, about who ends up paying for the missing jeans, about not being able to go back to the store since someone might recognize her or have camera footage. Both kids and teens, all of us actually, can get rigid in our thinking. It's just easier and limits short-term anxiety. But our kids need lots of practice seeing things from different points of view, reconsidering their actions, and learning from mistakes.

We have all received a crash course in the value of flexibility during periods of high and unanticipated challenge. While it's long been known that flexibility is related to mental health, we now know that it is protective of mental health even in extreme situations like the pandemic.[9] Under conditions of rapid change and great uncertainty, the exact conditions our children are likely to face, flexibility is a mandatory skill. Make sure you model alternatives calmly when your plans change. Encourage your kids to think through different options when considering challenges. Too often we feel that "everything" depends on one outcome. These are the kids I see in my office who are convinced that "it's the end of the world if I don't get into my dream school." It's not. Before that acceptance or rejection letter or email comes, kids need practice considering alternatives with interest and optimism.

EDUCATED RISK-TAKING

"Risk" is a word that tends to strike fear in a parent's heart. No matter what our child's age, we do quick calculations when they propose something we consider risky. Finding the right balance between oversight and freedom means knowing both ourselves and our children well. There are schools in Canada, the United Kingdom, and New Zealand where young children, with careful supervision, use power tools, build fires, and roam forests.[10] Large research studies are clear that this kind of play, where children test their boundaries and flirt with uncertainty, is associated with high social skills, confidence, resilience, and an ability to assess risk.[11] Of course, we worry about injuries. But they are rare and it's worth noting that children are more likely to need medical attention for an injury resulting from organized sports than from play.[12]

If we don't take risks, we miss opportunities. Taking risks inevitably means being wrong at times. James Gorman, chairman and CEO of Morgan Stanley, aims for about 80 percent certainty when making investment decisions.[13] His thinking is enlightening and important. "There are many reasons why we can't be a hundred percent right. It is recognition of that and moving forward notwithstanding that is leadership."[14] Gorman is not being frivolous or impulsive. He's taking educated risks that involve patience and persistence: you wait until you have *adequate* information, and then you forge ahead when others are still uncertain or fearful about taking action. This is a distinguishing feature of every CEO I spoke to.

Admiral Sandy Winnefeld, former vice chair of the Joint Chiefs of Staff, points to a Colin Powell principle called the "40/70" rule. Apparently, Powell believes that with less than 40 percent of information, we are bound to make wrong decisions. At the same time, if we keep looking for information beyond 70 percent, it will be so late that others will have made that decision and moved on. In our discussions, Admiral Winnefeld was clear that "paralysis by analysis" was not the way to teach military leaders how to be effective.[15]

I experienced this principle in action a few years back when I was doing a team-building exercise with a group of young executives.

They were mostly in their thirties; I was twice that. We'd been given a set of puzzles to complete, and when the guys (they were all male) had the puzzles about 75 percent finished, they started to shout, "We've got it!"

"No we don't!" I jumped in. "We're missing a bunch of information!" They laughed and said, "We've got most of it. That's close enough. If we're wrong, we'll just come back and do it again." It was a profound learning experience for me. These young men were willing to "fail," get new information or rethink earlier assumptions, and then move in a different direction if necessary.

Reid Hoffman, the founder of LinkedIn, famously said, "If you're not embarrassed by the first launch of your product, you've launched too late." Now, there's a good case to be made that this applies only to some sectors of commerce. "Sorry about that knee replacement, we've come up with a much better version" is not what any of us want to hear from our surgeon. But the fact is that even in medicine, many tries are needed before a product optimally delivers on its promise. However, because the pace of change is accelerating and products can be quickly replaced, it is likely that a more "virtuous" product, one that has been subject to scrutiny and revision, will do better in the long run than one that is simply viable. We have yet to see which approach will be more successful in the marketplace.

The more uncertain the environment, the greater the number of choices that will feel risky. The people who will thrive in this environment are those who can appreciate the excitement and opportunity in risk and not just feel threatened by it. So children need plenty of opportunities, under our guidance, to try risky things and calculate the risk-reward ratio. It's risky to try out for the lead in the school play and it's risky to drive after drinking. Parents, who are more experienced at the calculus of risk, need to help their kids distinguish an educated risk from a foolish risk. As we saw in the first part of this book, parenting styles that skew toward overprotection often result in anxious, risk-averse children. Teenagers, who are developmentally inclined toward risk-taking, may get a second chance to build those emotional muscles if parents can educate, set safe rules and boundaries when needed (i.e., driving, drinking) and applaud risk-taking when healthy and beneficial (running for office at school, going kayaking with friends). It's worth knowing that, since teens' brains are wired to take risks, encouraging healthy risk taking is not only a future workplace advantage, but is also a protective factor in the here and now against negative risk taking such as stealing, early sex, and substance abuse.[16]

COLLABORATION

In most fields, collaboration has always been a crucial element of success. In the near future, it will be even more so because of the fluidity of the workforce and the rapid evolution and increased capacity of work itself. Our children will need to be able to quickly engage with new colleagues and grasp their ideas; they'll need to be able to learn and to teach. Collaboration requires the ability to listen closely and ask thoughtful questions, the empathy to see another person's point of view, genuine curiosity about the ideas and opinions of others, an ego strong enough to acknowledge when someone else has a better approach than you do, patience, and the ability to synthesize many streams of information and accurately articulate them. Research shows that, under many circumstances, working in diverse groups makes for better decision making, faster innovation, quicker identification of mistakes, and better solutions.[17] In a complex world of "wicked" problems few of us can see the whole picture; we each see a part. Add those parts together and you get significantly better outcomes. No wonder collaborative activities in the workforce have ballooned by 50 percent over the past decade.[18]

Of all the nuanced skills that collaboration requires, listening is probably the most important. There's a saying that humans have been given two ears and only one mouth for a reason. On average, we spend about 75 percent of our day engaged in some form of communication, and about half of that time is devoted to listening.[19] Yet often we're really only half-listening: busy formulating that killer response in our mind. To encourage our kids to listen attentively, we can model it while we're talking with them. A few tips: Don't sneak peeks at your phone. Ask questions. To help my sons develop their listening skills, we used to play a game where we'd make up a story line by line—I'd say a sentence, and then we would each take a turn adding a sentence. That meant they had to listen to what every person said. Make it fun. They'll pay attention.

Increasingly, schools understand that one of the most effective ways to promote collaboration is through project-based learning. Small groups working together helps kids "own" their work while teaching them when to lead, when to follow, how to adjust their thinking, and what it means to be part of a team as opposed to an individual player. Since most of our kids are likely to end up working on teams, the earlier collaborative learning takes place, the more time they'll have to practice being an effective team member.

Kids learn from many sources, but they learn most quickly from their peers: be quiet—we've heard enough. Teachers or parents may gently suggest to an answer-hogging 8-year-old student that a little restraint is in order, but a peer's "Shut up—we've heard enough from you" is likely to get the job done faster. If this example seems harsh and feeds into some of the concerns about collaborative learning (my kid won't get credit for his work, the other kids will boss him around, why should my kid carry the load for other kids), consider that peers are often no-nonsense instructors around success in a group setting.

In our contentious era, developing a talent for collaboration has to include tolerating viewpoints different from our own. We've got to model for our kids how to express opinions without belittling, condescending to, or shouting down the other person. Childish grownups in politics, entertainment, and business are modeling exactly the opposite. In everyday non-celebrity life, behaving this way generally leaves a person exceedingly unpopular and socially isolated.

When someone disagrees with us, our brain perceives it as a threat. Even minor squabbles over things like where to go for dinner can set our heart pounding and make us feel surprisingly anxious. Sadly, our culture has moved into such a tribal mentality that our fear response now flares up over the pettiest of disagreements. The Thanksgiving dinner table has become so fraught that many families decree it a no-politics zone. But collaboration requires different muscles than agreeing to disagree or shutting down certain topics altogether. It requires empathy and compromise. It demands a sense of perspective: "Wait. Is this worth arguing about?" It requires pausing before we respond and asking ourselves, "Am I fully listening? Do I need to ask a follow-up question?" It's no exaggeration to say that our dinner table might be the only place our children get to practice this skill.

PERSEVERANCE

You can cultivate all kinds of positive qualities in your children, but if you don't add perseverance to the mix, you're liable to see only superficial gains. Perseverance (or grit or conscientiousness or just plain hard work) is the glue that makes things stick. Without it, kids are easily frustrated and quick to abandon difficult tasks. No matter how well your child works in a group, thinks creatively, or takes educated risks, without the desire and ability to keep trying even when the going gets tough, his or her progress will be limited. And in an environment where demands are most certainly going to be changing rapidly and continually, perseverance will be mandatory.

Life is tough. It's tough for us adults and tough for our kids. There are inevitable moments of loss, challenge, disappointment, and failure. For us that may be a missed promotion; for our kid it could be not getting the solo in the recital. However, we have a choice as to how we approach our challenges. My office sees more than its share of adults who feel they are inadequate or defective in some way: "I knew I wasn't really good enough for this job." There may be some truth in these assessments, but if we stay stuck in them (as opposed to using them to figure out how to improve), we are likely to lose motivation and become demoralized. Carol Dweck's concept of the growth mindset is important here: get into the habit of seeing life as a mix of successes and obstacles from which we can learn.[20] Dweck has a lovely way of dealing with all those times we haven't achieved mastery. She uses the word "yet" frequently and vigorously.

"I just can't figure out this problem!"

"Yet."

"I can't play the piano. I have no talent."

"Yet."

"Coach never puts me in at crunch time. I should quit, I'm not good enough at soccer."

"Yet."

This "yet" is a way of saying that when you're young you have a very long runway and lots of time to develop competence. It models enthusiasm for kids and encourages them to keep working at something—the very definition of perseverance.

Another thing parents can do to encourage perseverance is to keep their attention firmly focused on process as opposed to product. Of course we like to see those A papers and high test scores. The point is not to ignore our kids' good work. But you want to be interested in the process of learning. "Was that a good test?" "What did you learn from it?" "Were there other questions you thought should have been included?"

Finally, parents can teach perseverance by sharing our own experiences. I'm frequently on the road speaking, and when my sons were living at home, I'd always call them after I gave a talk. I used to joke about the inevitable flubs that would happen over two hours: the mic not working, my having difficulty getting my PowerPoint slides into presenter mode, the belligerent parent. This became a ritual, the point of which was not to tell my kids how often I screwed up, but to let them know that challenges arise and you have to be willing to adjust accordingly. As adults, most of us are so accustomed to the small accommodations we make every day as we hit bumps in the road that we don't think to share them with our kids. It helps to have a light touch and a serious purpose.

SELF-REGULATION

Self-regulation is the driving factor behind most of what differentiates a healthy life from one that isn't. I've spent many decades treating adolescents with problems. Every one of them has exhibited a failure to regulate their emotions, resulting in anxiety, depression, eating disorders, substance abuse, promiscuity, and shoplifting, to name some of the failures. If you can't regulate your emotions, you are unlikely to be a successful student, colleague, or partner. Since infants are not born preprogramed to regulate themselves, how do we teach this discipline?

An attentive, loving environment is the petri dish in which self-control begins to grow. Most of us are familiar with the idea that the optimal parenting style includes both love/support and demand/limits. And for most of us, support comes rather easily. We love our kids and want to see them happy. We know that they look to us to confirm a sense of competence and self-esteem. "You managed that tall slide all by yourself. What a big boy you are." We're also increasingly aware of not overplaying our hand in this direction. In general, we want our kids to be motivated internally because they want to learn, not externally because they will be rewarded by us. Notwithstanding this caveat, our children will learn a great deal about how to regulate their emotions by the way we guide and instruct them.

Many things will make our job more or less difficult. Some children take to self-regulation with little difficulty. Kids with easy temperaments pay attention, don't get overly emotional too often, and when they do, have effective strategies to calm themselves. Alternatively, there are kids who have difficulty paying attention, who sometimes seem incapable of modulating their feelings, and who have few strategies to help themselves calm down.

Self-regulation is the deliberate and conscious process of inhibiting emotions and behaviors that do not serve the goals of the individual under less emotional circumstances. It is of benefit in almost any circumstance, not just in a VUCA world. So why include it here? Without self-control, none of the other skills stand a chance. If you're inattentive, impulsive, and angry, it is unlikely to matter how well you program code, design websites, or diagnose physical problems, because you're unlikely to be valued. "A good attitude" has been cited as essential by every HR person I've spoken to regarding jobs ranging from tech to manufacturing to medicine to finance to the local grocer who is hiring baggers. There is no "good attitude" with poor self-control.

Parents foster self-control in their children when they set limits and ensure that their children honor those limits. "No candy" at the supermarket checkout means exactly that. Homework before video games couldn't be clearer. Home by eleven does not mean eleven-thirty. I think it helps greatly to be able to set a limit and then briefly explain what it takes to change that particular limit. "If you can come home by eleven for the next six months, we can then talk about eleven-thirty." Sometimes a simple "no" is good enough. But setting limits is also an opportunity to teach kids how they can work on progressing. Most things become habits when we do them often enough. If your kid can keep a curfew for six months, then she's had practice on many things, including keeping her word. This makes it more likely that she will continue to keep her word as her privileges are extended.

Ultimate Life Skills: Hope and Optimism

Of all the qualities parents can cultivate in their children, hope and optimism are the most precious. Without an enthusiastic outlook about both the present and the future, life seems drab and hopeless. (Yes, we all have bad days, or more recently bad months, but life is awesome and we need to communicate that, particularly in tricky, uncertain times.) We can nurture hope and optimism in our kids by demonstrating that we always have some control over our environment and ourselves. The future isn't a tide that's going to crush us, it's a wave we're a part of. If we're aware of how we fit in and the power we have to be ethical and active members of society, it's likely to turn out well.

We want our children to run toward adulthood eagerly, not cringe from it or burrow down in our spare room for years. We want to re-assure them that, even in our unpredictable era, there's always a way forward to a fulfilling life. And because nothing is more persuasive than the testimony of people who have followed an uncertain path and lived to celebrate it, I'm presenting some of the best true stories I know in the next chapter.

PART III

Thriving in the New Normal

CHAPTER 8

The Squiggly Line

We're sending the message that success is about precise allegiance to a painstaking script, when just as often it's about a nimble response to an unforeseen opportunity.

—Frank Bruni, journalist[1]

A 10-year-old boy sits quietly on the sofa in my office. Not yet in puberty, his legs dangle over the edge but don't quite touch the floor. It's our first meeting since he was referred by his worried mom, who thought he might be "losing his focus." She had noticed periods of "distractibility" and wanted her son evaluated. This concern, common in my community, is code for "Does my child have ADHD?" His high grades and lack of distractibility in my office suggest otherwise, as I try to engage him in that most awkward of encounters: a reluctant preadolescent boy being asked personal questions by a stranger with letters after her name.

Having raised three boys myself, I'm not surprised to find the youngster in front of me appropriately focused when talking about things that interest him, like sports or friends, and far less focused when talking about his sister or his homework. I wouldn't call him distractible, and I'm far more struck by his lack of enthusiasm than by any attentional issues. Ten-year-old boys should be squirmy, excitable, and after a few minutes of warm up, earnest if not ardent about their interests or passions. But even the fact that our home team, the

Golden State Warriors, has just won their sixth NBA championship and the city is awash in celebration doesn't elicit a fillip of emotion from this young man. He seems attentive but bland, and I make a mental note to myself to consider depression.

Casting about for something that might actually pique his interest, I ask if he ever thought about what he'd like to do when he grows up. Suddenly he perks up, and with no hesitation exclaims, "I want to run a startup." His animation, the forward-leaning posture, the spark in his eyes, tells me I've hit pay dirt. I want to know all about running a startup. In rapid succession I ask a lot of questions, the same kind of questions I ask when kids his age tell me they want to be a veterinarian or a firefighter. "Tell me more." "What do you know about startups?" "What's the most interesting thing about startups?" "What would you need to do to run one?"

Then I sit back and wait for the usual overwhelming amount of data I tend to get about wanting to be, say, a professional ball player. The endless statistics. The hero worship of this athlete or that. The plans to go to specialized camp. To play in high school and the certain (but actually highly unlikely) scenario of playing for a Division 1 college. Except this young man knows nothing at all about running a startup tech company. He doesn't even know what "startup" means. What he does know, in exacting detail, is the trajectory he believes he will need to take to become wildly successful in running one. Not yet finished with middle school, he has charted the next fifteen years of his life in impressive detail. He plans on applying to the most competitive high school in town, hoping that this will increase his odds of going to Stanford because he's heard that many startups are born on that campus. He knows he will have to serve time as an intern, preferably at Google, oblivious to the fact that Google is no one's idea of a startup anymore. He is intent on being a "winner," and here he surprises me with, "Like you said, the Warriors won the championship *six* times." But he shakes off this "distraction" and returns to his "lifelong goal" of running a startup. I suspect that I've just witnessed mom's concern about "distractibility." For a moment this boy was distracted by being ten years old. But this youngster is no longer a boy; he is a careerist. He is reverse engineering his life in a way that he believes is most likely to ensure his vision of success.

Unfortunately, he is wrong. Although my young patient's parents, teachers, and community are all likely to plant and then encourage this way of thinking, they are only making his future chances of being successful less likely. This is true whether he wants to work at Google or Teach for America. Whether he hopes to start his own business or work for an established company. The fallacy is his belief that in the coming decades, the most reliable way to get from Point A (being a kid) to Point B (being a successful adult) is to follow a straight line.

Life Is a Series of Detours

Too many of us tend to see success as static, something that is "one and done," when in fact success is dynamic, something that waxes and wanes. Success takes place over a long period of time. We're also mistaken if we believe that the trajectories which led to success in previous centuries continue to apply to the twenty-first century. I can say this with some confidence because I've spent more than fifteen years traversing this country, and sometimes the world, talking to rather large audiences about the intersection of child development, psychology, and education. What started out as an exercise in curiosity about how adults become successful has turned into an introduction to every talk I give. I have two PowerPoint slides. One is simply a straight line on a 45-degree angle. The other is a squiggly line with multiple ups and downs but that trends in an upward direction.

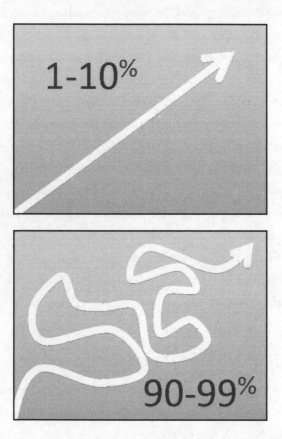

With the image onscreen, I ask the audience to raise their hands to one of these two questions: "How many of you who consider yourself successful have followed the straight path? How many have followed the squiggly path?" I have asked more than 100,000 people this question. Stunningly, whatever the composition of my audience—techies from Silicon Valley, cops and teachers from middle-class neighborhoods, the highest levels of management of some of America's biggest companies, Goldman Sachs recruits in

Hong Kong—the proportion of "straight arrows" and "curious wanderers" is always the same. Straight arrows make up 1–10 percent of people who consider themselves successful. The remaining 90–99 percent are folks who have taken risks, failed, changed course, recovered, often failed again, but ultimately found their stride.

We believe fervently that, given options, a straight line is a safer bet than a squiggly line. That staying "on track" beats wandering around. We are addicted to outcomes at a time when outcomes can't possibly be predicted. Rather than parenting for success, we are unintentionally parenting for disappointment by continuing to embrace a trajectory that has long since passed its "sell by" date.

To assume that success is best ensured by following a straight line is both anachronistic and dangerous. *The World Economic Forum estimates that 65 percent of today's children will end up in a job that doesn't exist as you read this.*[2] And if they work in jobs that are currently familiar, like teaching, nursing, or software development, those jobs are likely to be quite different than they are at present.

I live and work close to Silicon Valley. Communities here are often affluent, educated, and hyped up on technology. The pace of life is difficult and demanding despite a superficial laid-back California vibe. In fact, there is an almost relentless desire to be successful. It may be the only place in the country where "serial" refers to entrepreneurs and not killers. Like anyplace, it breeds a wide variety of children, some good, some not-so-good, but many carrying a disturbing sense of entitlement. Ditto their parents. The brilliant, risk-taking innovator is our model citizen. Money is overvalued and character undervalued. The 10-year-old sitting before me in my office is the logical outcome of this culture. He wants to be part of what appears to be highly valued but knows nothing about the kind of work he's signing on for.

Part of the culture, not only in Silicon Valley but in almost all enclaves of privilege in this country, is increasingly centered on a narrow notion of what success looks like and how to attain it. We are worried about how our kids will compete globally and are baffled by the desirability of jobs whose titles mystify us: Digital Overlord, Director of Insights, Growth Hacker, and Innovation Sherpa. While we overestimate the potential "value added" of certain educational institutions, more important, we are wildly off the mark about how most people actually become successful.

If a linear progression tightly tied to grades, schools attended, SAT scores, admittance to selective colleges, and high-powered internships in well-known companies were in fact the path taken by most successful people, we still would have to weigh its value against healthy child development, but at least there would be some evidence that our kids would one day benefit from all of the aggressive preparation, coaching, and tutoring. However, reality—that is, real people following real trajectories—suggests that this particular paradigm is, at best, only modestly accurate. What is far more accurate in terms of what it takes to be successful is that most successful people have trod a meandering and often unexpected path.

What exactly constitutes success is, of course, open to a world of meaning. Financial independence is one legitimate measure of success, a sense of doing meaningful and fulfilling work is another, and raising a healthy family and contributing to one's community yet another. Sometimes these varying definitions converge, sometimes they don't. One of the patterns that I see regularly among people who consider themselves successful, regardless of how it's defined, is real passion about the work they do. The kind of passion that makes them work harder than others, welcome mistakes and even failures as learning opportunities, and feel that what they do has impact. While money may be inherited, real success always has to be earned.

As human-interest stories go, there's nothing quite as compelling as a well-known person who has triumphed over difficult circumstances. We know that Oprah overcame poverty, parental neglect, and sexual abuse before becoming the world's first African-American billionaire. We know that Michael Jordan was cut from the high-school varsity team when he was a sophomore and that J. K. Rowling was a single mother living on welfare before the wild success of her Harry Potter franchise. Winston Churchill was persona non grata in his own political party for a decade before becoming prime minister, and Nelson Mandela was jailed as a prisoner of conscience for twenty-seven years before becoming South Africa's first democratically elected president and winning the Nobel Peace Prize. To say that any of these well-known celebrities or politicians followed a squiggly line would be an understatement. However, the drama of their lives can make us feel that, inspiring though they may be, they have little to do with how we think about preparing our own children for life.

Yet it's not just celebrities who followed squiggly lines. I first met Matthew at a fundraiser. He was one of "those guys" from Silicon Valley. Charming, exuberant, well informed, and "temporarily retired" at thirty-three. He had been an early employee at Facebook, one of just a handful of guys. I asked him how he had become so wealthy at such a young age and why he had chosen to work for Facebook when it was still being run out of Mark Zuckerberg's house. He laughed and asked if I wanted to know his story "before or after I was arrested." Like many of the early Silicon Valley success stories, his checkered history attests to the fact that a high degree of flexibility, creativity, and comfort with ambiguity are critical in a fast-moving and innovative environment. He had loved his years with Facebook and repeated a line I have heard from practically every successful person I've met: *"I never started out to make a lot of money. I just did what I loved."* The consistency of this observation should not be underestimated.

Success is not fixed. Every failure that precedes success (and there are always many) illustrates the squiggly line. Think of Steve Jobs being fired from his own company only to return and lead one of the most innovative companies in the world. In his commencement speech for the 2005 graduating class at Stanford University, Jobs offered one of the more novel examples of how the meandering path leads to unexpected accomplishment. He had dropped out of Reed College but was hanging around campus sitting in on classes that captivated him, including one on calligraphy:

> I learned about serif and sans serif typefaces, about varying the amount of space between different letter combinations, about what makes great typography great. . . . None of this had even a hope of any practical application in my life. But ten years later, when we were designing the first Macintosh computer, it all came back to me. And we designed it all into the Mac. It was the first computer with beautiful typography. If I had never dropped in on that single course in college, the Mac would have never had multiple typefaces or proportionally spaced fonts. And since Windows just copied the Mac, it's likely that no personal computer would have them. . . . Of course it was impossible to connect the dots looking forward when I was in college. But it was very, very clear looking backwards ten years later.[3]

The jagged resume is not reserved only for tech leaders or the affluent. I've talked to people from all walks of life whose stories confirm that it is rare in today's world to go from point A to point B without multiple detours. The pages that follow contain a few of my favorite stories from regular people—not millionaires or celebrities, but folks like you and me and probably your child as well.

Steven: The Most Important Play Is Always the Next One

Steven Kryger was the first in his family to attend college. His dad was a New York City fireman and his mom stayed at home until the kids were in high school, at which point she went to work in a factory. "My dad worked a lot of overtime to pay the bills. My mother was the rock of the family, balancing the lives of four kids and making sure we all had what we needed, emotionally and spiritually, as we grew up. She showed me what it meant to be resilient." Steven, a natural athlete, played on his public high school's football, soccer, and lacrosse teams and was recruited for lacrosse by a number of colleges. He says, "I fell in love with UPenn when I toured the campus. I didn't even realize it was an Ivy League school!" Their generous financial aid package sealed the deal.

Steven started out as a computer engineering major, "but after seeing the sunrise many mornings in the computer lab, I decided programming was not for me. So I transferred to the Wharton School of Business. I don't think I even knew what 'business' meant. I never had any firsthand experience because I didn't know people in the business world." He was not exactly a dedicated student. "I didn't see the value in the learning. As long as I got a C or higher, I was okay."

After graduation, Steven moved to the San Francisco Bay area, where one of his friend's father got the two young men positions in Macy's executive training program. "When I started working, a switch flipped and suddenly it mattered to me. I worked many long hours. But after a year or so, it became unrewarding and frustrating because there were a number of employees who were just collecting a paycheck, kind of like I had done in college. I started thinking, 'What would I really love to do?' I figured being a fireman or law enforcement officer would be a lot of fun. But firemen spend very little time fighting fires and way more time doing medical calls. That didn't interest me." So in 1988 he became an officer on the Oakland Police Force.

"It was an awesome experience. The group of people I worked with was very dedicated. It really was about trying to put bad guys in jail and clean up the streets so citizens could have a safe environment to live in. We dealt with some of the most hardened criminals. When I was working narcotics, we handled tens of thousands of dollars in cash, lots of drugs and guns, and every person I worked with was honest and ethical. It was a very fraternal, close-knit group. Like in any industry, some were lazy, but I was fortunate to work with a lot of great people. I loved going to work every day."

On January 20, 1993, Steven was working a street narcotics unit when one of his informants contacted him. "He told me a recent parolee from San Quentin was going to his grandmother's house and terrorizing her—locking her and her grandson up in a room and using her house to sell drugs."

After getting the okay from his supervisors, Steven and the narcotics team drove to the grandmother's house to search the premises. "As we were making entry into the house, which meant we had to rip off a security gate and use our battering ram to hit the door, the suspect fired off one round. It went through the wall of the house and hit me in the thigh, severing my femoral artery, vein, and nerve. My sergeant took a knife and cut open my jeans where the wound was and it immediately started squirting like a geyser. If it weren't for his efforts and the other guys in my squad, I would have died."

Surgery and months of rehabilitation saved Steven's leg, but he needed to wear a brace when doing physical activity. "The police department wouldn't let me go out on the streets in that condition. They offered me a whole bunch of other positions, but I knew I wouldn't be satisfied if I had to stay inside a building all day." At 32, he had to switch careers again.

"I thought about the amazing high-school coaches I had, as well as a calculus teacher I respected a lot. One coach, who was from Italy, had started a youth soccer club, and I had coached 6-to-8-year-olds for him. My high-school lacrosse coach was the guy who got me into college. There was always a part of me that wanted to give back."

Steven met with the assistant superintendent of his local school district, who advised him about the courses he'd need to complete in order to coach and teach math in the public-school system. It took three more years of college, plus another year when Steven was teaching high school during the day and completing his own studies at night—plus by then he was married and a father. But he kept at it.

Two decades later, Steven is the athletic director at Menlo-Atherton High School, where he also teaches four math classes and coaches the boys' varsity lacrosse team. Reflecting on his life, he says: "I've always been very fortunate. Even though we didn't have a lot of money growing up, I had a great childhood. I had a lot of fun. My parents were supportive of whatever I did. Every time I turned around, opportunity seemed to fall into my lap: I meet this guy in college who lives in California and his dad helps me get a job at Macy's. When I didn't want to be at Macy's anymore, the police department happened to be hiring and it was a place I wanted to go. Then when I couldn't be a cop anymore, the opportunity to teach opened up."

When I observe that some people might have reacted far less optimistically to events like getting shot and having to abandon a career he loved, Steven says, "Change doesn't bother me. I like change. Also, my dad has always been very resilient. He was forced to retire from the fire department after being injured, so he went to school and ended up becoming an instructor in the fire academy. When he couldn't do that anymore, he became a reporter for the local newspaper and covered high-school sports. So I've seen in action the idea that when one door closes, another opens up, and you've got to be willing to walk through doors.

"Initially your reaction is frustration and you wish these bad things didn't happen. But very quickly, you've got to move on with life. As we talk about in sports and I tell my kids, the most important play is always the next one."

Kathy: Seeing Opportunity

If you could see Kathy Fields, you would be struck by the energy and passion crammed into her five-foot-three-inch frame. She likes bright, sparkly clothes and wears stiletto heels in pack-a-punch colors. Kathy is a dermatologist and cofounder of two of the most successful women-created skin-care companies in the country: Proactiv Solution and Rodan + Fields. You might reasonably expect her to lead with self-importance or snooze-worthy medical details. Instead she leads with purpose, compassion, and big-picture concerns. Like all squiggly line stories. Kathy's success was not a straight shot to the top. It's much more interesting than that.

Kathy grew up on the tough side of Chicago in the blue-collar factory town of Waukegan. One of four children she was born into a household where the only choice of profession was *what kind* of doctor you would be. Her family was education focused and the kids were close and competitive. Born a twin, along with her brother Kenny, and a sister only 1.5 years older, she was happily part of a "team" from day one.

A straight-A student at her local high school, Kathy "hit a wall" her first year at Northwestern University. Her three-year high school education had left her ill-prepared to manage the rigors of a highly competitive university. Getting her first D ever on a chemistry quiz plunged her into a "dark hole." She attempted suicide. Yet, in what was to become a defining characteristic, Kathy opted to "become a warrior" and reversed course to do whatever was needed to get into medical school. She quit partying, transferred schools, and learned how to learn. While her school counselor suggested "marrying a doctor instead of becoming one," she was undeterred. Her perseverance paid off.

Kathy did well in medical school, and Stanford offered her a residency in dermatology. In the program she met Katie Rodan, another dazzle-dressed resident. Their friendship deepened while they studied for boards together, and they remained close even as they joined two different practices in the Bay Area. This was in the late 1980s in San Francisco; Kathy treated a large number of critically ill HIV patients with dire skin problems. She also saw a large number of adult women with acne severe enough that their lives were negatively impacted by it. In a time of insurance-managed care when specialist referrals were rationed, it was impossible for many of these women to get the treatment they needed for this condition. Acne is not simply a passing adolescent trial, but a stigmatizing condition capable of lifelong physical and emotional scarring. As Kathy says, "Your face is the most important real estate you will ever own. It's what you show to the world—when you go on a date, go to school, or go for a job. It's not simple vanity; it's the missed opportunities when you feel insecure in your skin. It is the evolutionary marker of health and fertility." Oddly, dermatology textbooks reported that only 3 percent of grown women in the United States had acne, yet both Kathy and Katie were both seeing many more women with this problem. They decided to take on a medical problem that "disinterested Big Pharma, the over-the counter world, and the beauty industry, which had had nothing new to offer sufferers for decades."

After a long day's clinical work, and with Katie's very young children skittering around their feet, the two women started experimenting in Katie's kitchen. Kathy is clear that she would have been unable to be successful without her teammates, which now included her husband, Garry. Unlike today's entrepreneurs fed by venture capitalists, all funds were written out of Kathy's and Katie's checkbooks, and in true team spirit, their (two line) contract specified that "all expenses over $50 must be approved by both parties prior to incurring expense." Young, stressed, and struggling financially, they were balancing diaper costs against the cost of the supplies they needed for their new venture. Like most "overnight" successes the two doctors worked for five years with a considerable number of disappointments and doors shut in their faces. Ultimately they developed a regimen, Proactiv Solution, which was a complete paradigm shift in the way acne was treated. It was effective and clinically tested, but how to get it into the hands of the consumer?

They decided to pitch the fledgling company to the leader in skin care at that time: Neutrogena. After a year of agonizing, Neutrogena turned them down. Then came the tears. But this "failure" paved the way to their success. One of the executives at Neutrogena suggested that they should try infomercials. It was a radical idea in the 1990s, but they saw its potential to reach a mass audience with a proven regimen to treat acne. They accepted the challenge in a leap of faith, both in themselves and in their product, and at the risk of professional disdain and failed sales. Their courage and conviction paid off massively.

Kathy likes to say "dermatologists don't sit on a beach," less as a reference to skin cancer than to the idea that passivity and lack of curiosity are not apt to lead to a satisfying career. So, flush with the success of helping millions of people with acne problems, the team turned their attention to helping even more people with other stigmatizing skin conditions such as dark spots, sensitive skin, and signs of aging. That work birthed Rodan + Fields.

Their new formulations led them to collaboration with Estée Lauder in 2003. In three years it was clear to Kathy and Katie that retail was wrong for them. Deeply frustrated they had the foresight to buy back their company and go up against the big skin-care companies. They set up a structure where the people who used and loved the products would earn the commissions. As early adapters in what today is known as a gig economy, they bet big that bricks and mortar stores were dead. R+F is now the leading skin care brand in North America.

Almost thirty years after mixing solutions in a kitchen sink, Kathy could have the luxury of sitting back and enjoying her success. But driven by curiosity, excellence, and responsibility she strives to do more as a doctor, entrepreneur, and philanthropist. Kathy muses about what comes next for her company. She's not sure what that will be, but I'd put my money on her figuring it out.

Harrison: Flexible Dreams

Growing up in Atlanta, Georgia, Harrison Siegal loved playing baseball. Luckily, he was a very good ballplayer. "I started playing competitive travel baseball when I was eight or nine, about fifty games a year. Once I got to high school and got ramped up, I was playing a hundred to a hundred twenty games between fall and the end of the school year. I played both second base and shortstop. It was my life." As high school progressed, Harrison's star rose. He and his dad traveled to colleges in Nebraska, Florida, Virginia, and Alabama, where the coaches looked at potential players they hoped to recruit. "My dream was to play in the majors, although just being on a college team was going to be great too."

Junior year is when high-school players meet with representatives from colleges with Division 1 teams, who will ask the chosen few to sign a letter of intent in the fall of their senior year. "In my high-school junior season, I started out superhot. I was on the front page of the local newspaper. It was my time to shine! I had interest from Division 1 schools like West Virginia U., Georgia State, and George Mason." It all screeched to a halt when Harrison shattered the bones in his knuckle and thumb and broke his right wrist. "I was in an immobile cast for ten weeks. So my high-school season was done."

As he slowly recovered, Harrison plotted how he could stay in the game. "I knew the Division 1 schools had pretty much written me off because they like to gobble up people early. So I played all summer and ended up getting my choice of eight schools. I picked Christopher Newport University in Virginia Beach. I went up there to play and I was superexcited. This was my ultimate goal."

Fall of freshman year, and the dream was finally realized: Harrison took his place in the team lineup. But then . . . "A bunch of ex–Division 1 players transferred in from another school. One of them played my position and was only a year older than me, so I had no shot at playing my freshman year. I got maybe a game's worth of playing time." Still, he stuck it out the rest of that season.

One other event occurred during Harrison's freshman year. At a cocktail party during Family Weekend, his parents met a chemistry professor who didn't know Harrison but impressed with his tenacity in sports urged them to tell their son about the research his lab was doing. Harrison's mom passed along the prof's business card. "I took it and threw it in my desk, and I was like 'Whatever. I'm never going to look at this. I'm a baseball player.'"

By the beginning of sophomore year, his thinking had changed. "Baseball was kind of pissing me off at that point. I thought, 'If this isn't going to be what I do the rest of my life, I've really got to get my act together and have a career.' So I met with the chemistry professor and he pitched me: 'You can join my research group, have an amazing career, travel. But there's no way you can do that and also play baseball. You have to decide what you ultimately want." So I thought about it and I made the decision. I quit the team after the fall of my sophomore year and started reading papers for his research over winter break."

Fast forward four years and, at 23, Harrison is in the doctoral program at Virginia Tech working toward a Ph.D. in analytical chemistry. He's candid about the factors that motivated him to shift careers. When asked what it was about the professor's research that clicked, he says, "I was so dejected with how the baseball was playing out that I didn't really care what the research was. It just felt so nice to be desired. I was expendable to my college coach. I was a nobody. Whereas I felt like this professor had a genuine interest in me and my success and he was giving me an opportunity. I came to a crossroads, and luckily I made the right decision.

"I always thought of myself as an athlete," Harrison reflects. "I was never a dumb kid—I graduated from high school with honors—I just never really thought of myself as an academic. With baseball I always had so much success, people were always complimenting me. Achieving awards and stuff like that, I loved it. It was like a drug almost. In college, I didn't have that success with baseball anymore. So I started doing the research, and it was cool, and I kept doing it, and I started getting summer internships and awards from chemical societies. I got a free trip to New Orleans my senior year when I presented the culmination of my three years of research at the American Chemical Society's national convention. All the recognition, the success and awards I was lacking in baseball, I was picking up in academics. I like having a purpose and being able to strive for something."

When Harrison describes the work he's now doing as a grad student, his enthusiasm clearly goes deeper than extrinsic motivations like awards. "Virginia Tech is a massive research institution. It's phenomenal here. The instrumentation my Ph.D. advisor has is one of a kind . . ." and he launches into a description of his specialty, the design of molecular quantification instruments. "It's the best of all worlds. A little bit of engineering, a little bit of math, a little bit of physics."

"If baseball had worked out," muses Harrison, "I'd probably either be in something minuscule in the sciences or I'd be a baseball hitting instructor, something like that. I'm so thankful that the right opportunity presented itself and I was smart enough to go down that path."

Harrison also mentioned an aspect of high-school sports about which his parents may be unaware: "Back then I might have felt like a nerd for devoting a lot of time to science, or my friends might have made fun of me." There's no way his parents could have foreseen their star shortstop's transformation into a doctor of analytical chemistry. That's the beauty of the squiggly line.

Thuy: Across Oceans to a Better Life

Thuy was born in 1972 and grew up in KienGian, a small town in South Vietnam. Her comfortable and industrious family owned a small store and lived above it. Her father grew pineapples, which were loaded onto trading boats and then sold in Saigon. One of seven children, Thuy recounts an affluent country life and having "the first television in the village." In spite of the war, life was relatively unremarkable when Thuy was young. One by one, her sisters and brothers dropped out of school to help the family business. But Thuy, generally acknowledged to be "the smartest and most capable one" in the family, was encouraged by her parents to keep attending school. She continued her studies until conditions in Vietnam deteriorated so badly, with over 2 million civilian casualties, that citizens who later came to be known as "boat people" began to flee the country by sea in the late 1970s.

With the economy and government run by communists, Thuy's family business could no longer prosper. Thuy's mother arranged for her daughter, then 15, to became a "boat person." With no one except a single aunt accompanying her, Thuy was smuggled onto a boat along with about seventy-five other people. The women were placed in the compartment reserved for fish at the bottom of the rickety vessel. The conditions were unbearable, hot, rank, and oxygen-deprived for three days and nights, with little food or water. Thuy recalls crying throughout the entire journey.

When the boat arrived at its destination, Malaysia, it was unable to dock on the beach. Everyone had to swim ashore. The five who could not swim drowned. For the next two years, Thuy lived in a refugee camp in Malaysia. To avoid being raped, Thuy and many of the young women darkened their skin, since the Thai pirates responsible for most of the rapes preferred fair girls. Held up by bureaucratic snafus and missing paperwork, Thuy "tried to make it work" for the two years she lived as a refugee. She volunteered at both the hospital and the temple, learned how to be a phlebotomist and a hairdresser, and studied English. Under unimaginable conditions and with no resources, Thuy was adaptable, flexible, and creative enough to not only survive, but to actually thrive. By the time she was released from the refugee camp, she had learned English and had found that she was particularly interested in the medical field.

After six months at an "education camp" in the Philippines, Thuy, now all of 17, was flown to the United States. There she found distant relatives who, despite having few resources themselves, took her in and helped her return to school. She worked any job she could find to help support herself and her relatives: McDonald's, cold calling for insurance companies, sewing, lab work.

Thuy went first to Laney College to make up credits so that she could graduate high school, then to Merritt College, and finally to the University of California at Berkeley, where she was offered a full scholarship and graduated with a degree in science. She found a life-altering tutor who knew and appreciated her story and helped her not only emotionally but also financially when she couldn't afford books or a computer.

According to Thuy, her story doesn't end as a resounding success. One by one, the rest of her family came to the United States and lived with Thuy. She had hoped to become a physician, but faced with the demands of supporting her family, she became a medical technician instead. She is married with two children and fiercely loyal to her employer, who gave Thuy her first professional job. We tend to think of squiggly lines as courageous leaps from one field of endeavor to another. The other kind of squiggly line includes adapting to the circumstances around us and "trying to make it work" in spite of fear, danger, challenges, and obstacles. Thuy's squiggly line is one of the bravest journeys I know.

Nate: A Sweet Commute

Nate McKinley grew up in a family that made different educational decisions for each of their children. Nate was sent to a private Catholic high school, while his older brother attended the local vocational high school. Although they both attended college, Nate's brother found success early in the programing field. Nate continued the path that had been laid out for him by his father, an international businessman, who had also influenced his major in global studies, with a concentration in business, and his class choices.

After graduation Nate worked at a financial institution and moved up the ladder. He met his wife Tessa and switched jobs to a small startup that was doing securities lending with international banks. At first he found the job exciting, but his enthusiasm waned after a year or so, and the three-hour round-trip commute seemed longer and longer. Nate recalls, "I craved some sort of personal interest and found it in gardening."

Nate and Tessa became such avid gardeners that after a few years they moved with their two young children from Lancaster to a rural town outside Boston. Nate was still working in finance and commuting two-and-a-half hours a day, but the couple spent their few precious quiet hours making jams, salsas, and other consumables with the vegetables and fruits from their garden.

Eventually, Nate decided he wanted to try something more challenging. "A friend brought me an old apple press, and I made my first batch of hard cider. It was revolting! So during my commute on the train I would read about yeast, fermentation, and the hundreds of varieties of apples. My next batch of cider wasn't gross, it was actually drinkable." Nate kept at it, and soon they had batches of 5-gallon jugs of fermenting cider in their basement. A year or so later, Nate was ready to let others try the brew: "At our annual Halloween party we had a tasting and encouraged the neighbors to bring apples to press and to have a taste. People liked it!"

One of the partygoers joked that Nate made his cider in the old pony shack behind his house—and Pony Shack Cider was born. That Christmas, Tessa bought him labels for his new, tasty hobby. He continued slogging away at his day job but bought increasingly large quantities of apples to press. He finished the family's garage and moved his now-incorporated business out of the basement. Nate would work in Boston from 7 A.M. to 7 P.M. and often stay up past midnight making cider. He was exhausted but happy. When he made his first sales, to a local farm stand and a local brewery, Pony Shack Cider was officially in business.

A year after Nate went retail, he leased a larger space that would allow the cider business to grow. Two months after that, he was laid off from his day job. "Although it was scary, it was a blessing in disguise. I could finally dedicate myself to my passion, and my commute was now only five minutes from home!" In another year, Nate's cider was on the menu at seven local restaurants and his retail sales had expanded beyond nearby liquor stores and specialty shops to stores on Cape Cod. Nate was producing 5,000 gallons of cider annually, with plans to double production the following year. Wife Tessa says, "He's happier than he's ever been, and as our kids make their way through school, I can't think of a better role model."

My Own Squiggly Line

My squiggly line starts in the home of my working-class family. My dad was a New York City police officer and my mother a housewife until Dad died suddenly at 47. On assistance and with no money, my mother took a job at Mount Sinai Hospital in New York as a social worker. My parents had a loving relationship and they adored me and my brother, so I was fortunate in that regard. At the same time, their protectiveness made them wary of my persistent curiosity and ambition. When I was a teenager, my mom used to say, "Madeline, don't have such big eyes." Her unspoken message: *Know your place.* There was the sense that kids from working-class families shouldn't shoot for the moon. They should aim a little lower. My parents hoped I might be able to be a teacher. I'm sure they had no idea that I could end up being a Ph.D. That simply wasn't their world.

One of my particular roles in the family was to serve as a kind of translator on topics that were complex or outside my parents' realm of experience. My parents were smart, but my father never went to college, and my mother hid her intelligence, worried about my marriageability, and counseled me, "Don't be so smart around the boys." Around the dinner table was fine. And my parents took great pleasure in both my brother's and my curiosity and academic achievement. It's the same for many working-class kids and children of immigrants: we're the bridge to the larger culture. In my family I had a lot of practice translating a more complex form of English to a simpler form of English. I learned how to synthesize ideas and information, explain them clearly, and make it entertaining enough to hold my parents' interest. Decades later I'd still be drawing on those same skills when I began writing and speaking in public.

There's serendipity in every squiggly-line story, from Steve Jobs taking a calligraphy class to Harrison Siegal's parents handing him a random chemistry professor's card. My first encounter with serendipity was at college. I applied to just one: the State University of New York at Buffalo. While my parents would have preferred me closer to home, at least Buffalo was in state, and I had earned a scholarship there. We couldn't afford anything else. In an unpredictable series of events, at the exact time that I entered college as an English major, the school happened to draw a group of teachers who would go on to become some of the most important literary voices in this country. Many years earlier the Black Mountain College in Ashville, North Carolina, had shut its doors. The faculty and student body at Black Mountain had comprised some of the most creative thinkers and artists of the day, including Allen Ginsberg, John Cage, Merce Cunningham, Buckminster Fuller, Robert Rauschenberg, and many others. After Black Mountain closed and these spectacularly creative and innovative individuals had wandered the country for a bit, a group of them and their friends migrated to SUNY Buffalo. And that's how I came to hang out on the quad with Allen Ginsberg and Leonard Cohen and take classes from people like literary critic Leslie Fiedler and poets Robert Creeley and Robert Hass (who went on to win a Pulitzer Prize and become the poet laureate of the United States not once, but twice).

By a stroke of good fortune, attending what would have been considered an ordinary state school gave me an extraordinary education. After graduation, I decided to get a master's degree in social work. I went to Columbia but never finished; I needed to do some personal work after the death of my father and a very rocky romance. So I returned to Buffalo, got a teaching credential, and taught adult education. The students, many of them minimum-wage folks who were desperate to get their GEDs, were highly motivated and I loved the job. "OK," I thought. "This works. I'll go teach high school in New York City." My experience in the South Bronx was not positive, to put it mildly. The students, who came from some of the most challenged and violent neighborhoods in New York, appeared unmotivated, and those who *were* motivated had to hide it or be ostracized by their peers. I spent a lot of time sitting at kitchen tables with those kids who were motivated and their aspirational moms trying to figure out schemes to sneak them books under the radar of their less-inspired classmates. I liked those kitchen-table talks and found that I was talented at coming up with novel solutions, like pilfering a second set of books from the school storeroom that these students could just keep at home.

However, I was awful at teaching. While I was feeling good about being able to work out individual problems, I was hopeless at figuring out how to motivate a class of thirty-five mostly disruptive teenagers. My classroom was chaotic and I had no idea how to bring my enthusiasm about literature to these kids who had been so ill-served by our education system and their communities. An outside observer would have said I was failing and failing badly. But the "failing" part of it didn't bother me particularly. I took it simply as a sign that I would probably never excel at teaching and needed to move on. When the school year ended, I quit the teaching position and took a job at Mt. Sinai Hospital in New York in the Department of Psychiatry. My job was officially titled "recreational therapist" and I worked on the inpatient adolescent psychiatry unit.

I wasn't bad at the group work, which wasn't therapy so much as keeping our teen patients busy with construction paper, glue, and macaroni. But I discovered that I was very good at talking one-on-one with teenagers, some of whom were depressed or anxious, others of whom had serious mental illnesses such as schizophrenia or bi-polar disorder. Their behavior could be extreme, and not everyone wanted to deal with them, but for some reason their intense feelings intrigued me. I was engaged and energized by these kids. I had never been uncomfortable with people's strong feelings, but it didn't cross my mind that this could lead to a career.

I had been at the hospital for about two-and-a-half years when my supervisor called me into her office and told me she was firing me. She said, "I don't want you in this job anymore. You need to go back to school and get a degree in psychology. You've got a talent for this." I was shocked at being fired and motivated by this woman who had such faith in me. She mentored me and I did get that Ph.D. in psychology, and went on to a career treating families and adolescents.

In retrospect, it's easy to trace the thread of what led to being a psychologist. I was a translator at home, a kitchen-table shrink in the inner city, and a capable companion to seriously disturbed young people at Mount Sinai. But it would have been a mistake to have known all this in advance. If my family had resources, perhaps they would have sent me to a career counselor who would have tested me and interviewed me and come to the conclusion that I should be a psychologist. But every step of the journey to figuring out what kind of work I would eventually fall in love with was necessary. I didn't "lose time" as so many parents fear; I gained wisdom, experience, and certainty.

After about twenty years in practice, I was moved to write a book about a cultural phenomenon I could see was impacting my young patients: *Viewing Violence: How Media Violence Affects Your Child's and Adolescent's Development*. I'd written a few articles by then and gotten positive feedback; the writing skill I had developed in my college literature classes was coming to fruition almost three decades later. I managed to snag a great literary agent, who sold the book to a prominent publishing house. But my editor quit her job and the book was orphaned—left without an editor who had a stake in its success. Although it got solid reviews, it sold very few copies. Another "failure."

It was six years before I returned to writing, and again it was because of symptoms I was seeing among young patients in the affluent suburb where I lived and practiced. *The Price of Privilege* struck a chord with parents across the United States and became a bestseller. I began to get requests to lecture in front of large groups. To my surprise, I was comfortable on stage—despite my lifelong struggles with anxiety and the fact that, other than the brief teaching stint in my early twenties, I had no experience with public speaking. If it took Steve Jobs ten years to connect the dots between a calligraphy class and the computer fonts it inspired, it took me forty years to connect the dots between regaling my parents with news of the outside world and being able to entertain and educate an audience full of parents.

My trajectory was not something I planned or ever could have predicted. The only constants in my squiggly line have been my curiosity, confidence, and willingness to take failure in stride. This book has tried to outline some of the ways we cultivate these particular characteristics, and while there's some hardwiring involved, we can do a better job of nurturing them in our children. I for one have always thrived on criticism, and even today I'm far more interested in my audiences' suggestions for improvement than in their praise. I want to keep learning, and feedback points the way.

When I think about what prompted me to write this book about accelerated change and adjustment, both for ourselves and our children, I realize that my curiosity about what I don't know is as great as my curiosity about fields that are my home territory. This was a chance for me to explore uncharted waters (I initially had to look up the meaning of AI!), to take a clear-eyed look at what I see as rather failed attempts to get parents to modify their parenting styles, and to take a deeper dive into not only psychology and education but neurology and social science in order to better understand what makes us move forward and what keeps us stuck. Besides, what's more fun and interesting than an unknowable future that is right around the corner? I hope the stories in this chapter give some real meat to the concepts this book has emphasized: curiosity, flexibility, creativity, resilience, and the nearly universal value of the squiggly path.

CHAPTER 9

A Revised Script

Moms and Dads in the Twenty-First Century

Having a kid conflicts with the gig economy unless you can have a gig kid.

—Josh, father of two

You'll be juggling a lot more balls. Figure out which are glass and which are rubber.

—Amanda, mother of three giving advice to a new mom

In this book we've looked at the ways uncertainty is negatively affecting the decisions we make about our children. We've seen how high rates of anxiety in our kids prevents them from developing resilience and risk-taking: the exact types of attributes they will need in order to thrive in a changing world. We've explored the array of academic, technical, and foundational skills that will best serve our children when they are grown. And we've seen that many adults have followed paths that were unpredictable yet led to fulfilling and successful lives. It's all been part of my full-court press to cultivate bravery in parents; to convince them to rethink and broaden their concept of what it means to prepare kids for the future. It also means taking care of ourselves in sympathetic and deliberate ways so that we retain the robustness and bandwidth needed to be loving and effective parents.

It's hard to ask moms and dads to think about parenting in a whole new way without acknowledging how much is already on their plates. Uncertainty influences our behavior every day on the micro level. Uncertainty on the macro level—about things like job security and the cultural expectations of men and women—forces us to regularly reconsider our roles as parents. That's a good thing: mothers and fathers experience parenthood differently and bring different strengths to parenting. Changes we make in our parenting approach can only be improved if we take some time to sort through and reflect on these differences.

However, it's disingenuous to talk about changing the way we parent without recognizing that many of our present hardships are institutional in nature: a hodgepodge of often inadequate state and federal support for children's services, inflexible work schedules or schedules that change at an employer's whim, the expectation that employees be accessible 24/7, no in-house child care at places of employment, miserly vacation and personal days, insufficient maternity leave, little or no paternity leave. Some companies boast about their generous employee perks—gyms, laundry services, yoga lessons, freeze-your-eggs compensation, and cafeterias with pick-your-favorite-international-food menus. But only 7 percent of U.S. employers offer child care at the work site or nearby,[1] even though that is by far the most important perk for parents. Creating a more joyful and functional family life is less about assorted fringe benefits and more about reforming our institutions. We'll all be better off if we actively promote such reform. But until those changes take place, we must do the best we can family by family.

A Snapshot of Today's Fathers

When I first began writing about parenting and child development, some twenty years ago, my audiences consisted almost entirely of moms. This has changed significantly, particularly over the past decade. While mothers still predominate, the number of men has increased to over 40 percent of my audience. And it's not simply that more men are attending, it's that much of the landscape of what constitutes a family has changed. While the majority of children (65 percent) live in traditional two-parent homes, that means that 35 percent don't.[2] Households with single parents, LGBTQ parents, grandparents, and foster parents have proliferated over the past few decades. My own three Millennial sons have peppered me with examples of how expanded the definition of family has become. They each know of households in which the dad is the stay-at-home parent or kids are being raised by two same-sex parents. But in most families, it is still Mom who shoulders a disproportionate amount of confounding pressures, expectations, and anxieties.

I see relatively few fathers in my practice, but, for this book, I actively sought out the new generation of involved dads and have delved into the limited research that exists on them. Many of these stay-at-home fathers or primary caretaker fathers are in consulting jobs or creative or tech fields that allow them to continue to do work from the house. Their comments reveal some misgivings about their new role, but also a spirited willingness to jump in. "The first week the baby is home, you learn eight million new things," said Ari, a musician whose wife is a sociology professor at Rutgers.

He mentioned trying to preserve his sanity and "prove that I could still be a human being" by taking the baby out a lot and visiting his friends, few of whom had kids. Although he deeply loves his little boy, "I don't really know what a dad is supposed to do. Men don't say, 'I always wanted to be a father.' Women grow up thinking, 'I want to be the best mom ever.'"

Many of the young dads I spoke with missed male bonding: "Hanging out with the guys, talking shit, going out with the guys for a beer." Since only about one in twenty at-home or primary caretaker parents is a dad, isolation can be a significant challenge.[3] Finding a group of similar dads can be difficult in some areas of the country. Many of the men I spoke with ended up in groups with stay-at-home moms, but often felt uncomfortable and stigmatized. A Washington, D.C., dad told me: "I was almost always the only dad. Most moms seemed completely fine with me being there, but lots of times I felt like a lot of people wouldn't actually talk to me, or just kind of avoided me. So in some respects it was a little lonely."

Another common experience these dads reported was how they were hailed as heroes merely for having a baby strapped to their chest out in public with no woman around. But they also got their share of momsplainers. Said Ari, "I'll get told by a strange woman, 'That baby is crying because he's hungry.'" Josh, whose wife works as a project manager for an advertising agency and who describes himself as a primary caretaker, said, "With my older daughter I got treated like a damsel in distress. So many women seemed compelled to tell me how to hold my baby and congratulated me on my shopping skills at the supermarket." When he showed up for his first PTA meeting a decade ago, the president said, "Oh, that's nice, I guess we can use a dad." Notes Josh, "They're more like MTA meetings."

Josh quickly realized that in order to be an effective primary caretaker he would have to "not care what other people think." His first daughter was born in 2002 and his two girls are now in middle and high school. He and his wife were early adopters of flexible parenting roles, but times are changing. Josh says that he now sees lots of dads on the streets, in the markets, and even at PTA events! Groups for stay-at-home dads and primary caretaker dads are starting to pop up and can be a good tonic for decreasing isolation and increasing camaraderie. While we have far less data, I think it's a reasonable assumption that, just like for moms, a father's mental health is a significant contributor to his children's adjustment.

Perhaps the most refreshing aspect of young fathers' attitudes is their general lack of anxiety compared to moms. If we're looking to help our children calm down, more dad time might be exactly what they need. Fathers don't have fevered conversations with one another about how much their kid ate or pooped. Jake, the father of 4-month-old Golda, is typical of the young fathers I've spoken with. "I'm not too anxious about making a mistake, and neither are the other dads I know. No matter how safe you try to keep your kids, you're going to mess up in some way. Everyone has different issues. Most of the guys I know who are doing this are treated like they're father of the year. The bar is much lower for us than it is for moms."

Men often bring a life-hack sensibility to fatherhood, and there's a relaxed sense of fun to it. The *At Home Dad Show* podcast is geared toward these guys and is the closest thing I found to a loose, nationwide daddy community. One episode featured fathers comparing tips on doing laundry. A dad who hates to fold explained that he keeps two hampers, one for dirty items and the other for clean, and lets his kids forage for their daily clothes. They love it. So did the other fathers, who agreed that this was a brilliant arrangement.

Another father on this show observed that there was a time when men didn't believe women really wanted to work outside the home. He mused, "Now maybe women don't believe that men really want to stay home with the kids." It is clear that we are in a time of accelerated change around roles—parenting roles, work roles, gender roles—to name a few. I urge you to consider these changes with enthusiasm and an open mind.

Dads in the Working World

Of course, the majority of fathers today are not the primary caretakers of their kids. Although dwindling, most still have the traditional role of primary breadwinner. One startling shift over the past decade has been the decline in the number of fathers who feel that it's in their child's best interest for Mom to stay home and not work at all. In 2009, 54 percent of dads felt that way. By 2019 it was down to only 37 percent. Forty-five percent of moms and 41 percent of dads thought that the ideal situation was a mother with part-time work.[4]

But economic realities continue to reshape those opinions and the choices about which parent can stay home with the children. With the housing crunch and the long list of financial pressures on most families, including previously unimagineable levels of school debt, it becomes ever more necessary for both parents to work full-time. Women, over a lifetime, earn between 49 and 80 cents for every dollar earned by men,[5] trends in the graduating classes at the nation's universities portend continued change. In 2016, women earned the majority of doctoral degrees for the eighth straight year and outnumbered men in graduate school 135 to 100.[6] With a new public focus on fairness in compensation, it's reasonable to hope that women's salaries will catch up to men's in the not-too-distant future.

This in turn will change the calculus of who works and who stays home for families that have these options.

A generation of overworked men may welcome the change. The Millennial dads I spoke with recoiled from what they called "hustle porn," the punishing brand of capitalism that urges employees to "sleep when you're dead" and "caffeinate to create." Stay-at-home dad Jake said, "Startup culture is very toxic. Men my age and younger are looking for more meaning in life and in work, not this culture of burnout."

It's hard to predict what will happen if significant numbers of stay-at-home fathers return to full-time work. In time, maybe the evolution of the employment landscape will enable both fathers and mothers to more easily move between active parenting and well-paying jobs, not only "gigs." A generation ago, employees who frequently job-hopped or had gaps in their résumés were viewed with suspicion. Not so much today. Résumé gaps—which often reflect time spent traveling, learning, or volunteering—can signal the type of flexible, curious job candidates employers claim to desire. Will taking time off to be a stay-at-home dad be met with similar admiration? Or will men face a Daddy Gap penalty in prestige, opportunities, and salary like the Mommy Gap that women have been battling since the 1970s? If men are welcomed back to the workforce without such a penalty, that could make the transition more equitable for women too. The jury is out. The trajectory of men who intentionally become integral parts of their children's upbringing is a field ripe for more research.

For Moms It's Harder to Find the Fun

Most of the mothers I see in my practice are trying to juggle challenging jobs and young children. It's a balancing act few can master because it leaves many of us feeling exhausted, overwhelmed, and guilty. "I should be able to do this," says a dedicated but depressed pediatrician and mother of three kids under the age of seven. Both she and I know that something has to give. A depressed mom carries risk for both herself and her children.

Research on parents in dual-income families reveals some possible reasons for her distress. It shows that in terms of the Second Shift—that is, work done in the service of the children and home—mothers are still the heavy lifters despite the fact that today's dads contribute much more than those of previous generations. The time fathers spend with their kids increased from 2.5 hours a week in 1965 to 8 hours a week in 2016, which is encouraging. But during the same period, moms' time with children increased from 10 hours a week to 18, so mothers are still clocking more than twice as many hours as dads and nearly twice as many as mothers did in the 1960s. On household chores, dads contribute about 10 hours a week while moms contribute 18.[7]

What does a mother's work consist of? It's not just the schlepping, shopping, cooking, and other household chores that most often fall to her. It's thinking about it all. Sociologists call the underpinning of family life "worry work," and it mostly remains the province of women. Additionally, research points to a particularly female aspect of human interaction called "emotional labor." One group studied the way female managers relate to colleagues. They found that the women "expressed optimism, calmness and empathy even when these were not the emotions they were actually feeling"—a repressive façade familiar to many a mom. This is emotional labor and it is debilitating: It leads to burnout at work, work-related rumination at home, and family conflict.[8] And it contributes to an enduring stress gap between men and women, as observed by Kristin Wong in the *New York Times*: "Circumstantial stress, like losing a job, may lead to these same issues, but emotional labor is not circumstantial. It's an enduring responsibility based on the socialized gender role of women."[9]

Cultural Expectations of Mothers

Mothers, especially those who work outside the home, have been studied and psychoanalyzed for decades. The popular term "intensive mothering," for example, was coined twenty years ago by sociologist Sharon Hayes in *The Cultural Contradictions of Motherhood*, in which she examined how working impacted women's relationship with their children. According to Hayes, working mothers face a paradox: they are expected to be competitive and ambitious at work yet nurturing and selfless with their children. It turns out to be incredibly difficult to integrate those two modes. And it often leaves moms with the feeling, "I can't seem to do anything right."

Hayes defined "intensive mothering" as labor centered on children's needs that involves costly, time-consuming, emotionally absorbing methods devised by parenting experts. This version of motherhood was gaining traction when Hayes published her book in 1998. She reasoned that the trend would fade as more women entered the workplace. A new model of motherhood would emerge: one that put less emphasis on micromanaging kids and more on an equitable division of labor between parents. But that never happened. Instead, cultural expectations kept rising for women both as mothers and as breadwinners.

Yet not all moms are caught in the web. The impossible-to-meet standards we've become accustomed to—be a good mom at home, a tireless advocate for our child at school, lean in at work, make good money, stay healthy, look young, feel sexy, be grateful—are hall-marks of the social class to which certain mothers belong. One study found that college-educated American mothers of 6-to-13-year-olds spend 130 percent more time in parenting "management" respon-sibilities than do their less educated counterparts.[10] Another study found that parents of "lower educational and professional status" tend to have a different style of interacting with their children than do middle- and upper-middle-class parents—setting more "nonne-gotiable limits," for example, and investing less in the cultivation of their children's presumably limitless emotional and intellectual un-folding. This is not only because working-class parents have differ-ent life demands pressing upon their time and resources; it's because they have a different idea of what it means to be a good mother, one that perhaps offers some protection against the perfectionist misery of so many middle- and upper-middle-class moms.

Within living memory, mothers across all social classes were not nearly so enmeshed in their children's lives as they are today. Nor were they as plagued by self-doubt. The mid-twentieth century had serious drawbacks: there were rigid gender roles, and the psychiat-ric community mistakenly blamed poor mothering for all sorts of childhood mental illnesses, everything from autism to schizophre-nia. At the same time, a positive aspect of the era was that moms didn't judge themselves or one another so harshly. There were good kids and "troubled" kids. Parents of the troubled kids were usually regarded with sympathy, not condemnation. Unless the family was severely dysfunctional, the assumption was that school-aged chil-dren were responsible for their own behavior. In contrast, today when we hear about a child's bad attitude or behavior, we reflexively think, "I wonder what's up with those parents?"

Another attractive aspect of twentieth-century parenting was that parents of the good kids didn't immediately broadcast every triumph. They couldn't—there was no social media. The social norms were different, too. It would have been considered weirdly neurotic to distribute weekly updates about your child or place a "My child is a star student!" sticker on your car. Whether you were the mother of a top student or of a troubled kid, there were limits to how much your reputation was tied to your child's deeds.

The daughters in those mid-century families grew up, had children of their own, and are grandmothers today. Their generation experienced it all—the thrill of greater access to work, political power, money, reproductive freedom, and also the reality that most of those advances came with strings attached. Fifty years on, our opportunities have blossomed, yet so have our parenting responsibilities and self-doubts. For too many women, the cultural contradictions of motherhood remain firmly entrenched.

Tearing Ourselves Apart

Recently a patient was telling me about her 3-year-old son's possible "learning disorder." He was restless and bored during story time at the preschool and showed zero interest in learning his ABCs. Out poured the lamentations: "According to the experts, kids should recognize letters between the ages of three and four! But I work, so maybe I'm not home with him enough. Maybe it's the cartoons I let him watch on Saturday mornings. I know I shouldn't, but I'm so tired. I read to him, but maybe he doesn't see me reading for pleasure enough."

Some of my patients are concerned about serious psychiatric and learning issues in their children, but many more are distraught about normal behaviors that will almost certainly resolve without intervention. I've come to expect mothers to overreact and blame themselves for any small lag in development or mildly disruptive behavior. Fathers as a group do not share in the self-flagellation. There is no single definitive reason for this. It could simply be that for millennia, child-rearing has been the mother's responsibility. It could have something to do with the "self-serving bias," a cognitive phenomenon in which males are slightly more apt to blame external forces for negative situations, thereby preserving self-esteem, while females are more likely to blame themselves, which negatively impacts self-esteem.[11] Whatever the reasons may be, in my experience fathers rarely overreact to or blame themselves for their children's (perceived) poor behavior or performance, while mothers routinely torment themselves over it.

There are lots of elements at play here aside from the tension caused by moms trying to balance being a competitive worker and a selfless nurturer. But one problem does have its roots in the worker/nurturer conflict. This has to do with the way most of us rate ourselves and our children. Parenting is an organic pursuit involving the passing on not only of knowledge but also of values, manners, traditions, and beliefs—things that can't be measured in numbers. Conversely, achievement at work is tallied in metrics. How much did you increase the value of your organization? How much do you earn? Just as women do "emotional labor" at the office, we've brought marketplace metrics home and into our parenting. Competition and striving for promotions are prized at work, and this has seeped into the way we evaluate our children—and by extension, our success as parents. This is a culture-wide shift affecting stay-at-home moms as well as those who work.

Motherhood has become professionalized for much of the middle and upper-middle class. I've often heard mothers describe what they do as an "Olympic sport," one that requires the best equipment, the best training, and the careful cultivation of talent in their children. The idea that we are competing with other mothers—we're thinner, sexier, more capable, our kids are more talented, we make more money—sets us up not for winning but for losing the very thing we need most, and that is the support of other women. While our work and the marketplace may demand competition, motherhood most certainly shouldn't.

Too often lacking the genuine support of other women, and often living far from family, we turn toward our children not only for emotional sustenance but also as markers of our own success. You may think your kids' success proclaims yours as well—all those bumper stickers about "My kid is an honor student" are really "I am an honor parent"—but most of us know that this is a false equivalency. Parents who have more than one child are very aware that, while we certainly have an impact on our child's development, it has as much to do with them as with us. "I can't believe how different my kids are" should inform us that child development is an uneven process only partly tied to parenting.

Competition breeds isolation, and in our current society there are fewer places to turn for companionship with people outside our children's sphere or our workplace. Over the past fifty years communities have fractured. Affiliation with organized religious groups is shrinking—one in five Americans, and one in three Millennials have no religious affiliation at all.[12] The ethnic communities that supported our immigrant grandparents are usually left behind when we make it to the middle class and upward. We all agree that "it takes a village to raise a child," but what does our typical village consist of? A few close friends. Some relatives, if we're lucky enough to live near them and also get along with them. Tutors and sitters—paid villagers. The school—a temporary community, not the kind that's going to have our back if our child gets seriously ill or we lose our job. And of course, our children graduate from school, one level after the other, putting an end to our involvement in that particular community.

In the end it's just us and our kids, and maybe our partner (35 percent of children live with an unmarried parent).[13] We squirrel away with our nuclear family. And we've come to see protecting that insular family as making sure our children will be "set for life" via good grades, a top college, and money. There is no question that some hunkering down with our family is the result of real economic forces. For many of us, the fear that our children will not reach our level of financial security is well-founded. But if we focus our kids solely on competing for grades and slots at brand-name colleges, they won't get exposed to a sturdy set of values that puts human relationships ahead of material gain. We all say we want "good" kids. While not mutually exclusive, "good" takes a different kind of parenting than "smart," "athletic," or "talented." We have dozens of verbal and nonverbal communications with our kids on a daily basis, hundreds on a weekly basis. What do we focus on, what are we curious about? If you want "good" kids, actively show them that while many things matter to you, goodness, compassion, and empathy matter most. When they come home from school, instead of asking, "How did you do on the test today?" or "Did your team win?" ask, "How's that new girl in your class getting along?"

There is another component that adds to mothers' emotional difficulties. It is the idea that the things we've had to sacrifice in our own lives during the active years of parenting (job advancement, friendships, alone time, going to the gym) will somehow be compensated for by the success of our children. After years of clinical discussions with moms about over-involvement with their kids, there seems to be an expectation, often clearly voiced, that "it was all worthwhile" because a child was a star athlete, became valedictorian, or made it into a top-tier college.

Parental involvement can help nurture a talented child. But it can also encourage resentment. Andre Agassi, generally considered one of the best tennis players of all time, says, "I hate tennis, hate it with a dark and secret passion and always have."[14] His father's obsessive and overbearing preoccupation with his son's career led to outward success and inward misery (Agassi was addicted to crystal meth). We can't trade the majority of our own needs in the hopes that one day we'll bask in the success of our children. Contracts need to be understood by both parties. Our kids never signed on for this exchange of goods.

To keep pace in our divided economy and earn enough to compete with other families, we believe we've got to keep striving, keep moving. In our rush, we've lost the capacity for introspection. We value busyness and disdain "laziness." No one can lead the kind of hectic lives that many of us are leading without building in some restorative time. We're often quick to take it when it's offered to us—by our partner or a friend or relative—but rarely feel comfortable asking for or even (imagine!) just taking our own "time-outs."

With very little support from our institutions and often not enough from our partners, mothers struggle to contribute to the family financially, nurture our children in the present, and prepare them for the future. We tell ourselves that we're smart—we should be able to handle this somehow. But rising rates of depression and anxiety among mothers suggest that we are overwhelmed and that our coping mechanisms are fizzling out.

The Jump from Active Mom to Empty Nester

When our children leave home, we finally have time to raise our heads from their schedules and return to ourselves. Who will we be returning to? Ready or not, we will need to recalibrate our identity from mother to "empty nester." Fathers don't experience the kids' departure in the same way. They may miss them, but for most men, their sense of self-worth and identity is not as dependent upon being a parent.

When my youngest son was about to graduate college, I found myself increasingly unmoored from my most fundamental view of myself: being a mom. It had been my core identity for three decades. For years, I had integrated stories about my own family into my talks. As my boys grew up, left for college, and then entered adulthood, I found myself increasingly flummoxed about when and how to say "I have three sons." It no longer felt like the most relevant part of me; certainly not for the fresh-faced, worried young parents in my audience. My career as a psychologist and author had been built on my belief that parenting is less about having "happy" children indefinitely tethered to us and more about preparing our kids to be independent and good adults. Yet I was blindsided by a sense of loss as my sons moved fully into lives of their own. Why wasn't I kicking up my heels and congratulating myself? Sometimes I did. But I was also taken aback by the melancholy that wafted around the edges of my pride in what our family had accomplished together.

I could see at the time that my sons would someday belong to a fraternity I would no longer be able to access. A world of work, friendship, and, most of all, other attachments. A separate sphere where I would be, for the most part, a welcome visitor but not an inhabitant. What I feared most was that their childhood selves would begin to feel distant, and that the woman I had been for thirty-plus years would slowly disappear. Recently, I was sitting in my kitchen with my youngest son, Jeremy, who had just become engaged. We were celebrating this happy event when I quite unexpectedly became somber. "I don't have kids anymore," I said to him. He quickly responded, "You don't have children anymore, Mom. You'll always have kids." I was touched to tears. That sentence is on a sticky note on my bathroom mirror. I see it first thing every morning and it's both reassurance and evidence of a job well done.

Over the span of decades during which infants grow into full-fledged adults, mothers change in profound ways. Part of our sense of disruption around identity comes not only from the loss of a particular kind of relationship with our children but also because this loss is temporally close to other losses in the life cycle. Our younger selves have dissolved into menopausal clouds. We are too old to realize certain dreams. We've made choices that are now irrevocable: not making partner because of the kids or making partner and always feeling guilty about the kids. Chickens tend to come home to roost at about the same time as our children grow up. The marriage that sputtered along, the career that never quite materialized, the friendships that couldn't be maintained and, most acutely, our own mortality. The chaotic diversions inherent in raising children cease, and we suddenly find ourselves with time to reflect. What did we do right? Where did we fail? How do we spend our remaining time? And who will show up to help with the transition?

Part of the price we pay for raising a family in such a child-centric era is that we haven't built a scaffolding to take us from one phase of our lives to the next. So the pain of our children's leave-taking is magnified and the shift in our identity is jarring. This is true whether or not we have careers. And the more all-encompassing our mothering has been, the harder it is. Which may be why the latest trend is to not let go at all.

Hanging On at What Cost?

A dramatic shift has occurred in the relationship between young adults and their parents over the past fifteen years. The change first showed up at college orientation. Parents who had become enmeshed in their high-schoolers' lives with the well-meaning goal of getting them into a good school were having difficulty stepping off that treadmill.

In the 1990s there was no such thing as an orientation for parents of college freshmen: the kids were dropped off at the dorm, and Mom and Dad hugged them goodbye and drove away. In the 2000s, colleges began offering the parents optional group discussions about the responsibilities of the parents and the school during freshman year. By 2010, parent orientation was mandatory at most institutions. Parents were firmly guided away from their kids and lectured on the importance of letting go so the newly minted freshmen could learn how to fend for themselves. By that time many parents had become skeptical that any school would provide the care and oversight they felt needed to be showered on their progeny. They had a point. Most institutions would expect 18-year-olds to have a basic knowledge of how to live life. Many incoming freshmen did not.

Today, colleges continue to revise their policies in order to appease anxious parents. Post–Great Recession and well into the age of uncertainty, we are reeling from the soaring price of tuition and housing, the lack of surefire career paths for graduates, and too much information via social media about what college students are up to.

With annual tuition running upward of $55,000 at some private colleges, parents are not about to back off. "You can bet your sweet ass that I'm calling that school. . . . If your children aren't getting what they've been promised, colleges are going to get that phone call from parents," declared one mom in an article in *The Atlantic*.[15]

Schools have responded by giving parents more access to campus events and resources, and in some cases establishing parent leadership councils so Mom and Dad can have a direct line to the administration. The result is that parents remain enmeshed in their adult children's lives on multiple levels: accessing their grades on the college website, intervening with professors and advisors, and high-volume texting and face-timing with their kids. Of this college intervention, sociologist Laura Hamilton observes: "The emotional demands of intensive parenting puts a strain on marriages and careers, especially for women. . . . There is also some truth to the notion that the helicoptered children are slow to adapt to adulthood."[16]

Research has been mixed regarding the impact on college students of communicating numerous times a day with their parents. But no one is asking how the distraction of recurrent texting and running interference affects a mother as she is making the transition to the next phase of her own life. This overwhelmingly applies to mothers more than to dads: it's rare to see a father deeply preoccupied with the college student's daily travails. Daughters, especially, will seek their mom's advice on the most minute decisions, and too many moms are reluctant to scale back the communication.

The overinvolvement doesn't necessarily end when the student graduates. According to a Michigan State University survey, almost a third of parents submitted job résumés on behalf of their recent graduate, close to 10 percent tried to negotiate their child's salary, and 4 percent of the time parents attended the actual job interview.[17] How awkward is that for the young applicant? And what is the mental state of the parent who's tagging along?

When our emotional lives have been tightly entwined with our children for eighteen years or longer, and our only community is the community of their school, team, or particular interest, how does it affect our own self-esteem, agency, and eagerness for a future in which our kids don't hold center stage? Intensive parenting can cause accumulated disability in young people. Does it cause accumulated dependency in their mothers? It stunts the development of teenagers. Does it do the same to their mothers? What are we missing out on when we cling so tenaciously to a role our kids are outgrowing? Is our longing to be not just loved but also needed by our adult children an unconscious bid to stave off the aging process by acting as if we're still the youngish moms of dependent teenagers?

The mother who is still editing the essays of her 25-year-old graduate student, paying the bills for her 26-year-old who is off "discovering himself," or washing the clothes of her 28-year-old because "being a young lawyer is so demanding" may look like a simple helicopter mom, when in fact she is fighting for her life by trying to maintain her primacy in the lives of her children. Mothers without a solid grounding in their own sense of self, independent of their role as mothers, are apt to find isolation and depression at the tail end of active mothering.

In an era when college graduates often return home for long periods (for many reasons, particularly economic ones), these issues are even more pressing. Moms who have difficulty separating from their college-age kids may be tested numerous times before the young person is completely launched. Even if we feel ambivalent about our twenty-something son or daughter moving back home, the cozy companionship can be hard to resist. But in all healthy scenarios, the adult child will eventually leave for good. Where will we be if we haven't been charting our own course with as much enthusiasm as we have charted our child's? We inhabit the same uncertain world as our children. Have we developed the skills we will need to confidently move forward?

Fair or not, these are a mother's challenges. It's true that a maddeningly unequal division of parenting labor persists; that raising very young children is exhilarating but also brutal; that ours is a culture of fiercely competitive parenting; and that it can all feel overwhelming. It's urgent that parents band together to fight for more institutional support for child-rearing. But right now no one's going to come to our rescue except us. Once our children enter the elementary school years, we mothers must make the effort to nurture our inner growth and adult relationships in addition to our kids and careers.

A Different Vision of Motherhood

Mothers too often give up personal aspirations and micromanage their kids while putting aside their own need for adult friendships, free time, and the pursuit of outside interests. There are times, especially when our children are young, that this is unavoidable. But we are not only mothers with careers, we are also women apart from those roles. Our own development didn't stop the day we gave birth. We need to continue to grow over the twenty or thirty years that we actively raise our children. If we neglect that growth, we are likely to be unhappy and stunted in the present and even more so in the future. This is not to place an additional set of demands on moms. Rather, it is to highlight the fact that by *continually* ignoring our own needs we skip over critical parts of our development, and that leaves us with scant resources (both internal and external) as our kids grow up, need us less, and ultimately leave home.

If it's hard to imagine being a good mom without all the enmeshment and self-sacrifice, the results of a 2015 study may alter your view. "Who Mothers Mommy? Factors that Contribute to Mothers' Well-Being," by psychologists Suniya S. Luthar and Lucia Ciciolla, found that four types of personal support were especially strong predictors of a woman's positive adjustment to her role as a mother. Those predictors are: feeling unconditionally loved, feeling comforted when in distress, authenticity in relationships, and satisfaction with friendships. "Being married in itself is not necessarily protective," they reported. "What benefits women more is that they feel loved and comforted when in need—whoever the source of those feelings. . . . As contemporary mothers strive so carefully to tend their children, therefore, they must deliberately cultivate and maintain close, authentic relationships with friends as well as family. These must be recognized as essential buffers against the redoubtable challenges of sustaining 'good enough' mothering across two decades or more."[18]

Close friendships are two-way affairs. Their cultivation requires time spent together in conversation, occasionally without kids running around making it impossible to focus on what the other person is saying. Of course, the easiest connection to make when we're new parents is with another new parent, and some of those turn into lifelong friendships. Meanwhile, relationships with people who don't have kids or whose kids are older can fall by the wayside. I encourage moms to make an effort to stoke the embers of these other relationships even during the tough early years of parenting. In this respect technology can be helpful. A quick text. A bit of social media that lets us shoot over a "thinking about you" message or post a picture on Instagram. These connections become part of the scaffolding we continue to build as our children grow older, which helps us move through the stages of their separation. Research shows that mothers are far less likely than non-moms to socialize with other adults, probably because of the intense busyness of their lives. Working moms may feel this most acutely and rely on "free" friendships such as going to Kindergym or attending soccer games.

Now that my children are launched, I often think about what I might have done differently during my three decades of active mothering. Even though I worked throughout those years, I never felt entitled to take time away from my kids or to become truly involved in something that was not part of family life. In retrospect, I would have allotted some time for individual pursuits and greater connection with friends. I think I would have been happier and that my kids would have barely noticed the few hours a week it would have required. Particularly once they were past being youngsters, their own lives were rich enough with friends, extracurriculars, and their own interests that my absence from soccer games, theater productions, or lacrosse tournaments would have been incidental and might even have been a relief. An image that often comes to mind when I reflect on this is the bleachers at my sons' various playing fields. How many hundreds of hours did I sit there, scrolling through my phone, bored to death much of the time? Those were hours I could have spent at an activity that had nothing to do with either children or career. My own son put it most eloquently one day when he loped over to me and the other parents before a practice: "Hey, there's an empty field over there. Why don't you guys go play?"

The other thing I regret is not having spent more time at my synagogue. My sons, who had years of religious education, didn't see me around much at temple, certainly not the way they saw me around at school—in the cafeteria, driving a field trip, being "class mom." As I write this section, I'm hit with one of those "aha" moments when something hidden becomes clear. I always thought that I should have been more involved at the synagogue because it would have been better modeling for my children. In fact, I should have been more involved because it would have been better for me. It would have given me a community of people who lived close by. It would have provided a break from both parenting and reading endless technical psychology books and journals. It would have enabled me to participate in the social justice activism in which the congregation was involved. And it would have given me the opportunity to connect with men and women over issues that didn't necessarily relate to children or even religion. Today, I'm increasingly immersed in those pursuits. It's too bad I waited so long.

Time Well Spent

There is one aspect of parenting about which moms and dads are in total agreement. Parents who think they're spending "the right amount of time" with their children are three times as likely to believe they're doing an excellent job as those who think they are spending too little time. On the surface it makes sense. But the Pew Research study that produced this data left a lot of questions unanswered.[19] How much time is "enough"? What sorts of activities do parents feel they ought to be sharing with their kids? It's pretty clear that parental guilt is fueling what one writer called "the quality family-time industrial complex"—expensive family vacation packages, theme parks, cinemas, gaming arcades, and more, all designed to make working parents feel less guilty by lavishing dollars on their children.[20]

The fear that our young children (ages 3–11) are suffering because we don't spend enough time with them isn't backed by reliable research.[21] There *is* research supporting a connection between family time spent with adolescents and lower rates of behavioral problems—the right amount of time in that case being about six hours a week, including activities like eating meals together.[22] Several new studies indicate that the quality of the time parents spend with their kids is more important than the quantity, but "quality" is not related to special occasions or expensive outings. It has to do with the tone and intimacy of the activities we share in the course of an average day—eating, driving somewhere, doing yard work, hanging out, shooting hoops—and the attitude of the parent involved. If parents enjoy the time they spend with their kids, that greatly contributes to the quality for everyone.[23,24] So it may be simpler than we think. Within our hectic and overscheduled days, salvation may lie in the small moments and casual conversations that add up to a deep and enduring relationship with our children. Like so much in this unprecedented era, it's counterintuitive, and we'll need to keep relearning it as we and our children grow.

Most important, we have to bear in mind that our own continuing development has a great deal to do with how well our children will be prepared for an uncertain future. The kinds of skills that have been emphasized in this book—creativity, curiosity, an open mind, a willingness to take risks—all depend on our children having enough resilience to muster the courage to meet the future with excitement and enthusiasm as opposed to anxiety and fear. Nothing prepares kids better for uncertainty than the stable, reliable base they construct inside themselves modeled on the stable, reliable base their parents have provided. This means that we protect ourselves from overwhelming stress and continue to build our own resources and interests. If the only way we can rationalize taking time for ourselves is that it's good for our kids, so be it. With all the attention paid to optimizing our child's development, it's time to fully appreciate how much of their development depends on our own.

CHAPTER 10

The Future-Proof Family

Building a Better Moral Compass
and Stronger Communities

If you want to go quickly, go alone. If you want to go far, go together.

—African proverb

When it comes to preparing our children for an unpredictable future, no conversation is complete without stating the obvious: many of the developments that feel frighteningly out of control are caused not by nature or technology but by people. An unstable health care system, an inequitable justice system, and shortsighted energy policies are the result of decisions made by the people we have elected. Imperfect as our democracy is, we citizens do determine who our elected officials are and the choices they make. By exercising our voting rights and highlighting compassion and justice in our homes, we and our children will have a strong voice in determining who has access to the bounty the future will hold and who will be most vulnerable to its unforeseen consequences. Nothing we teach our children will be more fundamental to an optimistic future than ethical values based on respect and concern for ourselves, for others, and for our planet. The only thing that can come close to guaranteeing a safe future for our children is a society grounded in such values. Even the most devoted, determined, and financially secure parents can't deliver that protection all by themselves.

Building a Moral Compass

Values are instilled in children and young people by the adults around them. Children simply don't have the cognitive capacity to grasp a set of abstract ethical standards; they need to see them in action. Values must be modeled by parents, examined in day-to-day life, nurtured through conversation, tested, and demonstrated. They are taught at home, but they are also taught by the culture, for good or ill. For the most part, values are caught not taught. We have to give our kids the opportunity to catch values by observing us putting into action what values mean. For instance, if you value respect, then you always speak to the person in the grocery store making your sandwich in the same way that you speak to your minister or physician. It doesn't matter if your kids are with you or not. Repetition is how we transform behavior into habit.

Over time, the set of values kids absorb creates a moral compass that will guide them throughout their life. I believe there are five core values that build a solid moral compass: honesty, compassion, civic engagement, personal accountability, and common decency. "Common decency" may sound old-fashioned, but I like it, just like I like "good attitude," because both imply courtesy toward everyone we meet, whether or not we agree with them, belong to their tribe, or hold them in high esteem. Empathy, which is also a critical value, is an element of compassion. Empathy alone doesn't necessarily move us toward helpful behavior; compassion does.

Over the past fifty years or so, there has been a cultural shift away from these fundamental values and toward a far greater emphasis on the individual and personal achievement. The message seems to be that if we concentrate on our family and our success, we'll be doing right by those we love and fulfilling our responsibilities. If along the way we skip a few elections, ignore issues in our neighborhood, dodge responsibility for our bad behavior, and dispense with the rules of civility, so what? Our current divisive society reveals the corrosive effect of this mentality.

A sturdy set of values requires us to occasionally put aside what we think of as our own best interests for the interests of the larger group, community, or country. Lower taxes for me? That sounds good. But what services will be cut as a result? Who wins and who loses? This calculus matters, because how we negotiate the difficult path of ethical behavior determines how our children will negotiate it. Most kids grow up with the values of their parents. They may have different haircuts, they may live differently, they may have piercings and tattoos, but the research is pretty clear that kids will grow up to be more similar to their parents than different from them.[1]

My own parents were born in this country, but my grandparents emigrated from Belarus at the turn of the twentieth century to avoid persecution. They never saw their families again, but they became active members of their new community in the Bronx. My grandfather, a bricklayer, was head of a local benevolent society that helped those who remained in the Old Country as well as those who had braved the difficult journey to America. My earliest memory of values in action were of Grandpa Sam collecting money for these efforts and asking all the children in the family to contribute. I remember how grown-up and proud I felt when handing him the few nickels and dimes I had been saving. I'm certain that no one ever asked me how I felt about contributing. Contributing was woven into the fabric of my immigrant family. If you want your child to exhibit good values, expect it. Kids want to live up to their parents' expectations and are eager to avoid parental disappointment. It's important to remember that moral development evolves as our kids grow up. For most of them, being "good" is motivation enough for doing the right thing. Your family is the first community that your children participate in. Make sure they understand that their contributions are expected and valued.

While I know that I've worked hard for my accomplishments, I also know that I stand on the shoulders of my family's sacrifice. The walls in my house display pictures of my grandparents' arrival at Ellis Island. They are not there for me. I knew them all. But my children didn't, and I want to make sure they never develop the mistaken impression that their accomplishments are solely the result of individual effort. I also want them to remember that their contributions, and the values they practice, will reverberate down the generations.

An Ethical Evolution

Now more than ever, it's up to parents to model ethical behavior. Where once we relied on schools and places of worship to deliver consistent and credible messages about ethics, today our trust, to varying degrees, in those institutions is eroding. Our research at Challenge Success at Stanford tells us that the vast majority of students at high-achieving schools are likely to be cheating, particularly as they approach senior year.[2] As we have seen, many academic institutions have fudged or outright lied about their student data in order to make the schools seem more selective. Communities often fail to offer strong unanimous guidance about how to make wise and ethical choices, and the broader culture has certainly been failing at it as well.

The good news is that we're finally experiencing a public reassessment about what constitutes ethical behavior. The universal outrage over the involvement of parents, coaches, and school officials in the 2019 Varsity Blues college admissions scandal brought the issue into stark relief.

Well-to-do parents had test scores altered, paid enormous bribes, and photoshopped pictures of their kids to make them appear to be competitive athletes in order to gain admittance to prestigious schools like USC, Georgetown, Stanford, and Yale. This story has continued to have legs as more parents are indicted, substantial fines are administered, and jail time is lurking. While there is no doubt that the children of privilege have always had advantages in the college admissions process, flagrant law-breaking crosses the line for most of us. The reality is, like many of the tough problems in this book, compromised behavior is endemic, complex, a reflection of the worst of our hyperindividualistic society, and unlikely to be solved by superficial attention. These kinds of ethical issues demand that we look deeply, wrestle with our values, and commit to solutions that take into account our long history of misplaced tolerance, looking the other way, and ignoring the factors that contribute to *even thinking* about this kind of behavior.

Things are even improving in tech, where for decades the credo has been to move fast, break things, and shrug off the fallout. I personally experienced this years ago when I was speaking with Google's director of research, Peter Norvig. "I use Google every day," I told him. "It's great for research. But I also have patients who learn how to cut their wrists on Google. Do you bear any responsibility for that?"

"No," he responded. "Go talk to the schools, the kids, the parents." That attitude has been fairly unanimous throughout my conversations with people in AI. At a Harvard event involving CRISPR, the genetic-engineering tool that alters DNA sequences, a friend asked one of the panelists about the moral implications of such research. The panelist replied, "Talk to an ethicist. I'm a scientist." The siloing of responsibility has been the norm, with ethics relegated to its own corner and scientists and engineers not willing or expected to concern themselves with it.

That abruptly changed after the 2016 U.S. presidential election, when it became clear that Russia had used fake accounts and false reports on Facebook to attempt to influence the outcome. Some of our top institutions—Stanford, Harvard, Cornell, and MIT among them—now offer or require courses on things like the ethics of computer science. Students are taught to consider questions such as: *Is the technology fair? How do you make sure that the data is not biased? Should machines be judging humans?*[3] "[The] one effective lever we have against tech companies is employee pressure," writes Irina Raicu, director of the Internet Ethics program at Santa Clara University's Markkula Center for Applied Ethics. "We should demand that technologists get some ethics training and recognize their role in defending democracy."[4] We saw this in action in 2018 when thousands of Google employees worldwide walked off the job to protest the tech giant's mishandling of sexual misconduct allegations against executives.

While parents have always wanted to raise trustworthy, socially responsible children, it's even more urgent when ethical decisions made by multiple people, not only CEOs, carry potential for widespread harm. A few examples: the scientists who develop genetic engineering of crops, the engineers who create and test driverless vehicles, the officials who rely on big data to determine public policy. Long before our kids enter the workforce and become these decision-makers, we need to instill in them a set of values and a way of thinking that will make them worthy stewards of our civilization and our planet. Of particular importance will be an increasing reliance on what is called design thinking. Basically, design thinking is about having an empathic, human-centered core at the heart of product development and problem solving. It is a way of thinking about things focusing first on the needs of the *people* that are affected by the problem. "Move fast and break things" had its day when rapid disruption meant soaring innovation and profits. We each, however, have grown weary of data breaches, lack of privacy, and unwanted intrusion. Hopefully, the generations leading us forward will value empathy, foresight, and transparency over "disruption."

Additionally, we can't expect our kids to build a better world when they aren't taught the first thing about what it means to be a thoughtful and engaged citizen. Robert Pondiscio, a former civics teacher and outstanding writer on education issues, nails it when he writes, "If we don't improve civics instruction, we must resign ourselves to our poisoned national politics."[5] In my opinion, this aspect of educating our children is starting about a decade late. Part of the school curriculum, beginning in middle school or earlier, needs to be considering the "big questions" around ethics, tech, government, democracy, and citizenship. Kids need to be thinking about these issues, discussing them, researching them, and understanding the implications from multiple points of view. By neglecting ethics and civics as core courses in middle and high school, we're not helping our kids develop the necessary skill set they will need to think deeply about complex and difficult problems. Critical thinking skills like an open mind, curiosity, flexible thinking, and awareness of one's own biases will be protective forces as our children face dilemmas we can't even imagine yet.

Impending technological and biological advances are sure to be thrilling, but they will also carry the potential for grave unforeseen consequences. Both Albert Einstein and Robert Oppenheimer came to question and rue their role in the development of the atomic bomb. Arthur Galston was the inventor of Agent Orange, the chemical weapon used extensively in Vietnam that wreaked havoc on the environment and caused untold illness and birth defects. Galston said, "Nothing that you do in science is guaranteed to result in benefits for mankind. Any discovery is morally neutral and it can be turned either to constructive or destructive ends. That's not the fault of science."[6] Genetically altered babies, artificial intelligence, drones, and robotics all have the potential for constructive or destructive uses. If we teach our children how to think critically and ethically about these developments, we have a better chance of reaping the benefits of technology while avoiding catastrophes. In the words of Alison Simmons, the Samuel H. Wolcott Professor of Philosophy at Harvard, "We want students to shape their technological future, not be shaped by it."[7]

Teaching Ethics at Home

Honesty, compassion, civic engagement, personal accountability, and common decency comprise a moral compass that will enable our kids to make thoughtful and ethically sound choices. We can teach these attributes by example, by repetition, and through conversation, adjusting our message as our child's capacity for understanding grows. We say to young children, "Never tell a lie." When they're older, we explain the nuances of social interaction—sometimes small white lies can be okay if you're trying to avoid hurting someone's feelings. It is also critical that we conduct ourselves with honesty. Kids are very quick to pick up on parental hypocrisy. A dinnertime conversation with our partner about the best way to get out of jury duty, lessen our tax obligation, or avoid contact with an unappealing family member is a surefire way to make our children suspicious of our own integrity. If we want kids with good values, we have to walk the talk.

Early on, children show a degree of empathy, the ability to understand and share the feelings of another. We try to expand that natural empathy into compassion—a desire not only to feel with another but also to be helpful and to alleviate the suffering of others. The words "How would *you* feel if . . ." are simple yet powerful tools. Walk your child through his or her feelings and solutions. "Owen's upset, he crashed my hoverboard. When I ride on his, I'm going to crash it and see how he likes it." Help your child to acknowledge his feelings—probably anger and disappointment with his friend. Then help him to see how his solution will only make his friend feel bad. What will he gain by this? Ask questions. Hold back on answers and solutions until your son has had a chance to calm down and acknowledge his own hurt feelings. Help him to stand in his distressed friend's shoes. It's unlikely that he will want his friend hurt. Help him walk through empathy—feeling that his friend is distressed— and toward self-regulation and compassion: "Maybe Owen can come with me to the store to have it repaired. We'll both feel better then."

Daily life provides lots of opportunities to model civic engagement: at our child's school, in local events, with neighbors, at our place of worship, in support of causes we care about. When our kids see us get involved, they learn how to do it. The same goes for personal accountability and common decency. Most of the lessons that stick are the tiny, recurring ones: how we treat the checker at the grocery store, relate to other parents and kids, behave when we make a mistake, speak about our relatives when they're not in the room. If we mock people or talk about how dumb they are, it's not only an attitude our children will absorb, it's a *value*: others don't deserve our respect.

Throughout the years our children are living with us, perhaps the most important thing we can teach them is how to reflect on their actions through an ethical lens. In this way we're demonstrating how to use their moral compass. The method? Asking questions, especially, "Why?" Say your preschooler just swiped a candy bar at the grocery store. You can snap at him and insist he return it immediately. The better course (with the same end result) is to ask why he took it and to spend a couple of minutes talking about what happens to a business when there is theft. Make it personal: tell him that the nice lady at the checkout counter might have to pay for the missing candy bar. If that's not true, let him know that her boss won't be happy. How would he feel in her shoes?

Perhaps your high-schooler is wondering whether to select math or graphic design as a college major. As you listen to her weigh the pros and cons, try not to favor one choice over the other. Then ask questions about what she values and why: *What's most important to you? Why do you care about those fields of study? Why would they be a good fit for you?* These can lead to larger questions such as *How would you define a good life?*

Conversations that touch on ethics and values don't need to involve big decisions like choosing a major. Most of these chats will crop up naturally, which is why you might want to keep a few value-oriented questions in your back pocket. Depending on the age of your child, expect different answers and encourage deeper thinking.

Younger kids see right and wrong in terms of what gets punished and what doesn't. Older kids and most adults strive to live up to being "good" and meeting social expectations. A smaller group of adults think about moral issues not in terms of rules but in terms of individual rights and justice. Our back-pocket questions should inspire reflection and move our children toward considering increased complexity: *What does it mean to be a good person? When should you apologize to someone else? What makes someone a hero? Is it ever okay not to follow instructions? Is it our responsibility to help others, or should they be in charge of helping themselves? Who might you want to be like when you grow up? Why?* Like any practiced habit, habits of ethical reflection will become second nature to your child.

We all know that sometimes doing the right thing isn't easy or especially pleasurable. In a "do your own thing," hyperindividualistic culture, parents can have second thoughts about forcing their kids into unpleasant duties. "He doesn't like going to church." "She's working so hard on homework, I just can't make her do the dishes." This kind of excuse-making (often because parents don't want their kids mad at them) diminishes the importance of every member of a family needing to be a contributing member. The outside world is unlikely to be forgiving when your kid has lapses in responsibility. I've thought about this quite a bit as my mom has unfortunately had advanced Alzheimer's disease for over a decade. I see her every week, for multiple reasons, but mostly because I believe it's the right thing to do. My middle son, Michael, lives in New York, but whenever he comes back to San Francisco (which is often) he asks to borrow my car and heads out to her skilled nursing facility. I've asked him why he always does this and his answer is "It's my duty Mom." Of course, it's a difficult visit and not fun. But a sense of duty, of obligation, is something we need to expect more of from our children. If we want our kids to be contributors—to themselves, to their eventual families, to the wounded world—they need to start at home. Give them opportunities. Make it easy for them to be good.

Values Need a Community

Values don't exist in a vacuum. They are behaviors: the way we interact with people face-to-face and the actions we take that we know will affect them. Values take on weight and meaning in the real world, in our community. Community is also where we can find solace for many of the ills we've discussed: our anxiety and alienation, our feelings of helplessness about the future, our kids' detachment and lack of agency. Historically, community is also where we have celebrated milestones, achievements, and a sense of belonging.

Over the past two decades, our near-exclusive preoccupation with our children has led to withdrawal from community life. Our lives have become contracted rather than expanded. This has not only distorted our value system, it has also left us increasingly isolated. And parents in the United States aren't the only ones feeling cut off. Social isolation is a global phenomenon affecting all ages and classes. The U.K. now has a Minister for Loneliness.[8] In Japan, where traditional households of multigenerational families are being replaced by Western-style nuclear families, there is an epidemic of *kodokushi*—people (not just the elderly) dying alone, whose bodies lay undiscovered for days because no one is checking in on them.[9] Junko Okamoto, a Japanese psychologist who has written about the phenomenon says, "Society is not doing enough to address loneliness and people don't want to admit how unhappy they are."[10]

Americans don't want to admit we're lonely or unhappy either. But scratch beneath the digital surface and the trend is unmistakable. Americans of all ages have gotten demonstrably lonelier over the past four decades."[11] Not surprisingly, the younger, digitally connected generation is most afflicted.[12] No selfie, Instagram, or Facebook post can produce the emotional revitalization of face-to-face contact. Loneliness feels bad and is bad for us: it is correlated with reduced lifespan similar to that caused by smoking, and is thought to be more damaging to a person's health than obesity.[13] Loneliness and lack of community exacerbates the stress of uncertainty. We need to be part of a larger project than supporting ourselves and promoting our children. While there is much talk these days about tribalism, joining a "tribe" isn't the same as joining a community. Unfortunately, as currently configured, a tribe is based on mutual distrust. Communities, on the other hand, are based on mutual trust and goodwill. We can't just be against other groups or ideologies. We must be *for* people and ideas because that's what sustains and inspires community members over time.

One of my favorite reminders of the strength of those communities that acknowledge the needs of all members comes from Erskine Bowles, former chief of staff under President Clinton and president of the University of North Carolina for five years. He's fond of telling a story handed down from his grandfather to his father about how, after you chopped wood for your family, you'd stop by the community woodpile on the way home and drop off a log or two. This was to make sure that all families in "sweet" Union County, North Carolina, had adequate heat over the winter. Every member of the community did this "whether you were to the left of Gore Vidal or the right of Jesse Helms." This was a time when taking care of your neighbors was more important than advertising the accomplishments of your own family or asserting your moral and political superiority over your neighbor. Think about what might constitute the community woodpile in your own neighborhood. Throw on a few logs.

From Bowling Alone to Angry Sports Dads

It was nearly twenty years ago that Robert Putnam published *Bowling Alone: The Collapse and Revival of American Community*, the first popular book to describe how dwindling community involvement in the United States is impacting us. A legion of authors and thinkers has tackled the topic since then. One recent contributor is Yuval Levin, whose *The Fractured Republic* contends that the individuality and personal expression so prized by Americans is a double-edged sword: "In liberating many individuals from oppressive social constraints, we have also estranged many from their families and unmoored them from their communities, work and faith. . . . We have also unraveled the institutions of an earlier era, and with it the public's broader faith in institutions of all kinds."[14] Our lack of trust in institutions has had a ripple effect on the public psyche, making suspicion and cynicism our default frame of mind, with the result that we trust only those in our small, immediate, and like-minded circle.

Prior to this century, the communities that sustained us were geographic locations (mainly cities and neighborhoods), organized religious groups, and ethnic enclaves. Our grandparents typically belonged to several such communities. We and our kids often belong to none, or take part in a watered-down version: religion on holidays, which might also be the time we enjoy favorite recipes passed down from Grandma and listen to family stories. These are lovely and worthwhile traditions, but they are echoes of community more than the actual experience. They're dessert without the main course—less demanding but also less nourishing.

Communities that deliver sustenance provide, at the very least, frequently recurring interaction with a group of people with whom we share some sort of common bond. But those communities require a level of participation many of us shy away from, such as putting our individual needs second to the needs of the group, socializing with people we don't always like, following rules or rituals we may find pointless or unfair, and contributing time and effort when it's not convenient or immediately rewarding. The organizations that most often seem to inspire such sacrifice and loyalty among today's parents are our kids' athletic teams.

The intense commitment of some parents to their child's team can be seen in hundreds of YouTube videos featuring out-of-control sports dads. Why are they so outraged over bad calls or a player's fumbled catch? At first we might think it's all about nurturing their child's talent and dreams. Dr. Stacy Warner, who heads East Carolina University's Sport Officiating Lab, offers another opinion: "Humans have an innate need to belong to community. Places where people meet are dwindling. What we have left is sport." A parent's membership in the community of their child's team is dependent on the kid's performance and the team's success. "Parents want their kids to constantly be involved, to make that 'A' team so they can continue to travel and do these things because it's their community. If their child is cut from the team, their social circle will look very different."

The phenomenon isn't limited to sports parents. The same thing happens with parents whose kids are in the performing arts or any competitive activity like debate or chess club. These are ready-built communities that parents can step into, and for some mothers it aligns with their conviction that any spare moment should be devoted to their child. Being a sports, theater, or debate parent checks all the boxes. But Dr. Warner echoed my son's earlier observation to "go play": "If parents had adult sport league practices, maybe they wouldn't sit around and watch their kids practice."[15]

The camaraderie enjoyed in places like Mommy and Me or the softball bleachers are sometimes called "free friendships" because parents automatically gain access to the group just by showing up. The community of parents cheering on their young players requires no special skill on the parents' part, but in a cruel twist puts a performance burden on the kids. Parents invest time and sometimes significant amounts of money in their child's team, which adds to the pressure. It's not surprising that a study in *Family Relations* found that the more money children perceive their parents have invested in a sport, the less they enjoy playing it.[16]

Ultimately, whether we do it subconsciously or with our eyes wide open, there are pitfalls to gaining community solely via our children's activities or schools. Not only does research show that too much parental involvement is unhealthy for kids,[17] these communities all have expiration dates unless you intend to stay involved after your child outgrows the activity. Becoming a little league coach at the local playing field is a viable choice. Hanging wistfully around the park remembering the "good old days" when your child played there is just plain sad.

Choosing Communities

If we decide to be supportive of our children in a more moderated way—for example, by attending big games or opening nights but not surrendering every weekend—we may open up some time to become part of a different community, one that speaks to other parts of our soul. Fathers have more of a tradition of simply hanging out—at sports games with a couple of buddies, throwing back a few beers, running or biking or shooting hoops with each other. Too often when I suggest to moms that they try something similar, the response is, "What could I do that's more important than spending time with my child?" For many, it's nearly impossible to fathom the idea that connecting with an outside community is as valuable to their children as accompanying the kids to another one of their activities. Moms are especially susceptible to the popular edict that when it comes to our offspring, we can never spend enough money on them or time with them.[18] That's a seriously flawed premise. By our engagement in the larger world, we show our kids what is worth cherishing *in addition* to our family. We demonstrate the value of broad interests, diverse friendships, and curiosity about the wide world. If we devote some time to volunteering, we show our kids that the community we live in is worth our time and effort. We model a version of adulthood that is deeper, more interesting, and more attainable than the one that implies that "life is all about our individual success and gratification."

As time-strapped adults who are actively parenting, how can we partake of community? One approach is to tap into two different types. The first might fulfill us on a moral or spiritual level, being an outlet for doing good deeds and making our community stronger. Organized religion is a natural choice. Religious groups offer structure, leadership, mission, support for life transitions, volunteer opportunities, spiritual education for young people, and much more. To the extent that adults want to engage, religion provides the depth and consistency that meet our human need to belong to a group. But this form of involvement is not for everyone. About half of Americans attend religious services only a few times a year, rarely, or never.[19]

For those not drawn to organized religion, there are loads of worthy organizations to connect with. We might bring food to a women's shelter once a month, or cheer up folks in an assisted living home. We could fundraise for a cause we believe in or join a community vegetable garden. The opportunities are there if we seek them out. Most nonprofit organizations need help with things like marketing, social media, and managing the books. It can be daunting to take the first step as a volunteer, so it helps if it's an activity you enjoy, an issue you care about, or a task with which you already have some experience.

Our second type of community activity could engage us on a personal level, generating friendships and allowing us to grow emotionally, creatively, or intellectually apart from our role as parents. The goal is to get into the habit of allotting time in our life for both communities, so that we contribute to the larger world, nurture our own growth as individuals, and make meaningful connections with people outside our family.

The amount of time we engage in these two communities would have to fluctuate depending on our kids' ages and our other commitments, but ideally we would devote at least a few hours every month to both spheres. Our child's part would simply be to witness our involvement and participate when appropriate. One of my friends recalls that when she was growing up, her mother took a course to learn Braille and volunteered to transcribe books into Braille for the vision-impaired. The mom was an avid reader, and she told her kids that she couldn't imagine not having access to the world of literature (audio books didn't exist back then). When my own children were young, I used to deliver meals to shut-ins who were ill. I'd sometimes take the boys along, but I mainly did it because it was meaningful to me. A fundamental precept in Judaism is *tikkun olam*—acts of kindness performed to heal the world. Delivering the meals was mine, as I explained to my sons at the time. Today they all volunteer for good causes. Would they have been inclined toward volunteerism if they hadn't seen me making my rounds? Maybe. No way to know. But the tenor of a home is set not so much by what we say as by what we do. And here's part of the payoff. My oldest son, Loren, volunteers at a family camp where there's a terminally ill parent. He recently recruited me to help at the camp. It's out of my wheelhouse and feels very challenging. But it is a terrific opportunity to learn, to be of service, and to share a meaningful experience with my grown son. There are very few promises I've made in this book. But I can promise you this, whatever pleasure you may currently get from your children's academic or athletic successes won't hold a candle to the pride and pleasure of seeing them grow into generous and kind adults.

Activism

Shortly before I finished writing this book, a mom in my neighborhood approached me with a request I'd never had before: "Would you be willing to come to my house and talk to a group of parents about teaching their kids activism?" I agreed. Then I had to ponder what, exactly, I would advise them to do. I concluded that building community, volunteering, and political activism are overlapping spheres, like circles in a Venn diagram. You can place yourself anywhere on the diagram you feel comfortable. Begin with what strikes a personal chord. Maybe it's the environment, a topic children are drawn to. Involvement can be organizing a day to clean up the beach, the beach-cleaning day itself (community in action!), and if you want to take it to the "political activism" level, you can help your child compose a letter to your local representative describing the beach cleanup and asking if the rep is currently sponsoring any beach-related legislation. Investigate with your kids. Show them how to research the representative's voting history, navigate the website, and use the "Contact" page. The Internet and social media have made activism accessible to everyone. Witness the 1.6 million students in 2019 who, by connecting to other students around the world, staged a walk out to protest against the greatest threat to their well-being, the lack of action on climate change.

Part of good parenting is about making the world a better place for all children, not just our own. Our kids don't live in isolation and neither should we. Instead, we can teach them that civic engagement is normal and expected and involves more than helping at the Thanksgiving food bank or going to a big march, although those activities are energizing and worthwhile. Activism that's interlaced with our regular routine helps both adults and children feel empowered and positive about the future. Instead of cursing the darkness, we can light candles as big as running for office or as small as actually reading the voter education pamphlet that comes to the house. We can model what it means to be a citizen by discussing issues at the dinner table and taking our kids along when we vote, and by working with schools to reinstate civics courses.

Toward the end of reviewing the manuscript for this book, I noticed how many times I'd invoked the dinner table. I'm curious about this. I know that the dinner table isn't the only place where we talk to our children. But I also know from decades of raising my three sons that it was the place where we reliably gathered. That family assembly ended more than a decade ago. Yet it is probably my fondest parenting memory and the place where the issues of the day, and much of what I've highlighted in this book about values, was talked about, debated, argued, and occasionally even resolved. It was the incubator of conscience and action, not only for my children but for myself and my husband as well. I know that since I've raised my sons, the pace of life has quickened and the demands have increased. My guess is that few of you have the luxury of nightly family dinners. And much discussion does take place in the car or at the breakfast table. But not with the sense of predictability and relative leisure that dinner can afford. A writer can only ask her audience to read what she has written. I'm going to go one step further and ask you to consider fashioning this corner of your life in a way that, at least most of the time, allows your family to gather, to share, to explore, and to grow. I do believe that if you can modify this one aspect of our current rushed, hectic, and often impossible day you will have given both yourself and your children a gift that will reap great benefits.

Some of this may feel abstract, even irrelevant, if you're in the midst of juggling a fussy baby, a recalcitrant toddler, a work deadline, family responsibilities, and an hour a week of yoga. But here's the thing. We can lavish all kinds of attention and remediation and accelerated coursework on our kids, but if they don't have a chance to use their advantages in a reasonably sane and stable world, then it's a whole lot of wasted time and energy. We simply cannot disconnect from the world our kids will inherit. Our continued involvement is a greater part of their future than any advantage we think we might be bestowing with specialized camps, homework therapists, or AP courses.

Romancing the Future

As Americans, we're fortunate to live in a country that has many flaws but many more graces. For better and worse, there is a rootlessness that has accompanied the digital revolution that we're still trying to figure out. One thing is clear: pouring some of the time, attention, and resources we have devoted to our children into strengthening our communities and our country will benefit our kids and ourselves. When I was young, I had a love affair with America—the stories my grandparents told of escaping from unimaginable persecution and horror made me certain I was living in the best country on earth. As I matured, my assumptions about my country were challenged. My vision grew sharper and I saw more depth and more shadows. The world at the moment seems rather broken to me, with incivility, bias, and bigotry taking center stage. Yet if my lifelong practice as a psychologist has taught me anything, it is to put my faith in the power of insight and self-awareness to change behavior.

We are not lost. The robot apocalypse is not upon us. Our children will most likely have jobs and marriages and children that, while different than ours in some ways, are apt to be similar in many ways. There is no question that both the amount and velocity of change have accelerated and we can't predict the future, but that doesn't mean we can't prepare for it. We most certainly can. And we must. Our children will need greater freedom, both cognitively and emotionally, as well as greater optimism and stability at home in order to craft the kind of resilience that our uncertain future is likely to demand. The dozens of military, business, and thought leaders I've spoken to over the past few years, while differing on details, are unanimous in their opinion that an appetite for challenge and the interest and capacity to remain an agile and active learner will be mandatory. Different metrics are likely to signal success. An A in the expectable may well be less valuable than a B in the difficult, idiosyncratic, or unexpected.

As parents, we must stay intrigued and optimistic about the unsettled world we are living in. We will have plenty of our own challenges to meet in the coming decades, including familiar ones like balancing work and child-rearing, aging, caring for parents, and retirement, as well as challenges we can't begin to anticipate. Just like our children, we will need to continue developing what has traditionally been called "an open mind." For our kids, we must model concern for the common good—other people, our country, and our earth. Hunkering down will not serve us well. Neither will continuing to cultivate the kind of anxiety that gets in the way of the enthusiasm and openness needed to meet unknowable challenges. Our children have had enough of how special they are. They've had enough of parental preoccupation. And they've had enough of being pressured to achieve a standard of success that will be reexamined multiple times before they actually enter the work world. If I had just one piece of advice for parents in our age of uncertainty? Spend half the amount of time you now spend on hounding your children about grades and test scores and twice as much time cultivating a strong moral compass and an appreciation for the common good. We will all be called upon to be our best selves in the breathtakingly unpredictable, exciting, and yet-to-be-written future.

ACKNOWLEDGMENTS

It always takes a battalion of people to write a book; this one took an army.

Sometimes it really helps to step back. Years spent writing and lecturing on the damage done by an overreliance on grades, test scores, and college admissions simply hadn't moved the needle enough. I'd exhausted my own echo chamber and needed new ideas and fresh perspectives. To my original group of non-psychologist, free-thinking, design-thinking, divergent-thinking pals: Pam Scott, Tim Koogle, Jeff Snipes, and Dave Whorton, thank you for all the afternoons of discussion and all the scribbling on poster-board-covered walls that eventually led to the formulation of this book.

Thank you to the many additional experts who were willing to talk with me and offer the alternative points of view that I needed to see these seemingly intractable problems through a different lens. Thank you to "Sandy" Winnefeld, former vice chairman of the Joint Chiefs of Staff; Bob Burton, neurologist and author; William Damon, director of the Stanford Center on Adolescence and author; James Gorman, chairman and CEO of Morgan Stanley; Byron D. Trott, founder, chairman, and CEO of BDT and Company; Peter Norvig, director of Research at Google; Jason Rubin, head of studios at Oculus; Blythe Yee, vice president, Employee Communications at LinkedIn; and Christina Hall, chief people officer at LinkedIn. And to Erskine Bowles, too many titles to list, but mentor par excellence, who always helps to keep my thinking gracious, optimistic, and ethically grounded.

To my diligent teachers and editors on neurology: Elliot Stein, head of the neuroimaging lab at the National Institute of Drug Abuse and Catherine Madison, director of the Brain Health Center at California Pacific Medical Center. Thank you both for your expertise and patience in talking to a profoundly interested but also modestly educated "newbie" about the awe-inspiring complexity of the human brain.

Most particularly to my colleagues, mentors, and good friends John Walkup, director of the Child and Adolescent program at Lurie Children's Hospital in Chicago and Susan Friedland, also at Lurie Children's Hospital. Without your wisdom, experience, and generosity I doubt that this book would have been completed. Most certainly it would not have been as rich, layered, or well-informed. And to my pal Tony Wagner, author and co-director of the Change Leadership Group at Harvard University, thank you for always injecting a blast of curiosity and creativity into my thinking and writing.

To my dear, funny, brilliant, and generous colleagues, Michele Borba and Catherine Steiner-Adair. Our weekly talkfests helped me get through a year of Covid isolation and the necessary recrafting of *Ready or Not* for the paperback edition.

To the amazing Challenge Success crew at the Stanford Graduate School of Education. Led by my co-founder and senior lecturer Denise Pope and our boundlessly competent executive director Kathy Koo, this little educational startup has morphed into an important and effective change agent across the country. Thank you co-founder Jim Lobdell. And thank you all for giving me so many passes while I've been writing and on the road.

To Dagmar Dolby, Bonnie Caruso, Michelle Wachs, Phyllis Kempner, and David Stein, thank you for your friendship and years of stalwart support both when I'm around and when I'm not (which is too often). To Lauren Taddune, my daughter-in-law and all-around connector to things "tech," thank you for your endless patience with this technology immigrant. And finally, to my dear friends Kathy Fields, Garry Rayant, Wendye Robbins, and Craig McGahey. You all positively astound me. Thank you for lighting up my dark corners with your relentless talent, optimism, and resolve. Most of all, thank you for inviting me in.

To Sharon Doyle, my assistant and auxiliary brain. The luxury you afforded me by taking care of all the details and detritus of my life allowed this book to come into existence. And to the ever-extraordinary Maga who takes care of my mother with the same kind spirit that she helped take care of my kids—words will never be enough. To Tom Hutchman, my trainer extraordinaire, who has spent nearly two decades patiently working, cajoling, and insisting that the job of my body is to be more than a transport system for my head. To Scott Wood, the only IT guy in the world who not only answers the phone and takes my panicked questions at two in the afternoon but also at two in the morning—there is no way to thank you enough.

To Lynette Padwa whose thoughts, words, and logic permeate this book. Thank you for your generous sharing of time, effort, and talent. I'd still be working on it a decade from now if it wasn't for your conviction that it needed to see the light of day.

To Eric Simonoff, my agent since he was a twenty-something and I was an untested writer. Thank you for your faith in me and your conviction about the importance of my work. And to Gail Winston, my HarperCollins editor who, through three different books, has helped to keep me on track and clearer than I would be without her. Thank you to the rest of the HarperCollins team: Heather Drucker, Tom Hopke, Emily Taylor, Nathaniel Knaebel, and everyone else who had a hand in bringing this book to life. And, of course, to the many individuals who were willing to share their stories, sometimes uplifting, sometimes mortifying, that put meat on the bones of this book. Thank you for your courage and generosity.

To my husband of four-plus decades, Lee Schwartz, thank you for your support, your boundless curiosity, and for generously allowing me the time and space for the intense focus and endless late nights of writing that a book demands.

And finally, to my three grown sons Loren, Michael, and Jeremy. Thank you all for the discussions, corrections, and attempts to help me see the world through your younger, more tolerant, more optimistic eyes. In one of those extraordinary shifts/gifts in life you are no longer my charges, but have become my teachers. This is a fresher, better, and more relevant book because of your contributions.

NOTES

INTRODUCTION

1. U.S. Department of Health & Human Services, "Common Mental Health Disorders in Adolescence," https://www.hhs.gov/ash/oah/adolescent-development/mental-health/adolescent-mental-health-basics/common-disorders/index.html. Retrieved Sept. 14, 2018; https://www.nimh.nih.gov/health/statistics/any-anxiety-disorder.shtml.

CHAPTER 1: WHY THE NEEDLE HASN'T MOVED: DOUBLING DOWN ON THE PAST WHEN WE FEAR THE FUTURE

1. "Common Mental Health Disorders in Adolescence." https://www.hhs.gov/ash/oah/adolescent-development/mental-health/adolescent-mental-health-basics/common-disorders/index.html

2. R. Mojtabai, M. Olfson, and B. Han, "National Trends in the Prevalence and Treatment of Depression in Adolescents and Young Adults," *Pediatrics* 138, no. 6 (2016).

3. "Common Mental Health Disorders in Adolescence."

4. Benjamin Shain, "Suicide and Suicide Attempts in Adolescents," *Pediatrics* 138 (July 2016), 1.

5. Jerusha O. Conner and Denise C. Pope, "Not Just Robo-Students: Why Full Engagement Matters and How Schools Can Promote It," *Journal of Youth and Adolescence* 42, no. 9 (Sept. 2013): 1426–1442.

6. C. Farh, M. G. Seo, and P. E. Tesluk, "Emotional Intelligence, Teamwork, Effectiveness, and Job Performance: The Moderating Role of Job Context," *Journal of Applied* Psychology 97, no. 4 (July 2012): 890–900.

7. M. Berking and P. Wupperman, "Emotional Regulation and Mental Health: Recent Findings, Current Challenges, and Future Directions," *Current Opinion in Psychiatry* 25, no. 2 (2012): 128–134.

8. L. A. Sroufe, "From Infant Attachment to Promotion of Adolescent Autonomy: Prospective, Longitudinal Data on the Role of Parents in Development," in J. G. Borkowski, S. L. Ramey, and M. Bristol-Power, eds., *Parenting and the Child's World: Influences on Academic, Intellectual, and Social-Emotional Development* (Mahwah, NJ: Lawrence Erlbaum Associates, Inc., 2002).

9. Peter Dockrill, "America Really Is in the Midst of a Rising Anxiety Epidemic," *Science Alert*, May 9, 2018, https://www.sciencealert.com /americans-are-in-the-midst-of-an-anxiety-epidemic-stress-increase.

10. Greg Toppo, "Why You Might Want to Think Twice Before Going to Law School," *USA Today*, June 28, 2017, https://www.usatoday.com /story/news/2017/06/28/law-schools-hunkering-down-enrollment -slips/430213001/.

11. Association of American Medical Colleges, "Medical Student Education: Debt, Costs, and Loan Repayment Fact Card," October 2017, https://members.aamc.org/iweb/upload/2017%20Debt%20Fact%20 Card.pdf.

12. Neil Patel, "90% of Startups Fail: Here's What You Need to Know About the 10%," *Forbes*, Jan. 16, 2015, https://www.forbes.com/sites /neilpatel/2015/01/16/90-of-startups-will-fail-heres-what-you-need -to-know-about-the-10/#28351bb66792.

13. Phil Haslett, "How Much Did Employees Make per Share in Recent Startup Acquisitions?" Quora (website), Sept. 17, 2013.

14. Ryan Carey, "The Payoff and Probability of Obtaining Venture Capital," 80,000Hours.org, June 25, 2014.

15. Steve Lohr, "Where the STEM Jobs Are (and Where They Aren't),"

New York Times, Nov. 1, 2017, https://www.nytimes.com/2017/11/01/education/edlife/stem-jobs-industry-careers.html.

16. Jean M. Twenge, Gabrielle N. Martin, and Keith W. Campbell, "Decreases in Psychological Well-Being Among American Adolescents After 2012 and Links to Screen Time During the Rise of Smartphone Technology," *Emotion* 18, no. 3 (Jan. 22, 2018), 765–780.

17. Frank Newport, "The New Era of Communication Among Americans," Gallup news.gallup.com/poll/179288/new-era-communication-americans.aspx., Nov. 10, 2014.

18. A. Lenhart, "Teen, Social Media, and Technology Overview," Pew Research Center, 2018, http://www.pewinternet.org/2018/05/31/teens-social-media-technology-2018.

19. C. Auguer and G. W. Hacker, "Associations Between Problematic Mobile Phone Use and Psychological Parameters in Young Adults," *International Journal of Public Health* 57, no. 2 (2012): 437–441.

20. Jean M. Tweng, "Have Smartphones Destroyed a Generation?," *The Atlantic*, September 2017.

21. Monica Anderson and JingJing Jiang, "Teens, Social Media & Technology 2018," Pew Research Center, May 31, 2018 https://www.pewinternet.org/2018/05/31/teens-social-media-technology-2018/.

22. K. Eagan et al., "The American Freshman: Fifty-Year Trends," Cooperative Institutional Research Program, Higher Education Research Institute, University of California, Los Angeles, 2014, https://heri.ucla.edu/publications-tfs/.

23. Eagan et al., "The American Freshman."

24. "Cheat or Be Cheated? What We Know About Academic Integrity in Middle & High Schools & What We Can Do About It," http://www.challengesuccess.org/wp-content/uploads/2015/07/ChallengeSuccess-AcademicIntegrity-WhitePaper.pdf.

25. L. Taylor, M. Pogrebin, and M. Dodge, "Advanced Placement–Advanced Pressures: Academic Dishonesty Among Elite High School Students," *Educational Studies: A Journal of the American Educational Studies Association* 33 (2002): 403–421.

26. https://nces.ed.gov/programs/coe/indicator_cgg.asp. Retrieved April 23, 2021.

27. Arthur Allen, "Flag on the Field," *Slate*, May 16, 2006, https://slate.com/technology/2006/05/taking-the-sat-untimed.html.

28. Alia Wong, "Why Would a Teacher Cheat?," *The Atlantic*, April 27, 2016, https://www.theatlantic.com/education/archive/2016/04/why-teachers-cheat/480039/

29. Larry Gordon, "Claremont McKenna College Under Fire for SAT Cheating Scandal," *Los Angeles Times*, Jan. 31, 2012, http://latimesblogs.latimes.com/lanow/2012/01/claremont-mckenna-college-sat-cheating.html.

30. Adam Brown, "Why Forbes Removed 4 Schools from Its America's Best Colleges Rankings," *Forbes,* July 24, 2013, https://www.forbes.com/sites/abrambrown/2013/07/24/why-forbes-removed-4-schools-from-its-americas-best-colleges-rankings/#62401a343521.

31. M. Herrell and L. Barbato, "Great mangers still matter: the evolution of Google's project Oxygen," Google re:Work, Feb 27, 2018.

CHAPTER 2: YOUR BRAIN ON UNCERTAINTY: WHY WE MAKE DUBIOUS DECISIONS

1. J. Hawkins and S. Blakeslee, *On Intelligence* (New York: Times Books, 2004).

2. Andres Molero Chamis and Guadalupe Nathzidy Rivera-Urbina, "Researchers Identify Area of the Amygdala Involved in Taste Aversion," University of Granada, April 5, 2018, https://study.com/academy/lesson/the-amygdala-definition-role-function.html.

3. U. Neisser, "The Control of Information Pickup in Selective Look-ing," *Perception and Its Development: A Tribute to Eleanor J Gibson*, ed. A. D. Pick (Hillsdale, NJ: Lawrence Erlbaum Associates, 1979): 201–219.

4. https://www.theatlantic.com/health/archive/2015/03/how-uncertainty-fuels-anxiety/388066/ retrieved May 16, 2019.

5. Daniel Kahneman and Amos Tversky, "Prospect Theory: An Analysis of Decision Under Risk." *Econometrica* 47 (2) (March 1979), 263–291.

6. K. Starcke and M. Brand, "Effects of Stress on Decisions Under Un-certainty: A Meta-Analysis," *Psychological Bulletin* 142 (2016): 909–933, DOI:10.1037/bul0000060.

7. Paul G. Schempp, "How Stress Leads to Bad Decisions—and What to Do About It," *Performance Matters,* August 26, 2016, http://www.performancemattersinc.com/posts/how-stress-leads-to-bad-decisions-and-what-to-do-about-it/.

8. Howard Kunreuther et al., "High Stakes Decision Making: Norma-tive, Descriptive, and Prescriptive Considerations," *Marketing Letters* 13, no. 3 (August 2002): 259–268, https://link.springer.com/article/10.1023/A:1020287225409.

9. Christopher R. Madan, Marcia L. Spetch, and Elliot A. Ludvig, "Rapid Makes Risky: Time Pressure Increases Risk Seeking in De-cisions from Experience," *Journal of Cognitive Psychology* 27, no. 8 (2015): 921–928, http://dx.doi.org/10.1080/20445911.2015.1055274.

10. http://www.washington.edu/news/2007/08/07/baby-dvds-videos-may-hinder-not-help-infants-language-development/.

11. Diane Whitmore Schanzenbach and Stephanie Howard Larson, "Is Your Child Ready for Kindergarten?: Redshirting May Do More Harm than Good," *Education Next* 17, no. 3 (Summer 2017), http://educationnext.org/is-your-child-ready-kindergarten-redshirting-may-do-more-harm-than-good/.

CHAPTER 3: ACCUMULATED DISABILITY: THE REAL DANGERS OF OVERPROTECTION

1. "Prevalence of Any Anxiety Disorder Among Adults," National Institute of Mental Health, https://www.nimh.nih.gov/health/statistics/any-anxiety-disorder.shtml#part_155094.

2. Ibid.

3. Alex Williams, "Prozac Nation Is Now the United States of Xanax," *New York Times*, June 10, 2017, https://www.nytimes.com/2017/06/10/style/anxiety-is-the-new-depression-xanax.html.

4. J. M. Hettema, M. C. Neale, and K. S. Kendler, "A Review and Meta-Analysis of the Genetic Epidemiology of Anxiety Disorders," *American Journal of Psychiatry* 158, no. 10 (Oct. 2001): 1568–1578, https://www.ncbi.nlm.nih.gov/pubmed/11578982?mod=article_inline.

5. V. E. Cobham, M. R. Dadds, and S. H. Spence, "The Role of Parental Anxiety in the Treatment of Childhood Anxiety," *Journal of Consulting and Clinical Psychology*, Dec. 1998, https://www.ncbi.nlm.nih.gov/pubmed/9874902.

6. Kyle Spencer, "Homework Therapists' Job: Help Solve Math Problems, and Emotional Ones," *New York Times*, April 4, 2018, https://www.nytimes.com/2018/04/04/nyregion/homework-therapists-tutoring-counseling-new-york.html.

7. Ibid.

CHAPTER 4: LEARNED HELPLESSNESS AND DELAYED ADOLESCENCE: A STALLED GENERATION

1. Holly H. Schiffrin et al., "Helping or Hovering? Effects of Helicopter Parenting on College Students' Well-Being," *Psychological Science* 7 (2013), https://scholar.umw.edu/psychological_science/7.

2. Ibid., 548–557.

3. Suniya S. Luthar, "Vulnerability and Resilience: A Study of High-Risk Adolescents," *Child Development* 62, no. 3 (June 1991): 600–616.

4. "Suicide Rising Across the US," Centers for Disease Control and Prevention, last updated June 11, 2018, https://www.cdc.gov/vitalsigns/suicide/.

5. "Suicide Rates for Teens Aged 15–19 Years, by Sex—United States, 1975–2015," *Morbidity and Mortality Weekly Report*, Centers for Disease Control and Prevention, August 4, 2017, https://www.cdc.gov /mmwr/volumes/66/wr/mm6630a6.htm.

6. R. Weissbour, S. Jones, et al., "The Children We Mean to Raise: The Real Messages Adults are Sending About Values," Making Caring Common Project, Harvard Graduate School of Education, 2014.

7. Hanna Rosin, "The Silicon Valley Suicides," *The Atlantic*, Nov. 2015.

8. https://www.theguardian.com/society/2012/oct/21/puberty-adolescence -childhood-onset. Retrieved Dec. 23, 2018.

9. Laurence Steinberg, *Age of Opportunity: Lessons from the New Science of Adolescence* (Wilmington, MA: Mariner Books, 2015).

CHAPTER 5: UNLEARNING HELPLESSNESS AND RESTORING CAPABILITIES

1. "How Many People Attended March for Our Lives? Crowd in D.C. Estimated at 200,000," CBS News.com, March 25, 2018, https:// www.cbsnews.com/news/march-for-our-lives-crowd-size-estimated -200000-people-attended-d-c-march/.

2. A. J. Willingham, "Some of the Most Powerful Quotes from the #NeverAgain Rallies," CNN.com, February 21, 2018, https://www .cnn.com/2018/02/21/us/neveragain-parkland-shooting-rallies -quotes-trnd/index.html.

3. Bureau of Labor Statistics, U.S. Department of Labor, "Employment Characteristics of Families—2017," 2–3.

4. https://www.census.gov/newsroom/press-releases/2016/cb16–192. html. Retrieved July 30, 2018.

5. National Sleep Foundation, https://www.sleepfoundation.org/articles /what-happens-when-my-child-or-teen-doesnt-get-enough-sleep. Retrieved May 11, 2019.

6. *Desk Reference to the Diagnostic Criteria from DSM-5* (Washington, DC: American Psychiatric Association, 2013).

7. "Age-Appropriate Chores for Children," LivingMontessoriNow.com, https://livingmontessorinow.com/montessori-monday-age-appropriate -chores-for-children-free-printables/.

8. Lenore Skenazy, founder, LetGrow, Letgrow.org. Retrieved Dec. 5, 2018 https://letgrow.org/resources/really/.

9. Secretary Colin Powell, opening remarks before the Senate Governmental Affairs Committee. https://fas.org/irp/congress/2004_hr/091 304powell.html. Retrieved Mar. 15, 2019.

10. Sonja Lyubomirsky et al., "Thinking About Rumination: The Scholarly Contributions and Intellectual Legacy of Susan Nolen-Hoeksema," *Annual Review of Clinical Psychology* 11 (2015), https://www.annual reviews.org/doi/abs/10.1146/annurev-clinpsy-032814–112733.

11. Martin E. P. Seligman and Mihaly Csikszentmihalyi, "Positive Psychology: An Introduction," *American Psychologist* 55, no. 1 (2000): 5–14, DOI:10.1037/0003–066x.55.1.5. PMID 11392865

12. H. Zhao, J. Xiong, Z. Zhang, and C. Qi, "Growth Mindset and College Students' Learning Engagement During the Covid-19 Pandemic," Frontiers in Psychology, February 19, 2021.

13. "Father of Student Killed in Parkland Shooting Discusses School Safety," interviewed by Mary Louise Kelly on NPR, *All Things Considered*, August 15, 2018, transcript on NPR.com, https://www.npr.org /templates/transcript/transcript.php?storyId=639001302.

CHAPTER 6: DEMYSTIFYING TWENTY-FIRST-CENTURY SKILLS

1. https://eric.ed.gov/?id=ED519462. Retrieved Sept. 12, 2018.

2. *P21 Framework Definitions*, Partnership for 21st Century Skills, Copyright © 2009.

3. Benjamin Herold, "The Future of Work Is Uncertain, Schools Should Worry Now," *Education Week*, Sept. 26, 2017, https://www.edweek.org /ew/articles/2017/09/27/the-future-of-work-is-uncertain-schools.html.

4. Dom Galeon, "Our Computers Are Learning How to Code Themselves: Human Coders Beware," Futurism.com, Feb. 24, 2017, https:// futurism.com/4-our-computers-are-learning-how-to-code-themselves.

5. Leigh S. Shaffer and Jacqueline M. Zalewski, "Career Advising in a VUCA Environment," *NACADA Journal* 31, no. 1 (Spring 2011), http://www.nacadajournal.org/doi/pdf/10.12930/0271–9517–31 .1.64?code=naaa-site.

6. David Brooks, "Amy Chua Is a Wimp," *New York Times*, Jan. 17, 2011, https://www.nytimes.com/2011/01/18/opinion/18brooks.html.

7. Jeffery R. Young, "How Many Times Will People Change Jobs? The Myth of the Endlessly-Job-Hopping Millennial," EdSurge.com, July 20, 2017, https://www.edsurge.com/news/2017–07–20-how-many -times-will-people-change-jobs-the-myth-of-the-endlessly-job-hop- ping-millennial.

8. Young, "How Many Times Will People Change Jobs?"

CHAPTER 7: ACADEMIC AND FOUNDATIONAL SKILLS IN AN AGE OF UNCERTAINTY

1. https://www.ncbi.nlm.nih.gov/pmc/articles/PMC1324783/. Retrieved Nov. 18, 2018.

2. Cameron Kasky, personal response, Nov. 15, 2019, Common Sense Media Award for Advocacy.

3. Prachi E. Shah, Heidi M. Weeks, and Niko Kaciroti, "Early Child- hood Curiosity and Kindergarten Reading and Math Academic Achievement," *Pediatric Research*, 2018.

4. Francesca Gino, "The Business Case for Curiosity," *Harvard Business Review*, Sept.–Oct. 2018, https://hbr.org/2018/09/curiosity#the-business-case-for-curiosity.

5. Ibid.

6. "Not My Job: 'Stay Human' Bandleader Jon Batiste Gets Quizzed on Robots," transcript from *Wait, Wait . . . Don't Tell Me!* July 28, 2018, https://www.npr.org/templates/transcript/transcript.php?storyId=633019196.

7. Elizabeth Svoboda, "Cultivating Curiosity," *Psychology Today*, September 2006.

8. https://www.latimes.com/health/la-xpm-2012-oct-02-la-heb-teens-risk-averse-20121001-story.html. Retrieved May 12, 2019.

9. K. Pakenham, G. Landi, G. Boccolini, A. Furlani, S Grandi, E. Tossani, "The Moderating Role of Psychological Flexibility on the Mental Health Impact of the Covid-19 Pandemic and Lockdown in Italy," https://www.ncbi.nlm.nih.gov/pmc/articles/PMC7370913/. Retrieved March 13, 2021.

10. Patrick Barkham, "Forest Schools: Fires, Trees, and Mud Pies," *The Guardian,* https://www.theguardian.com/education/2014/dec/09/the-school-in-the-woods-outdoor-education-modern-britain, Retrieved Nov. 14, 2018.

11. Mariana Brussoni et al., "What Is the Relationship Between Risky Outdoor Play and Health in Children? A Systematic Review," *International Journal of Environmental Research and Public Health* 12, no. 5 (2015): 6423–6454.

12. Joske Nauta et al., "Injury Risk During Different Physical Activity Behaviours in Children: A Systematic Review with Bias Assessment," *Sports Medicine* 45, no. 3 (March 2015): 327–336.

13. James Gorman, personal communication, Sept. 25, 2017.

14. James Gorman, personal communication, Jan. 16, 2019.

15. James "Sandy" Winnefeld, personal communication, Jan. 18, 2019.

16. https://www.psychologytoday.com/us/blog/youth-and-tell/201107 /risky-business-why-teens-need-risk-thrive-and-grow. Retrieved 5-12-19.

17. Marco Casari, Jingjing Zhang, and Christine Jackson, "When Do Groups Perform Better than Individuals?" Working Paper Series, Institute for Empirical Research in Economics University of Zurich, revised April 2012, http://www.econ.uzh.ch/static/wp_iew/iew wp504.pdf.

18. Rob Cross, Scott Taylor, and Deb Zehner, "Collaboration Without Burnout," *Harvard Buiness Review*, July–August 2018, https://hbr .org/2018/07/collaboration-without-burnout.

19. https://listen/org/Listening-Facts. Retrieved Nov. 22, 2018.

20. Carol Dweck, *Mindset: The New Psychology of Success* (New York: Ballantine Books, 2007).

CHAPTER 8: THE SQUIGGLY LINE

1. Frank Bruni, "The Moral Wages of the College Admissions Mania," *New York Times*, March 16, 2019.

2. http://reports.weforum.org/future-of-jobs-2016/chapter-1-the-future -of-jobs-and-skills/-view/fn-1. Retrieved Dec. 16, 2018.

3. "'You've got to find what you love,' Jobs says" (a prepared text of the commencement address delivered by Steve Jobs, CEO of Apple Computer and of Pixar Animation Studios, on June 12, 2005), *Stanford News*, June 14, 2005, https://news.stanford.edu/2005/06/14/jobs-061505/.

CHAPTER 9: A REVISED SCRIPT: MOMS AND DADS IN THE TWENTY-FIRST CENTURY

1. Kenneth Matos, Ellen Galinsky, and James T. Bond, "National Study of Employers," Families and Work Institute, 2016 Copyright © 2017, Society for Human Resource Management.

2. Gretchen Livingston, "About One-Third of U.S. Children Are Living with an Unmarried Parent," Pew Research Center (analysis of U.S. Census Bureau data), April 27, 2018, https://www.pewresearch.org/fact-tank/2018/04/27/about-one-third-of-u-s-children-are-living-with-an-unmarried-parent/.

3. Gretchen Livingston, "Stay-at-Home Moms and Dads Account for About One-in-Five U.S. Parents," Fact Tank, Sept. 4, 2018, Pew Research Center, https://www.pewresearch.org/fact-tank/2018/09/24/stay-at-home-moms-and-dads-account-for-about-one-in-five-u-s-parents/.

4. "Modern Parenthood: Roles of Moms and Dads Converge as They Balance Work and Family," Pew Research Center; Social & Demographic Trends, March 14, 2013, https://www.pewsocialtrends.org/2013/03/14/modern-parenthood-roles-of-moms-and-dads-converge-as-they-balance-work-and-family/.

5. Annie Lowrey, "Women May Earn Just 49 Cents on the Dollar," *The Atlantic*, Nov. 28, 2018, https://www.theatlantic.com/ideas/archive/2018/11/how-big-male-female-wage-gap-really-is/.

6. Mark J. Perry, "Women Earned Majority of Doctoral Degrees in 2016 for 8th Straight Year and Outnumber Men in Grad School 135 to 100," American Enterprise Institute (AEI), Sept. 28, 2017, http://www.aei.org/publication/women-earned-majority-of-doctoral-degrees-in-2016-for-8th-straight-year-and-outnumber-men-in-grad-school-135-to-100/.

7. Kim Parker and Gretchen Livingston, "7 Facts About American Dads," Pew Research Center, June 13, 2018; "How Mothers and Fathers Spend Their Time," Pew Research Center, Social and Demographic Trends, March 14, 2013.

8. "When Work Takes Over: Emotional Labor Strategies and Daily Ruminations About Work While at Home," *Journal of Personnel Psychology* 16 (2017): 150–154.

9. Kristin Wong, "There's a Stress Gap Between Men and Women. Here's Why It's Important," *New York Times*, Nov. 14, 2018, https://www .nytimes.com/2018/11/14/smarter-living/stress-gap-women-men.html.

10. A. Kalil, R. Ryan, and M. Corey, "Diverging Destinies: Maternal Education and the Developmental Gradient in Time with Children," *Demography* 49, no. 4 (Nov. 2012): 1361–1383.

11. Anne Maass and Chiara Volpato, "Gender Differences in Self-Serving Attributions About Sexual Experiences," *Journal of Applied Social Psychology*, May 1989.

12. "Event Transcript: Religion Trends in the U.S." Pew Research Center, Aug. 19, 2013, http://www.pewforum.org/2013/08/19/event-tran script-religion-trends-in-the-u-s/.

13. "Fewer than Half of U.S. Kids Today Live in a 'Traditional' Family," Pew Research Center, Dec. 22, 2014, http://www.pewresearch.org /fact-tank/2014/12/22/less-than-half-of-u-s-kids-today-live-in-a -traditional-family/.

14. Andre Agassi, *Open* (New York: Knopf, 2006).

15. Laura McKenna, "The Ethos of the Overinvolved Parent," *The Atlantic*, May 18, 2017, https://www.theatlantic.com/education/archive /2017/05/the-ethos-of-the-overinvolved-parent/527097/.

16. Laura Hamilton, "The Partnership Between Colleges and Helicopter Parents," *The Atlantic*, May 13, 2016, https://www.theatlantic.com /education/archive/2016/05/the-partnership-between-colleges-and -helicopter-parents/482595/.

17. https://www.forbes.com/sites/amymorin/2017/08/29/parents-please -dont-attend-your-adult-childs-job-interview/-7ab0b92e2a31. Retrieved Dec. 15, 2018.

18. Suniya S. Luthar and Lucia Ciciolla, "Who Mothers Mommy? Factors That Contribute to Mothers' Well-Being," *Developmental Psychology*, Dec. 2015, https://www.ncbi.nlm.nih.gov/pubmed/26501725.

19. "Modern Parenthood: Roles of Moms and Dads Converge as They Balance Work and Family."

20. Lila MacLellan, "Research Shows Daily Family Life Is All the 'Quality Time' Kids Need," Quartz at Work, Nov. 5, 2017, https://qz.com/work/1099307/research-shows-daily-family-life-is-all-the-quality-time-kids-need/.

21. Melissa A. Milkie, Kei M. Nomaguchi, and Kathleen E. Denny, "Does the Amount of Time Mothers Spend with Children or Adolescents Matter?" *Journal of Marriage and Family*, March 4, 2015, https://onlinelibrary.wiley.com/doi/pdf/10.1111/jomf.12170.

22. Brigid Schulte, "Making Time for Kids? Study Says Quality Trumps Quantity," *Washington Post*, March 28, 2015, https://www.washingtonpost.com/local/making-time-for-kids-study-says-quality-trumps-quantity/2015/03/28/10813192-d378-11e4-8fce-3941fc548f1c_story.html?utm_term=.ce0f193211b8.

23. Ibid.

24. Charles Opondo et al., "Father Involvement in Early Child-Rearing and Behavioural Outcomes in Their Pre-Adolescent Children: Evidence from the ALSPAC UK Birth Cohort," *BMJ Journals*, Nov. 2016, https://bmjopen.bmj.com/content/6/11/e012034.

CHAPTER 10: THE FUTURE-PROOF FAMILY: BUILDING A BETTER MORAL COMPASS AND STRONGER COMMUNITIES

1. https://journals.sagepub.com/doi/10.1177/0192513X20943914. Retrieved March 15, 2021.

2. "Cheat or Be Cheated," Challenge Success white paper, 2012, www.challengesuccess.org. Retrieved Nov. 25, 2018.

3. Natasha Singer, "Tech's Ethical 'Dark Side': Harvard, Stanford, and Others Want to Address It," *New York Times*, Feb. 12, 2018.

4. Irina Raicu, "Rethinking Ethics Training in Silicon Valley," *The*

Atlantic, May 26, 2017, https://www.theatlantic.com/technology /archive/2017/05/rethinking-ethics-training-in-silicon-valley/525456/.

5. https://www.usnews.com/opinion/knowledge-bank/articles/2016 –11–22/donald-trumps-election-is-civic-educations-gut-check. Retrieved Jan. 7, 2019.

6. Quoted by Jeremy Pearce in "Arthur Galston, Agent Orange Researcher, Is Dead at 88," *New York Times*, June 23, 2008, B6.

7. Personal communication, July 1, 2019

8. Ceylan Yeginsu, "U.K. Appoints a Minister for Loneliness," *New York Times,* Jan. 17, 2018, https://www.nytimes.com/2018/01/17/world /europe/uk-britain-loneliness.html.

9. Marc Prosser, "Searching for a Cure for Japan's Loneliness Epidemic," *HuffPost*, Aug. 15, 2018, https://www.huffingtonpost.com/entry /japan-loneliness-aging-robots-technology_us_5b72873ae4b05307 43cd04aa.

10. https://www.ft.com/content/e4d15154-6a31-11e8-b6eb-4acfcfb08 c11. Retrieved May 14, 2018.

11. Fiza Pirani, "Why Are Americans So Lonely?" *Atlanta Journal-Constitution,* May 1, 2018, https://www.ajc.com/news/health-med -fit-science/why-are-americans-lonely-massive-study-finds-nearly -half-feels-alone-young-adults-most-all/bbIKsU2Rr3qZI8WlukH fpK/. Retrieved Jan. 7, 2019.

12. Ibid.

13. Ibid.

14. Yuval Levin, *The Fractured Republic: Renewing America's Social Contract in the Age of Individualism* (New York: Basic Books, 2017).

15. Emilie Le Beau Lucchesi, "Why Sports Parents Sometimes Behave So Badly," *New York Times*, Nov. 1, 2018, https://www.nytimes .com/2018/11/01/well/family/why-sports-parents-sometimes-behave -so-badly.html.

16. C. Ryan Dunn et al., "The Impact of Family Financial Investment on Perceived Parent Pressure and Child Enjoyment and Commitment in Organized Youth Sport," *Family Relations: Interdisciplinary Journal of Applied Family Sciences*, May 24, 2016, https://onlinelibrary.wiley.com/doi/abs/10.1111/fare.12193.

17. Chris Segrin et al., "Parent and Child Traits Associated with Over-parenting," *Journal of Social and Clinical Psychology* 32, no. 6 (2103): 569–595.

18. Claire Cain Miller, "The Relentlessness of Modern Parenting," *New York Times*, Dec.25, 2018, https://www.nytimes.com/2018/12/25/upshot/the-relentlessness-of-modern-parenting.html.

19. Miller, "The Relentlessness of Modern Parenting."

INDEX

public transportation, 112
Putnam, Robert, 234

racism, 39
Raicu, Irina, 226
Rauschenberg, Robert, 190
rebelliousness, 75–76, 90
recess, 128
redshirting, 38
Reed College, 174
relaxation, 100, 105
religion, 207, 217–18, 237
resilience, 49, 143, 177–78, 194, 219
  cultivating, 99, 155
  optimism and, 121
responsibilities, 71, 77, 84
  age-appropriate, 107–11
  moral values and, 226, 231
résumé gaps, 201
retail, 181
reward, 32, 34, 35, 43, 51
risk and risk-taking, 5, 8, 12, 17, 88, 90–91, 150, 193
  anxiety and, 53
  assessing, 111–15, 155
  brain and, 33–34, 81–82
  cultivating, 138–39, 155–56
  fear and, 24, 34
  growth mindset and, 123
  reward vs., 43, 51, 156
robotics, 228
Rodan + Fields, 178, 181
romantic relationships, 17, 89–90
Rosin, Hanna, 80
Rowling, J.K., 173
rule-setting, 21, 77, 156
Russia, 130, 226
Rutgers, 197

sadness, 32
same-sex parents, 197
Santa Clara University, 226
SATs and ACTs, 21–22, 37, 45, 73, 117, 119, 172
school, 21, 57, 80, 132, 208. See also academic success; education; learning; and specific levels

separation anxiety and, 68–70
skills vs. arts and, 128
school gardens, 143
school shootings, 40. See also gun violence.
Schwartz, Jeremy, 211
Schwartz, Loren, 239
Schwartz, Michael, 231
science, 9–10
scooters, 112–13
Second Shift, 202
self
  authentic, 76, 90
  false, 12, 14–15
self-awareness, 56, 153
self-care, 71
self-efficacy, 111
self-esteem, 15, 21, 73, 162
self-regulation, 4, 30, 74, 115
  adolescents and, 81
  college and, 77
  cultivating, 161–63
  middle school and, 71
self-reliance, 83
self-sacrifice, 216
Seligman, Martin, 119–21
separation, 17, 70
  adolescence and, 76, 78, 90
separation anxiety, 57, 59, 68, 103
Sephora, 50
setbacks. See failure
sex, 157, 226
sexism, 39
Siegal, Harrison, 181–84, 189
Silicon Valley, 11, 170, 172, 173
"Silicon Valley Suicides, The" (Rosin), 80
Simmons, Alison, 228
single parents, 99, 197, 208
Skenazy, Lenore, 112
sleepaway camp, 65, 104
sleeping with child, 57–58, 64–65
sleep needs, 46, 57–59, 79, 71, 102
sleepovers, 62, 65–66, 134
smartphones, 17, 54, 70, 71
Snapchat, 15, 17
social anxiety, 68–69, 84, 103. See also friendships; isolation